D0850408

Hysterical Fictions

Also by Clare Hanson

THE CRITICAL WRITINGS OF KATHERINE MANSFIELD (*editor*)

KATHERINE MANSFIELD (*with Andrew Gurr*)

RE-READING THE SHORT STORY (*editor*)

SHORT STORIES AND SHORT FICTIONS, 1880–1980

VIRGINIA WOOLF

Hysterical Fictions

The 'Woman's Novel' in the Twentieth Century

Clare Hanson

First published in Great Britain 2000 by
MACMILLAN PRESS LTD
Houndmills, Basingstoke, Hampshire RG21 6XS and London
Companies and representatives throughout the world

A catalogue record for this book is available from the British Library.

ISBN 0–333–63889–1

First published in the United States of America 2000 by
ST. MARTIN'S PRESS, LLC,
Scholarly and Reference Division,
175 Fifth Avenue, New York, N.Y. 10010

ISBN 0–312–23529–1

Library of Congress Cataloging-in-Publication Data
Hanson, Clare.
    Hysterical fictions : the "woman's novel" in the twentieth century / Clare
Hanson.
        p.   cm.
    Includes bibliographical references (p.) and index.
    ISBN 0–312–23529–1
        1. English fiction—Women authors—History and criticism. 2. Feminism and
    literature—Great Britain—History—20th century. 3. Women and literature–
    –Great Britain—History—20th century. 4. Feminist fiction, English—History
    and criticism. 5. Mind and body in literature. 6. Body, Human, in literature. 7.
    Women—Books and reading. 8. Femininity in literature. 9. Sex role in
    literature. 10. Women in literature. I. Title.

    PR888.F45 H36 2000
    823'.91099287—dc21
                                                                    00–033344

This book is printed on paper suitable for recycling and made from fully managed and sustained
forest sources.

10   9   8   7   6   5   4   3   2   1
09   08   07   06   05   04   03   02   01   00

Printed and bound in Great Britain by
Antony Rowe Ltd, Chippenham, Wiltshire

For Antonia and Jack

Contents

Acknowledgements

I would like to thank Nicola Bradbury, Catherine Burgass, John Hughes and Marion Shaw for reading draft material for this book and for offering many astute and helpful comments on it. I am most grateful to Nicole Ward Jouve for her imaginative responses to my ideas, and to Judy Simons for inviting me to speak at the 1995 conference 'Literature: A Woman's Business' at Sheffield Hallam University, which provided me with an opportunity to try out some arguments. Thanks also to Avril Horner and Sue Zlosnik for sharing their thoughts about non-canonical women's writing, and to Ozlëm Gorey, Ayako Mizuo and Andrea Peterson for many enjoyable conversations about feminist theory. I am grateful to members of the Feminist Research Group at Loughborough University for their encouragement, and in particular to Gill Spraggs for sharing her knowledge of classical literature. Charmian Hearne at Macmillan has been the most helpful of editors: I am grateful for her support and advice.

Introduction

In 1980, Rosalind Coward wrote an article in *Feminist Review*, subsequently widely reprinted in anthologies of feminist criticism, entitled '"This Novel Changes Lives": Are Women's Novels Feminist Novels?'.[1] She concluded that they were not, arguing that 'it is just not possible to say that women-centered writings have any necessary relationship to feminism' and that it would be misguided 'to mark a book of interest to feminism because of the centrality it attributes to women's experiences'.[2] The effect of this article has been effectively to close off discussion of 'women's novels', which is unfortunate, as two separate arguments are conflated in the article, and arguably only one of them is defensible. Coward is right to point out that there is no necessary relationship between women's novels and feminist novels: in other words, *women's novels* are not necessarily feminist – although they can be so. However, it is wrong to argue that women's novels are not of interest to *the feminist critic*: they are of interest precisely because of the centrality they attribute to women's experiences. Maroula Joannou makes exactly this point in her book *Ladies, Please Don't Smash These Windows*. She argues that in dismissing woman-centred texts, feminist critics may, consciously or not, be perpetuating 'the dominant cultural view of femininity as trivial, marginal, or otherwise unworthy of serious consideration'.[3] As an example, she takes Elizabeth Wilson's influential survey of women in post-war Britain, *Only Halfway to Paradise*, in which the work of Elizabeth Bowen, Rosamond Lehmann and Elizabeth Taylor is treated unsympathetically. As Joannou writes, in Wilson's study:

> Elizabeth Bowen is characterised as manifesting 'a "woman's" sensibility taken to excess'; Rosamond Lehmann in *The Echoing*

Grove is said to be 'successful in connecting the general atmosphere of retreat to a special sense of women's peculiar situation'. One wonders why women's situation is deemed 'peculiar'? and whether or not a novel that *'successfully'* linked the mood of the times to a sense of man's situation would be damned with faint praise as merely a limited success? (p. 132)

Joannou takes the opposite view from Coward and Wilson, arguing that 'woman-centred texts ... must always be of interest to the feminist critic as the essential building blocks of a politics of feminist change' (p. 158). Indeed, it could be argued that texts with a coherent feminist agenda ('feminist novels', in Coward's terms) will be of *less* interest to feminist criticism than woman-centred texts, as it is in the latter that the complex and contradictory elements which go to form 'feminine' identities are more fully explored.[4] Without an understanding of that femininity with which so many women readers and writers identify (at least in part), a viable and inclusive 'politics of feminist change' is indeed difficult to envisage.

The term 'woman's novel' gained critical currency in the 1980s with the publication of Coward's article, which was followed in 1983 by Nicola Beauman's *A Very Great Profession: the Woman's Novel 1914–1939*. In her introduction to this study, Beauman defines the woman's novel between the wars as one written by middle-class women for middle-class women, and goes on to argue that these novels:

> all have an unmistakably female tone of voice. They generally have little action and less histrionics – they are about the 'drama of the undramatic', the steadfast dailiness of a life that brings its own rewards, the intensity of the emotions and, above all, the importance of human relationships.[5]

Beauman's comments point to the ways in which the woman's novel constructs its reader as feminine, interpellating her, in Althusser's phrase, calling on her to recognize a shared identity and shared knowledge. While Beauman's book is confined to the inter-war period, Olga Kenyon, in her 1988 study *Women Novelists Today*, traces the line of development of the woman's novel through from Rose Macaulay to Anita Brookner, singling out Jean Rhys, Rosamond Lehmann, Elizabeth Bowen, Barbara Pym and Elizabeth Taylor as key figures. Kenyon argues that these writers display 'what might be termed a "feminine" sensibility in the subtle descriptions of appearance, textures, social nuances', and also that they have the ability 'to represent the social frustrations and intimate thought-processes of gifted, undervalued women'.[6]

Women writers, too, began to discuss the category of the woman's novel. Some wished to distance themselves from the form. A. S. Byatt, for example, expressed reservations about it in a 1986 review of Barbara Pym's *An Academic Question*, and has written of her own early 'fear of the "woman's novel" as an immoral devouring force'.[7] As she acknowledges, her resistance was connected with the suspicion that if she wrote women's novels, she would be classified as a lesser writer: 'I wanted my harvest, both in my life and in my work, and I was afraid that my light was a lesser one.' On the other hand, Anita Brookner has endorsed the form. She has said in interview that the women novelists she really admires in the English tradition are Rosamond Lehmann and Elizabeth Taylor, and that she doesn't mind being described as a woman's novelist 'in the least'. In contrast to Byatt, she has defended the specificity of the woman's novel, arguing that:

> Women have devoted themselves to a certain kind of storytelling, which is extremely valid and extremely absorbing; mainly to other women, but to men as well, I think. It's a quite different genre. It does limit itself, but it tends to go deeper. Also it's full of information. Women tend to read novels for information – and to learn about other women, so the novel fulfils a particular function if it's written by a woman for other women.[8]

These different responses from Byatt and Brookner point to an anxiety about the cultural status of the woman's novel which is picked up in Hilary Radner's discussion of the genre in 'Extra-Curricular Activities: Women Writers and the Readerly Text' and '"Out of Category": the Middlebrow Novel'. Together, these essays offer the most sustained analysis to date of the woman's novel. Radner (like Nicola Beauman) defines the 'woman's novel' as the novel written by educated women for women like themselves. Such women are, she argues, at a point of intersection between two contradictory worlds, because they choose to define themselves by their intellect and educational status, while also maintaining a 'feminine' identity constructed through 'their role in the home, in relation to children, lovers, friends and family'.[9] The texts which they write reflect and reproduce this contradiction, which Radner discusses in terms of the reading positions which such texts offer. She suggests that 'two distinct, rhetorically inscribed regimes of pleasure, two different ways of producing pleasure for the reader' may be offered by a text. Borrowing from Freud, she suggests that we see these two different ways of reading as 'two different symptom formations, hysterical and obsessional'. These two symptom formations define what Radner calls (after Freud and Lyotard) two different 'libidinal economies': a pleasure in the symptom, generally associated with hysteria, and a pleasure in repression or deferral, generally associated with obsessional neurosis. Radner suggests that the first of these economies is usually present in the reading of a popular cultural text. In the reading of Harlequin or Mills & Boon romances, for example, the process of reading has 'no ostensible goal except its own replication' (p. 253). Because the romance reader knows the formulaic plot, she does not read for the plot but to enjoy the *process* of reading. Similarly with soap-opera, in which the open-ended plot emphasizes pleasure in the process of viewing. Popular forms, then, encourage a mode of reading which is 'hysterical', sensationalist rather than intellectual, generating pleasure through the experience of textuality rather than through the pursuit of closure and the resolution of an enigma. In using the term 'hysterical' Radner does not mean to imply that such a reading process is mistaken or delusive. Nodding ironically at the etymology of the word (*hystera* = Greek for womb, hysterical = morbidly emotional), she suggests that it is a process involving the generation of feeling and empathy, and that it is a two-way process involving both reader and text.

Literary or high cultural texts, by contrast, offer pleasure as a goal rather than as a process – 'a pleasure in deferral and displacement, rather than a pleasure in the symptom itself' (p. 254). They invite a regime of reading that privileges interpretation, in which the reader is encouraged both to solve the immediate enigma of plot ('who did it') and to solve the critical enigma in the wider sense, finding out what it all means. The reader of literature (or Literature) is invited to analyse the text, reworking and rewriting the narrative in his own image, 'reinscribing the enigma in his own terms as a sign of his position of mastery' (p. 254). Such a reading process involves deferral, and repression of the experience of the text as pleasure in and of itself.

Radner suggests that textual consumership (reading the text 'for pleasure') is characteristic of the type of novel that Roland Barthes has called the readerly text.[10] Popular fiction and formula romance represent extreme forms of the readerly text, offering themselves for consumption as a product, by brand name. At the opposite end of the spectrum, Barthes places the writerly text, which offers the reader the impression of writing his own narrative. The writerly text demands a reader initiated into those cultural codes which will enable him to reinscribe the text for himself 'as a sign of his position of mastery'. This kind of reading is, Radner suggests, characteristic of textual studies in academia. 'Within the academic institution the text is always used as an instrument that empowers the scholar with a position of mastery over his own discourse' (p. 255). Such 'interpretive reading' is at the other end of the spectrum from 'reading for pleasure'.

Radner goes on to argue that there is one genre which confounds the distinction between these two regimes of reading: the woman's novel. The woman's novel, producing a discourse that is both public and private, offers the possibility of reading in both ways, looking in two directions. As she writes:

[The woman's novel] stubbornly rejects the status of high art. It is adamantly not against interpretation and demands to be understood in terms of its content. The woman's novel says, by and large, what it means to say, refusing to reveal its secrets under the scrutiny of the analyst by displaying these last for all to see, literati and nonliterati alike. Yet the richness of its language, the subtlety of its arguments, and its undeniable intelligence and self-consciousness defy the classification of popular culture. The woman's novel may be read either as popular culture or as literature, challenging the categories of High Modernism, reflecting the ambiguous social position of its preferred reader – the educated woman. (p. 256)

In her second essay, '"Out of Category": The Middlebrow Novel', Radner uses the metaphor of a picture in a gestalt experiment to suggest the way in which the woman's novel functions, offering two possibilities of structuration, two possibilities for reading.[11] On the one hand, the woman's novel offers a discourse of mastery and a regime of pleasure modelled on obsessional rather than hysterical structures. The intelligence, the psychological and sociological acuity of the novel, its 'high' cultural references, all reflect/create a discourse of mastery. However, this kind of novel also works in the identificatory mode, allowing the reader to give herself over to the novel as a process, reading (hysterically) for the pleasure of the text.

Radner suggests that the duality of the woman's novel is most clearly illustrated by a 'subgenre' that she terms the dissertation novel. Radner discusses Rebecca Goldstein's *The Mind–Body Problem* (1983) as an example, but one more appropriate to this study of the British 'woman's novel' might be Margaret Drabble's *The Millstone* (1965), which exemplifies many of the points Radner makes in relation to Goldstein's novel. In Drabble's novel as in Goldstein's, the heroine has to work through her experiences of conflicting systems of value. Rosamund Stacey is a highly educated postgraduate student working in the British Museum on a thesis about Elizabethan sonnet sequences. She is thus firmly placed within a dominant academic discourse of which she has complete mastery – she is good at her work and enjoys it. However, when she accidentally becomes pregnant, she discovers the limitations of the culturally legitimate discourses of academia. The novel charts the progress, side by side, of her thesis and her pregnancy, and shows how the pregnancy brings knowledge and experience which cannot be articulated within the terms of academic discourse. The pregnancy brings specificity, limitation, a realization of the contingency of existence. The first-person narrator underlines this point, writing of the difference the pregnancy makes:

> I did not go over from the camp of logic to the camp of intuition; it was rather that I became aware of facts that I had not recognised or even noticed before. There is nothing logical about ignorance. I am sure that my discoveries were common discoveries; if they were not, they would not be worth recording... I had always felt for others in theory and pitied the blows of fate and circumstance under which they suffered; but now, myself no longer free, myself suffering, I may say that I felt it in my heart.[12]

At the end of the novel, the importance of such knowledge is again affirmed. The narrator comes to the conclusion that there is only one thing in the world that she truly knows about, and that one thing is her daughter. This complete knowledge has made her lose her taste for all other 'half-knowledge'.

Rosamund has her baby, who is beautiful and flourishes, although only after a heart operation (analogous to the 'operation' on Rosamund's heart). She also finishes her thesis, successfully: it is regarded as 'an exceptional piece of work'. Like the author, Rosamund has demonstrated her mastery of dominant discourses, but we are also made keenly aware of her 'feminine' experiences. Drabble thus manipulates two discourses, academic discourse (present especially in the extended use of literary allusions and parallels in the text), and the 'feminine' discourse of domestic realism. The latter enables her to make visible that which is meaningless in terms of dominant cultural discourse, and generally occluded by it. The text dramatizes the tension between the two forms of discourse/experience, often to comic effect. For example, on one occasion when she is visiting the ante-natal clinic, Rosamund fails to notice that a shabbily dressed two-year-old is standing on her foot, because she is too much engrossed in an interesting point about the poetry of George Herbert. The different experiences/discourses collide in the text, jostling each other, so that the reader is forced to consider their separation and supposed opposition. It could be argued that what Drabble's text does is to deconstruct the binary opposition between dominant cultural and occluded feminine discourses, revealing them to exist in a relationship of 'both/and' rather than 'either/or'.

Hilary Radner takes a less optimistic view, arguing that the writing and reading of women's novels is a practice that can be easily 'circumscribed and contained within dominant discourse'. Yet these novels do not simply *write about* the collision of different discourses or different 'life narratives': they are *made up of* different discourses, moving between 'undeniable intelligence and self-consciousness' and simple, direct, almost folkloric elements. They thus not only raise crucial questions about women's lives but also offer a powerful critique of cultural assumptions about what 'art' should be.

As Nicola Beauman's study suggests, the 'woman's novel' as a novel written by and for educated middle-class women emerged as a significant form in the 1920s and 1930s. Its emergence can be linked with the expansion of women's education in the early twentieth-century. Women began to enter higher education in increasing numbers after the establishment of the first women's colleges at Girton and Newnham in the 1870s. In 1878 London University awarded degrees to women on the same terms as men. Improvements in girls' schooling followed parliamentary investigations in the 1870s, and by 1900 the Girls' Public Day School Company had established 30 schools for girls, while girls constituted almost a quarter of the total number of pupils in endowed schools. Progress was not rapid, but by the early twentieth century, a liberal (as opposed to a domestic) education was available for a significant proportion of middle-class girls. This was true to a much lesser extent for working-class girls. While the 1870 Education Act had made elementary schooling compulsory for all, there was a strong bias towards domestic subjects such as domestic economy, cookery and laundry for girls in elementary schools. And needless to say, working-class girls rarely attended university.[13]

Between the wars there was a steady increase in the numbers of girls who obtained a secondary education, the numbers rising from 185 000 in 1920 to 500 000 in 1936. However, while the Education Act of 1918 provided elementary schooling for all children up to the age of 14, beyond that age education remained a privilege open almost exclusively to fee-paying, middle-class girls, the 'daughters of educated men', in Virginia Woolf's phrase. University education also remained the preserve of a very few, although teacher training, involving a two-year college course, offered an important educational and professional route for women of all classes.[14] It was not until the 1944 Education Act that all children were given the right to free secondary education, up to the age of 15. The act was not entirely successful in increasing access to education because of the continuing bias towards domestic subjects in secondary schools for girls; nonetheless, girls' grammar schools offered a significant route to higher education for women after 1944. The story of women's education after the war is indeed one of steady progress, with developments especially in the higher education sector. The expansion of universities, colleges and polytechnics in the 1960s and 1970s led to a significant increase in women students: the percentage of women students in universities rose from 29.2 per cent in 1956 to 38.4 per cent in 1981/2.[15]

In the twentieth century, in consequence of women's increased access to academic education, a distinct reading public of educated women grew up. There were two periods of especially marked growth, the first between the wars, and the second in the 1960s and 1970s. The expansion of the reading public between the wars can be linked with changing patterns of leisure as well as with increased educational opportunities. As Nicola Beauman has shown, the circulating library was especially important in bringing books to middle-class women in this period. The turnover of the circulating library gives some impression of the level of demand: 25 million volumes were exchanged among Boots libraries in 1925 and 35 million by the time of the outbreak of the Second World War.[16] In the post-war period, the expansion of the reading public in the 1960s and 1970s can be linked with increased access to higher education, and with the 'second wave' of feminism, which brought the establishment of feminist publishing houses. A. S. Byatt has described (with some ambivalence) the 'flowering of Virago and the rehabilitation of the library novel and good read' in this period.[17]

The changes in women's lives in the period from the 1920s to the 1980s have been profound. The two most significant factors have been the widespread reduction in family size due to increased access to contraception, and middle-class women's gradual entry into the labour market. Birth control was pioneered by Marie Stopes, who set up her first clinic in Holloway in 1921 and established a Society for Constructive Birth Control in 1922. Contraception was at this time widely associated with immorality and illicit sex, and both the church and the medical profession opposed the circulation of information about it. Nonetheless, the practice of birth control spread steadily through the 1920s, and in 1930 local authorities were given limited powers to give contraception advice to nursing and expectant mothers 'in whose cases further pregnancy would be dangerous to health'. The birth rate fell consistently through the inter-war years, and continued to fall during and after the Second World War. In 1967 the Family Planning Act made contraception advice available to single women, and the introduction of the contraceptive pill in the 1960s gave women the opportunity to take complete control of reproduction.

The decline in family size which began in the 1920s brought freedom for the middle-class woman which she was unable to use for some time. As Cate Haste has shown, in the inter-war years social and economic pressures pushed women firmly back into the home. In consequence of these pressures:

> Marriage was portrayed as a career for women, houswifery was elevated to a craft, the management of family and home became a professional activity demanding scientific skills to which women, by their nature, were deemed particularly suited.[18]

This was also a period of unprecedented growth in the women's magazine market: 60 new titles were launched between 1920 and 1945. These focused intensively on selling the domestic ideal, much to the dismay of feminists like Vera Brittain. 'Happy and lucky is the man whose wife is houseproud ... who likes to do things well, to make him proud of her and her children' is a typical policy statement from *Housewife*, quoted by Haste (p. 91).

During the Second World War, things changed dramatically. Manpower shortages meant that women had to take over in almost all areas of industry, eventually replacing men in engineering, shipbuilding and aircraft production, in chemical production, in transport and in the civil service. According to Haste, by 1943 women made up 57 per cent of the total workforce, with nine single women out of ten and 80 per cent of married women aged 18–40 in the Services or working in industry or civil defence (p. 100). When the war ended, however, it became clear that, just as after the First World War, women would have to return to the home in large numbers. Wartime nursery facilities were closed down almost immediately, and the ideology of houswifery was brought back into play. Haste quotes the novelist Monica Dickens, for example, explaining in *Woman's Own* that women are born to love, 'to be partners to the opposite sex, and that is the most important thing they can do in life . . . to be wives and mothers, to fix their hearts to one man and to love and care for him with all the bounteous unselfishness that love can inspire' (p. 152). It was the economic boom of the mid-fifties which enabled women to return to paid, mainly part-time, employment. In 1947 18 per cent of married women worked outside the home, while by 1957 this had risen to one in three. By 1962 over half of all women workers were married women (p. 153).

The lives of the writers discussed in this study reflect the changing patterns of middle-class women's lives. All but one (Anita Brookner) have married, and all but two (Bowen and Brookner) have had children. Those who grew up before the Second World War (Lehmann, Bowen and Taylor) had no career other than their writing, and indeed Bowen in particular disliked the idea of the 'professional woman', celebrating instead the work of the non-professional woman in the private sphere (she was also the president of her local Women's Institute).[19] Of those who grew up after the Second World War, Drabble has had a literary-academic career as well as a career as a novelist, and both Byatt and Brookner have had successful academic careers. Their work has been in an area (education/higher education) in which women have had considerable success over the last twenty or thirty years. Such work is very different from that of the majority of women, who continue to work part-time for low pay in the service industries, in a country which has extremely inadequate state-funded childcare provision. Nonetheless, what is striking about these 'high-flying' women is their sense that they are divided beings, and it is this division which is the principal subject of this book.

In 1988 the writer Amanda Craig wrote of her feeling that she was being 'crucified by the competing demands of intellect and economics, and those of instinct and emotion'.[20] She was writing as a high-flying woman in a post-Thatcherite, post-feminist era. In 1973, in her feminist study *Woman's Consciousness, Man's World*, Sheila Rowbotham described the effect then on female students of their induction into higher education:

> Girls who go to university encounter capitalism in one of its most sophisticated forms, but their socialization in the family has prepared them for marriage and motherhood, traditional production at home. Temporarily co-workers with boys in the knowledge industry, the contrast between their traditional feminine role and competitive academic life is extreme ... The way in which these female knowledge workers are absorbed into production means that they continue to be aware of their contradictory social position.[21]

In her autobiography *The Swan in the Evening*, Rosamond Lehmann writes of the difficulty she had in the 1920s in coming to terms with what she thought of as 'the dual responsibilities of my destiny', that is, the difficulty of balancing her obligation to be a wife and mother and her role as 'one of the new post-war young women writers, product of higher education (Girton College), a frank outspeaker upon unpleasant subjects'.[22] What all these accounts foreground is an opposition between the intellect and femininity which takes us straight back to the 'mind–body problem' which Radner sees as central to the woman's novel.

What I want to suggest is that this opposition cannot be understood simply in terms of changing social roles or in terms of the all-pervasive influence of popular ideology like that promoted by *Woman's Own*. While it is true that in the twentieth-century women have combined intellectual work and family responsibilities in far greater numbers than ever before, there is no *intrinsic* reason why this juggling act should be experienced in terms of a conflict between mind and body. There is no evidence that men working in similar circumstances experience such a conflict. And as many critics have argued, it is a mistake to assume that readers of popular texts like women's magazines accept the ideology embedded in them uncritically. On the contrary, the adoption of a position of critical distance is for many an essential element in the pleasure of reading.[23] I would argue that the 'mind–body problem' is far more deeply rooted than this, and that its origins lie within the very cultural system with which the 'educated woman' is invited to identify.

For the most sustained analysis of this cultural system we must turn to the work of Luce Irigaray. Irigaray has been under-utilized by Anglo-American feminists, who have seen her as a mystical essentialist promoting an elusive femininity not yet represented within the symbolic order. While there are difficulties with some aspects of Irigaray's thought (difficulties to which I will return), her critique of Western philosophical thought is unrivalled in its scope and in its trenchancy. In *Speculum of the Other Woman* and in *An Ethics of Sexual Difference* Irigaray examines the ideas, metaphors and myths which structure Western metaphysics and which support cultural production. What she discovers is that, as Christine Battersby puts it, '[i]n the tradition of philosophy that reaches from Plato and Aristotle to Freud and Lacan, woman falls both inside and outside the boundaries of the human, the genus, the self itself'.[24] One might put it another way and suggest that what Irigaray discovers is that thought itself, in the Western tradition, is gendered. For example, in her analysis of Plato's allegory of the cave in *The Republic* and of the *Timaeus*, Irigaray traces the complex role in Plato's thought of metaphors of sexual difference. Plato sets up an opposition which is at the foundation of Western philosophy between what is intelligible and unchanging (the world of Forms or Ideas) and what is sensible and subject to change: this can also be couched as an opposition between the ideal and the material, the divine and the mortal. As Irigaray points out, in Plato's scheme the intelligible is identified with the masculine, with the father, and the sensible with the feminine, and what Plato does is try and sever the link between the two, in order to elide the significance of the sensible/material. As Irigaray writes:

> No proper sense, proper noun, proper signifier expresses the *matrix* of any discourse, or any text, even the legal text. The necessity of its (re)production is absent from what it lays out. Eclipse of the mother, of the place (of) becoming, whose non-representation or even disavowal upholds the absolute being attributed to the father.[25]

Plato's argument is complex and involves the introduction of the *chora* as an enigmatic category which is superimposed, as it were, over that of the sensible in order to distract our attention away from the dependence of the intelligible on a material support. The *chora* is that unthinkable foundation which supports everything and yet is so neutral as to 'be' nothing. Irigaray quotes this passage from the *Timaeus*:

> "Wherefore, the mother and receptacle of all created and visible and in any way sensible things, is not to be termed earth, or air, or fire, or water, or any of their compounds, or any of the elements from which these are derived, but is an invisible and formless being which receives all things and in some mysterious way partakes of the intelligible, and is most incomprehensible." (p. 307)

Both matter and *chora* are, paradoxically, 'formless' (void) and feminine.

In *Speculum* and in *An Ethics of Sexual Difference* Irigaray discovers a similar gendering of spirit and matter, mind and body in the philosophy of, among others, Aristotle, Descartes, Kant, Hegel, Merleau-Ponty and Levinas. In *An Ethics of Sexual Difference* she also offers a critique of Christian theology in which, she argues, 'the gender of God, the guardian of every subject and every discourse, is always *masculine and paternal*'.[26] In a move which echoes uncannily Plato's identification of the feminine with a 'facilitating' *chora*, Christianity postulates 'a God-father who engenders a God-son by means of a virgin-mother', the maternal function serving only 'to mediate the generation of the son' (p. 68). Body and soul, sexuality and spirituality are dissociated, and only the male mind has access to God, in a 'transcendental realm where all ties to the world of sensation have been severed' (p. 15).

Irigaray's work allows us to define the problem that the educated woman faces. She is offered access to a philosophical and cultural tradition that defines her as an anomaly, even a monstrosity, in that she identifies with transcendent male reason yet is confined within the immanence of the fleshy female body. Irigaray's work also, however, offers an answer to the problem, an answer which has been overlooked by Anglo-American feminists, with the notable exception of Christine Battersby. In *The Phenomenal Woman*, Battersby distances herself from the Lacanian undertow in Irigaray's work, in other words, from her apparent endorsement of the Lacanian view that 'woman' does not exist within the symbolic order, that she is unrepresentable within it. As Battersby argues, 'it is a mistake to interpret the 'feminine imaginary' (and female identity) as something which has not existed in patriarchal modernity' (p. 119). However, as Battersby also sees, the paradox in Irigaray's work is that while she continually displaces the realization of feminine identity onto the future, she also, via her critique of her philosophical 'masters', begins to map out more innovative possibilities for thinking identity otherwise, particularly in relation to what Battersby calls 'that sticky boundary between self and other' (p. 36). Irigaray shows us that subjectivity in the West has been identified with masculinity, singularity, and a project of transcendence. By implication (especially in view of the reproductive capacities of the female body), feminine subjectivity can be conceptualized in terms of multiplicity/division and an acceptance of immanence and corporeality. Such a conceptualization might offer a more productive model for thinking about *all* (inter) subjectivities, as Irigaray suggests in a critique of the ethics of Emmanuel Levinas:

> For Levinas, the distance is always maintained with the other in the experience of love. The other is 'close' to him in 'duality'. This autistic, egological, solitary love does not correspond to the shared outpouring, to the loss of boundaries which takes place for both lovers when they cross the boundary of the skin into the mucous membranes of the body . . . abandoning the relatively dry and precise outlines of each body's solid exterior to enter a fluid universe where the perception of being two persons (*de la dualité*) becomes indistinct . . .[27]

'Mucosity' is an important metaphor: like Battersby's image of the 'sticky boundary' it points to a subjectivity which does not fear contact with or invasion by the other.

I want to suggest that the women writers discussed in this book are engaged in a project which is analogous to that of Irigaray, that is, they are engaged in a revaluation of the feminine, of that which has been derogated in patriarchal culture. To propose this is to invite the time-honoured charge of essentialism, that is, of assuming a female sameness or 'essence' based on biology or shared experience. I want to counter this charge by invoking the model of a 'non-essential essence' developed by Battersby in order to support her argument for a feminist metaphysics.[28] Like Battersby, I would take issue with the idea that all metaphysics is necessarily complicit with patriarchy, just as I would take issue with the idea that the feminine cannot/has not been written in our culture. Both positions depend on a semi-mystical and indeed essentialist view of 'the feminine'. Against such positions, I would support Battersby's Bergsonian notion of a 'feminine essence'. Tracing the history of the concept of essence back to Aristotle and his idea of 'species-forms', Battersby points out that there is no need to accept the Aristotelian definition of essence, as so many feminists have done. Many philosophers, including Wittgenstein and Derrida, have understood essence differently, but it is Bergson's account which Battersby finds most helpful. She quotes the following passage from *Creative Evolution*:

> What is real is the continual *change of* form: *form is only a snapshot view of a transition* . . . When the successive images do not differ from each other too much, we consider them all as the waxing and waning of a single *mean* image, or as the deformation of this image in different directions. And to this mean we really allude when we speak of the *essence* of a thing, or of the thing itself. (pp. 33–4)

'Essence' in this formulation is a rule or norm that can itself fluctuate under the pressure of historical change.

I would also agree with Battersby in her identification of the problematic of embodiment as a key feature of female lives. As she suggests, the fluidity of female lives and female experience does not mean that a series of Bergsonian 'snapshots' cannot emerge that will provide the notion of a (shifting) essence that in western modernity has only been established by 'the positioning of the female relationship to her body as "abnormal" and as an inappropriate starting point for thinking self and personhood' (p. 36). As she also writes:

> the (white) male body is frequently represented as a thing that is capable of being transcended – or as ennobled by forms of agency ('manliness') in which full humanity is expressed. Women's flesh is, by contrast, monstrous – with a materiality which is more fully immanent, and yet with the capacity to birth new selves from within the embodied self. (p. 19)

It is my contention that the problematic of female embodiment is at the very heart of the fiction discussed in this book. Like Irigaray, the women writers considered here are engaged in a double manoeuvre. On the one hand, they must resist the symbolic distribution of functions whereby the mind and spirit are ascribed to man while woman is identified with the body (and matter, and death). They must claim their right to intellectual and spiritual identity. However, they must also 'defend' that which has been identified with the feminine, if they are not simply to replicate a masculine subject position. Characteristically, then, they interrogate the identification of the intellect solely with the masculine, but also explore the positive aspects of a (female) subject position closely tied to embodiment. For example, Rosamond Lehmann explores the connections between the experience of female embodiment and an acceptance of death as, in Irigaray's phrase, 'the other face of life'; Margaret Drabble explores the possibility of a different ethics, which I have called an 'ethics of labour', based on an understanding of bodily interconnectedness at different stages of life.

If female embodiment is a central issue for these writers, how does one define embodiment, or indeed the body? This has been one of the most hotly contested areas of recent feminist debate, particularly after the publication of Judith Butler's *Gender Trouble* (1990) and *Bodies that Matter* (1993). Butler's critique of the feminist distinction between sex and gender, her suggestion that sex may have been 'always already gender', and her enormously influential concept of 'gender as performance' have fostered a widespread understanding of the body as discursively constructed and thereby open to (voluntary) resignification and change. It could be argued that such an understanding rests on a misinterpretation of Butler's work. I will return to the significance of her intervention, but want first to sketch something of the history of feminist thinking about the body, taking Elizabeth Grosz's helpful account in *Volatile Bodies* as a point of departure.[29] As Grosz suggests, there are three broad positions which feminists have taken in theorizing (or retheorizing) the body. The first category is that of egalitarian feminism and includes figures such as Mary Wollstonecraft and Simone de Beauvoir. Thinkers in this tradition regard the specificities of the female body (its capacities for menstruation, pregnancy, lactation and so on) as limiting women's access to the rights that patriarchal culture accords to men. The female body from this perspective is a hindrance to be overcome, and motherhood in particular is viewed with suspicion as something inherently in conflict with a public or civic role for women. The aim of such feminism is to eliminate, as far as possible, the specific effects of women's biology: thus, as Grosz puts it, 'biology itself requires modification and transformation' if women are to become the equals of men (p. 16).

The second category is that of social constructionism, which includes Marxist feminists such as Michèle Barrett and psychoanalytic feminists such as Julia Kristeva. This group is less interested in the body than in the social construction of subjectivity. The focus is on changing beliefs and attitudes and on attaching new cultural meanings to biological differences. Psychoanalysis, in particular, is mobilized in order to explore the social construction of gender. The body is considered to be naturalistic and pre-cultural, in a base/superstructure model in which, Grosz writes, 'biology provides a self-contained "natural" base and ideology provides a dependent parasitic "second story"' (p. 17). For constructionists – and this is crucial for Judith Butler's critique – the sex/gender opposition, which is a recasting of the distinction between the body and mind, is still operative. The body is given meanings, but the meanings can be distinguished from a material base which remains, on some level, uncontaminated by them.

The third category Grosz considers under the rubric of 'sexual difference'. The theorists in this category include Luce Irigaray, Hélène Cixous, Moira Gatens, Judith Butler and indeed Grosz herself. For these thinkers, the body is no longer understood as a biologically given or pre-cultural entity. They are concerned with the *lived* body, and for them 'the body is neither brute nor passive but is interwoven with and constitutive of systems of meaning, signification, and representation' (p. 18). It is, paradoxically, a 'production of nature'. The body is not conceived of as a blank screen onto which cultural meanings are projected: it is viewed instead as 'always already' bound up with systems of cultural production. Thus, for these theorists, the sex/gender distinction is called into question. Access to a 'pure', pre-cultural, pre-linguistic body is an impossibility, as is access to the 'neutral' body presupposed by some medical discourses. The body is a social and discursive object, which is precisely why it is a site of struggle.

The sex/gender distinction brings us back to Butler and her contribution to thinking about the body. The passage which has given rise to so much 'trouble' in feminist circles is this, from the 'Preface' to *Gender Trouble*:

As a strategy to denaturalize and resignify bodily categories, I describe and propose a set of parodic practices based in a performative theory of gender acts that disrupt the categories of the body, sex, gender, and sexuality and occasion their subversive resignification and proliferation beyond the binary frame.[30]

This passage does seem to presuppose an inert (and largely irrelevant) material body which can be assigned new meanings and identities very much as the social constructionists suggest: an unreconstructed sex/gender division seems to underpin it. However, in the chapter to which Butler looks forward in this passage, she is at pains to argue *against* a Cartesian dualism which would, as in the thought of Sartre and Beauvoir, figure the body 'as a mute facticity, anticipating some meaning that can be attributed only by a transcendent consciousness' (p. 129). In *Bodies that Matter*, mindful of the dangers of misinterpretation, she is more explicit about her understanding of the relationship between mind and body. In a helpful passage which looks back to the question of the 'discursively constructed' body she writes:

To claim that discourse is formative is not to claim that it originates, causes, or exhaustively composes that which it concedes; rather, it is to claim that there is no reference to a pure body which is not at the same time a further formation of that body... In philosophical terms, the constative claim is always to some degree performative.[31]

In other words, while there may be a material body which exists 'outside' or 'before' language, we can never have access to it. And to name such 'a' body is always to shape it, to map it in the context of a pre-existing (though always changing) linguistic and cultural system.

Elizabeth Grosz takes a similar line, arguing in *Volatile Bodies* that:

The body must be regarded as a site of social, political, cultural, and geographical inscriptions, production, or constitution. The body is not opposed to culture, a resistant throwback to a natural past; it is itself a cultural, *the* cultural, product. The very question of the ontological status of biology, the openness of organic processes to cultural intervention, transformation, or even production, must be explored. (p. 23)

However, she also emphasizes the interplay between bodies and minds, acknowledging the ways in which the body, in its changes (many of which may have nothing to do with sexual difference, but which might involve illness, for example), challenges and extends our understanding of the world, constantly forcing new inscriptions. As she puts it, bodies 'are not inert; they function interactively and productively. They act and react. They generate what is new, surprising, unpredictable' (p. xi).

Grosz also explores the specificity of female embodiment, understood precisely in terms of inscription. For example, she points out the widely divergent ways in which male and female bodily fluids are coded in Western culture. Seminal fluid, for example, is either elided or solidified:

> Seminal fluid is understood primarily as what it makes, what it achieves, a causal agent and thus a thing, a solid: its fluidity, its potential seepage, the element in it that is uncontrollable, its spread, its formlessness, is perpetually displaced in discourse onto its properties, its capacity to fertilize, to father, to produce an object. (p. 199)

By excluding their own body fluids from representation, men are able to establish their bodies as clean and proper. They distance themselves from an unwanted aspect of corporeality which is then projected onto women. Grosz suggests that the female body is thus constructed 'as a leaking, uncontrollable, seeping liquid; as formless flow; as viscosity, entrapping, secreting'. She continues:

> My claim is not that women have been somehow desolidified but the more limited one which sees that women, insofar as they are human, have the same degree of solidity, occupy the same genus, as men, yet insofar as they are women, they are represented and live themselves as seepage, liquidity. (p. 203)

Invoking Irigaray, Grosz suggests that such representations can, however, be challenged and overturned. A 'mechanics of solids' which works in complicity with Cartesian dualism and the metaphysics of realism and self-identity can be complicated and 'befuddled' by an Irigarayan 'metaphorics of fluids'. The way in which female embodiment has been culturally produced (not the 'fact' of female embodiment) can be turned from something negative into something

positive, generating a new way of looking at subjectivity and corporeality. Such a perspective would problematize, in particular, the
automatic assumption of a clear-cut separation between subject and
object.

Christine Battersby similarly focuses on the specificities of female
embodiment. Her philosophical project in *The Phenomenal Woman*
is to ask 'what happens if we model personal and individual identity in terms of the female', what happens if we take seriously 'the
notion that a "person" could normally, at least always potentially,
become two'. She asks:

> What would happen if we thought identity in terms that did
> not make it always spatially and temporally oppositional to other
> entities? Could we retain a notion of self-identity if we did not
> privilege that which is self-contained and self-directed? (p. 2)

Such an emphasis on the cultural significance of the body that can
give birth risks (again) the charge of essentialism. However, I would
suggest that Battersby is isolating one acute example (pregnancy as
it is produced and experienced in the West) in order to make points
about subjectivity/identity which are as relevant to men as to women.
As she points out, '[w]e carry on idealizing autonomous "individuals"
who have equal rights and duties, and look away from the fact
that "persons" only become such by first moving out of a state of
foetal and childhood dependency on others' (p. 3). Dependency,
interdependency, the splitting of the subject: these are aspects of
experience which affect us not only through pregnancy, but also as
a result of, for example, external trauma and injury, and through
illness. Like Grosz, Battersby argues that such experiences can give
rise to new perspectives on identity and subjectivity. And like Grosz,
she mobilizes an Irigarayan 'metaphorics of fluids' to underpin her
argument, thus subverting and troubling Cartesian metaphysics. She
argues that:

> Recognizing natality – the *conceptual* link between the paradigm
> 'woman' and the body that births – does not imply that all women
> either can or 'should' give birth. Instead, an emphasis on natal-
> ity as an abstract category of embodied (female) selves means
> that we need to rethink identity. The 'self' is not a fixed, permanent
> or pre-given 'thing' or 'substance' that undergoes metamorpho-
> sis, but that nevertheless remains always unaltered through change.

Instead, we need to think of identity as emerging out of a play of relationships and force-fields that together constitute the horizons of a (shared) space-time. We need a metaphysics of fluidity and mobile relationships; not a metaphysics of fixity, or even of flexibility. (p. 7)

It is in the context of such feminist thought that the problematic of female embodiment is explored in this study. The most constant point of reference throughout is the work of Luce Irigaray, especially in *Speculum* and *An Ethics of Sexual Difference*, but I have also drawn on other thinkers, not all of whose work is by any means compatible with that of Irigaray (Deleuze and Guattari spring instantly to mind). I have, in other words, adopted a 'perspectival' approach, in order to draw out the specificities, the particular emphases and interests, of the writers considered. So in the first chapter, the fiction of Rosamond Lehmann is discussed partly in relation to Irigaray but also in relation to Simone de Beauvoir's analysis of 'The Woman in Love' in *The Second Sex*. Lehmann was one of Beauvoir's favourite writers, and it is tempting to suggest that Beauvoir's analysis of 'love as religion' owes something to her reading of Lehmann. In this chapter, it is argued that Lehmann affirms her female characters' need for romantic love while at the same time disclosing the limitations, and indeed the inauthenticity, of love as they understand it. Lehmann's heroines seek transcendence by proxy: they seek to be redeemed from their own immanence (what Beauvoir would call 'facticity'), by the love of a man who is viewed as a godlike, superior being. It is only in Lehmann's last novel, *A Sea-Grape Tree*, that she presents a love in which both woman and man understand themselves in relation to both the sensible and the transcendental (what Irigaray would call the 'sensible transcendental').

In Chapter 2, the fiction of Elizabeth Bowen is read in relation to the work of Deleuze and Guattari, and especially in relation to their controversial concept of 'becoming woman'. Many feminist theorists have viewed Deleuze and Guattari's project with concern, suspecting that their interest in intensities, flows and becomings rather than in subjectivities or identities may be unhelpful for feminism. In a version of the standard feminist question to (male) post-structuralists, Rosi Braidotti thus asks:

Can feminists, at this point in their history of collective struggles aimed at redefining female subjectivity, actually afford to let go of their sex-specific forms of political agency? Is the bypassing of gender in favour of a dispersed polysexuality not a very masculine move?[32]

Deleuze and Guattari certainly see 'becoming woman' as a stage on the way to something else, i.e., 'becoming imperceptible', and argue for the rejection of 'molar femininity' in favour of a molecular formation open to new and unexpected (bodily) connections. In this sense, their work does 'bypass' the feminine. Nonetheless, it is argued in this chapter that their understanding of the body as excessive to hierarchical control and in tension with the reproduction of social identities is uncannily close to the understanding of the body expressed in Bowen's discreetly subversive fiction.

In Chapter 3, Elizabeth Taylor's critique of 'the classical tradition' is explored. Taking Irigaray's argument in *Speculum* (particularly in 'Plato's Hystera') as a starting point, it is argued that Taylor's allusive fiction engages with the Western philosophical tradition in order to subvert it. While Platonic philosophy disavows both the material conditions of being and the female body which stands in for this materiality, Taylor continually writes the female body – and particularly the maternal body – back into cultural history. Her work is particularly unusual in its focus on the pregnant body, which is widely seen as an excess within and a threat to culture. The work of Julia Kristeva is invoked in order to shed light on this aspect of Taylor's fiction: in Kristeva's terms, pregnancy is a threat because 'the heterogeneity that cannot be subsumed in the signifier nevertheless explodes violently with pregnancy'.[33] It is also suggested that in her allusions to both popular cultural texts (*Brief Encounter*) and high cultural texts (*The Waves*), Taylor foregrounds the hybridity of her own art and opens up the whole question of what 'art' should be.

In Chapter 4, the fiction of Margaret Drabble is discussed in relation to the philosophy of Hannah Arendt. Seyla Benhabib, in *The Reluctant Modernism of Hannah Arendt*, has shown just how productive a reading of Arendt 'against the grain' can be. In this chapter, Arendt is cast as a reluctant feminist, whose analysis of the different spheres of human activity can be enormously helpful in thinking through the implications of woman's (culturally constructed) role. It is argued here that the central issue in Drabble's fiction is that of the relationship between the private and the public spheres, between, in Arendt's terms, the spheres of labour and those of work and action.

From their confinement in the sphere of labour, Drabble's female protagonists develop an understanding that humans do not enter the world as free and equal beings, but develop in and through relationships of inequality and dependency. In this space, her heroines develop an 'ethics of labour' founded on an understanding and experience of mutual and shifting relationships of dependency. In the (usually male) spheres of work and action, by contrast, it is assumed that human beings are free and equal, unconstrained by obligations to children, the sick, the dispossessed. Drabble's fiction works away at this contrast/contradiction, exploring the ways in which an ethics of labour might be brought into the public and political world.

In Chapter 5, A. S. Byatt's engagement with literary tradition and with post-structuralist theory is considered. It is argued that her fiction is structured around two interlocking 'fall' myths, the first being the biblical myth of the Fall, expressed most resonantly for Byatt in *Paradise Lost* and *Paradise Regained*. Byatt engages critically with this myth, with its emphasis on death and resurrection, invoking alternative myths, particularly the story of Ceres and Proserpine, in order to read the 'fall' into sexuality and death in more positive and generative terms. The second 'fall' is the fall into language, which Byatt links with Foucault's discussion of the fusion between word and thing in the Renaissance period and with T. S. Eliot's account of the 'dissociation of sensibility'. For Byatt, just as there never was a space of innocence before the biblical Fall, so there never was an Edenic fusion between words and things. Nonetheless, her characters are haunted by dreams of wholeness and completion, of 'breaking through' into a state in which mind and body, word and thing, would be one. Needless to say, the attainment of such a state is extremely difficult for the 'intellectual woman' who is at the centre of her fiction.

Finally, in Chapter 6, Anita Brookner's particular perspective on the mind–body problem is explored. Brookner's protagonists are, typically, academic women who are torn between their investment in intellectual life and their investment in an ideal of romantic love. Brookner's fiction emphasizes the ways in which 'structures of feeling' which developed in earlier periods still remain closely woven into our culture and continue to structure our imaginative lives. In the case of the ideal of romantic love, this is, in Brookner's view, no bad thing. The ideal of romantic love involves a relationship in which each partner loves the other 'without strategy', in

Brookner's phrase, without any intention of use or exploitation. In this sense, 'real love is a pilgrimage',[34] defended *as an ideal* by all her heroines. The work of Ernst Bloch is drawn on in order to highlight the idealist and utopian elements of Brookner's fiction, while the theory of Melanie Klein, Melitta Schmideberg and Julia Kristeva sheds light on its more sombre aspects, in particular the treatment of female eating disorders.

These women's novels subject the experience of their female protagonists to intense and critical scrutiny. The question of whether or not they are therefore feminist novels remains an open one. None of the writers considered here, with the exception of Margaret Drabble, has explicitly identified with the feminist movement. Rosamond Lehmann seems to have been largely indifferent to it, taking her nineteenth-century precursors as role models and 'assuming (or half-assuming), with Mrs Gaskell, that "a woman's principal work in life is hardly left to her own choice; nor can she drop the domestic charges devolving on her as an individual, for the exercise of the most splendid talents that were ever bestowed"'.[35] Elizabeth Bowen identified with femininity rather than with feminism. As Victoria Glendinning writes, 'She was no feminist in the usual sense . . . She did not think women ought to be rated highly only in so far as they did things that men traditionally did.'[36] Elizabeth Taylor, a rationalist and lifelong Labour voter, hints at feminist sympathies. In the only article by her reprinted by Virago she writes, for example, that 'Of present-day writers my favourites are I. Compton-Burnett (one of the greatest writers in our history), Elizabeth Bowen, Colette, Eudora Welty. I am sure there are many men whose books I have enjoyed, but their names do not seem to come readily to mind'.[37] Margaret Drabble identifies wholeheartedly with feminism: for her 'feminism is a new light'.[38] A. S. Byatt is more equivocal, not wanting to be a 'spokeswoman': she feels that women writers 'don't want to have to be believers and to have to make other people believe'.[39] Anita Brookner distances herself more sharply from feminism, which she sees as combative and partial. She thus criticizes Germaine Greer's *Sex and Destiny* for its 'selective moral blindness'.[40]

These ambivalent responses to feminism suggest that we might turn Rosalind Coward's question round and ask, not whether women's novels are feminist novels, but whether feminism has attended sufficiently to the values expressed in women's novels. As I have tried to show, one of the most crucial elements that links the writers considered in this study is their revaluation of aspects of experience which have traditionally been linked with femininity. In this sense, I would argue that their novels *are* feminist novels. At stake, of course, is the definition of feminism. As we move into a new millennium, will feminism incorporate those perspectives which may have developed out of a female subject position, but which theorists such as Irigaray, Grosz and Battersby see as crucial for the reconfiguration of *all* identities?

1
Rosamond Lehmann and the Woman in Love

Rosamond Lehmann's first novel, *Dusty Answer* (1927) has claims to be one of the earliest examples of a genre, the woman's university novel. It documents a rite of passage, following the heroine Judith Earle's life at Cambridge, which has many parallels with Lehmann's own experiences at Girton in the 1920s. The book was a *succès de scandale*, attracting a good deal of criticism because of its open treatment of sexuality. As Lehmann herself commented, 'it was discussed, and even reviewed, in certain quarters as the outpourings of a sex-maniac'.[1] It also has an interesting intertextual relationship with the most famous discussion of higher education for women in the 1920s, Virginia Woolf's *A Room of One's Own* (1929). Lehmann's vivid evocation of the impact of college life on her heroine ('ugly and noisy and crude and smelly') seems to anticipate, and may well have influenced, Woolf's description in *A Room of One's Own* of the rigours of life at 'Fernham', complete with prunes and custard for dinner.[2] Woolf's diary records in more detail her impressions when she first visited Girton to give a talk on women and fiction. She wrote of the students as 'starved but valiant young women... Intelligent, eager, poor; & destined to become schoolmistresses in shoals'.[3] For both Lehmann and Woolf, the students' intelligence is inseparable from their poverty and plainness. By contrast, Woolf herself seemed to the students who heard her speak the embodiment of wealth and beauty as well as intelligence. Katherine Raine, for example, wrote that '[w]ith Virginia Woolf had come her friend Victoria Sackville-West: the two most beautiful women I had ever seen. I saw their beauty and their fame entirely removed from the context of what is usually called "real" life, as if they had descended like goddesses from Olympus'.[4]

It is interesting to see both Lehmann and Woolf associating higher education for women with poverty and plainness, a point to which I will return, for it is central to the unfolding dialectic of Lehmann's novel. *Dusty Answer* is concerned with Judith Earle's education – intellectual and sentimental. The novel is divided into five parts, and opens with a flashback which shows Judith's childhood. She is an isolated figure: an only child from a privileged background, educated at home. Her imagination is caught by the family of cousins who spend their holidays in their grandmother's house next door. The Fyfes seem to Judith magical creatures – 'beautiful and mysterious', 'mysterious and thrilling', their London background giving them a sophistication and glamour which Judith lacks. After a gap of some years, when Judith is eighteen, the Fyfes return to the house next door. Charlie, the favourite, has been killed in the First World War, but Judith takes up the threads of her relationships with the other three boys. The central part of the novel is concerned with Judith's years at Cambridge, and in particular with her passionate involvement with another undergraduate, Jennifer Baird. This is succeeded by more or less disastrous relationships with each of the Fyfe brothers. The novel concludes with Judith's recognition that a cycle of development is now complete: she must move on, though 'not quite yet'.[5]

One of the most significant features of *Dusty Answer* is the tension between Judith's intellectual and her emotional life, or perhaps more accurately the tension between her intellect and her femininity. In this respect, Judith is like the 'educated woman' described by Hilary Radner,[6] placed at a point of intersection between two contradictory worlds because she chooses to define herself by her intellect while maintaining her position as feminine. To do this is to attempt to reconcile positions which the whole system of Western culture tries to keep apart. Despite its alleged lack of attention to social and cultural issues, it is French feminism which has provided the fullest account of the workings of culture in this respect. Hélène Cixous's account of the binary oppositions which structure cultural life makes it clear that in Western culture it is always the father, or the masculine principle, which is associated with intellectual life: the list of binary oppositions in *The Newly Born Woman* (1975, tr. 1986) famously includes the pairs 'Father/Mother; Head/Emotions; Intelligible/Sensible; Logos/Pathos'.[7] Luce Irigaray, too, has argued that the whole system of Western thought rests on the identification of reason with the masculine principle. Her analysis

of phallocentricity shows how a unitary notion of masculine identity is inextricably intertwined with unitary notions of truth. The
feminine is the 'dumping ground' for all that is excluded from such
concepts of identity and truth.

In such a cultural system, it is no wonder that the 'intellectual
woman' should figure as a problem, or as an impossibility, and this
is an issue which is central throughout Lehmann's fiction. In *Dusty
Answer*, Judith is a clever girl from a cultivated home, whose education is taken extremely seriously by her parents. However, it is
made clear that she is also attractive, even beautiful: in a series of
set pieces, Judith is watched admiringly by the Fyfe boys as she
skates, swims and dances, embodying feminine grace and desir-
ability. These two aspects of Judith – her intellect and her femininity
– are echoed in the characters of Mabel and Jennifer, whom she
meets at Cambridge. Mabel is a rather unkindly drawn scholarship
girl, one of those who has 'got to depend on their brains for a
livelihood' (p. 114), that is, one of those whom Woolf described as
'destined to become schoolmistresses in shoals', see above. Her most
striking features are her earnestness and her physical repulsiveness.
When Judith first meets her she is repelled by her eyes beaming
and glinting behind thick glasses, and by her greasy skin and lank
hair. She fails her final examinations, and so it becomes apparent
that she may not really be very clever, but she functions in the
text as an awful warning of what can happen to a woman if she
concentrates on the life of the mind and neglects the life of the
(feminine) body. By contrast, Jennifer represents a very physical
femininity, which attracts Judith from the moment when she first
catches sight of her:

> There was a light there, flashing about: the tail of her eye had
> already caught it several times. She looked more closely. It was
> somebody's fair head, so fiercely alive that it seemed delicately
> to light the air around it: a vivacious, emphatic head, turning
> and nodding; below it a white neck and shoulder, generously
> modelled, leaned across the table. Then the face came round
> suddenly, all curves, the wide mouth laughing, warm-coloured . . .
> It made you think of warm fruit, – peaches and nectarines mel-
> lowed in the sun. (p. 110)

Just as Mabel pursues Judith, Judith pursues Jennifer, in a passionate friendship which suggests the indeterminacy and fluidity of gender

boundaries and identifications. Jennifer's femininity is stressed: she represents a kind of ideal femininity, associated with colour, warmth, and fruitfulness. Although she is a brilliant student, she pays little attention to her work, being in this the exact obverse of Mabel. Eventually she has to leave college, having fallen in love with Geraldine Manners, a woman whose sexual orientation is clearly signalled by her short hair and 'heavy and masculine' jaw. Mabel and Jennifer, then, represent two undesirable extremes (for a woman) of devotion to the mind and devotion to the body. At the time when she leaves Cambridge, Judith seems to have walked the fine line between the two extremes. She is successful academically, aquitting herself with distinction in the tripos, but retains all her feminine charms – her mother, dispassionately observing her on her return from Cambridge, calls her a 'lovely young creature' (p. 193). Yet in Part Four of the novel, it becomes clear that Judith does not really value her academic success: as she puts it, '[o]ne doesn't much value that sort of success' (p. 205). Rather than using it as a springboard for self-development, she repudiates her intellectual achievements, and seeks fulfilment instead through love.

Judith commits herself wholeheartedly to the romance plot which, Judy Simons has argued, is essential to Lehmann's fiction.[8] In virtually all her novels, Lehmann uses the mechanisms of traditional romance in order to offer a critique of a patriarchal social order. Her heroines characteristically attain some degree of self-understanding through the experience of a love affair, but at the same time are deeply undermined by it. Because of its implication in the existing structures of patriarchal power, romance can only limit their real freedom. Simone de Beauvoir has written illuminatingly on this aspect of romance, and it is intriguing to speculate on her debt to Lehmann in this respect. In her study of Beauvoir, Toril Moi notes her 'lifelong admiration' for Lehmann's work.[9] *Dusty Answer* (translated into French as *Poussière*) remained one of Beauvoir's favourite books, and there are several references to Lehmann's fiction in *The Second Sex*.

Lehmann's novels seem to disclose exactly the structures described by Beauvoir in the section of *The Second Sex* entitled 'The Woman in Love'. In a key passage, Beauvoir distinguishes between the male drive to transcendence and the 'inauthenticity' of the woman who can only seek transcendence *through him*:

The individual who is a subject, who is himself, if he has the courageous inclination towards transcendence, endeavours to extend his grasp on the world: he is ambitious, he acts. But an inessential creature is incapable of sensing the absolute at the heart of her subjectivity; a being doomed to immanence cannot find self-realization in acts. Shut up in the sphere of the relative, destined to the male from childhood, habituated to seeing in him a superb being whom she cannot possibly equal, the woman who has not repressed her claim to humanity will dream of *transcending her being towards one of these superior beings*, of amalgamating herself with the sovereign subject. There is no other way out for her than to lose herself, body and soul, in him who is represented to her as the absolute, as the essential.[10]

Drawing on existentialist ideas, Beauvoir describes a world in which *only* the masculine can be identified with freedom and transcendence. Anticipating the arguments of Irigaray (mentioned above), she exposes a symbolic universe which is structured according to the 'law of the self-same', in which the alterity of women is denied, leaving them in a state of '*déréliction*' (absence of God, of grace).

For Beauvoir, 'an authentic love' must be based on a human interrelation between two beings who each have economic independence and each move towards ends of their own, transcending themselves towards the social whole. Such a love is possible only in theory, for the social and economic structure prevents women from existing *pour-soi*. 'Most often woman knows herself only as different, relative; her *pour-autrui*, relation to others, is confused with her very being' (p. 678). This is exactly the situation in which Judith Earle finds herself in *Dusty Answer*. From childhood, she has idealized and romanticized one of the Fyfe brothers, Roddy, an enigmatic and silent figure, who is seen by her as godlike, transcendent. In a key childhood moment, he comes to stand for the possibility of transcendence, merging with the beauty and mystery of the natural world – 'he seemed mingled with the whole mysterious goldenness of the evening, to be part of it' (pp. 26–7). When Judith meets him again after coming down from Cambridge, he is presented again as god-like – '[i]n the moonlight she worshipped his dark head and moon-blanched features' (p. 221). She declares her love for him in terms which recall, again, Beauvoir's account of the pathology of romantic love. Just as Beauvoir writes of the woman in love that she 'chooses to desire her enslavement so ardently that it will seem to her the expression of her liberty', so Judith tells Roddy that '[t]he more my love for you annihilates me, the more it becomes a source of inexhaustible power' (p. 224).

The sub-text of all Lehmann's fiction is that this kind of love must come to grief precisely because, for the woman, it is based on misrecognition of the other and on an inadequate sense of self. The structure of romance is thus *inherently* flawed: there is no possibility of there ever being a happy ending. In a sense, Lehmann's fiction shows that 'the woman in love' will always want too much, her exorbitant desire being a measure of her sense of lack or inauthenticity. In *Dusty Answer*, none of the three Fyfe brothers can give Judith what she needs. As Simons has pointed out, the three men correspond to three archetypal heroes from the world of romantic fiction – Roddy the 'rhapsodic' lover, Martin the 'boy next door', Julian the 'glamorous but dangerous seducer'.[11] Only Roddy, the most distant and opaque of the three, can function as Judith's object of desire, but Lehmann emphasizes the way in which *his* desires are directed away from Judith and back to the world of men. For Roddy is bisexual, and at the end of the novel Judith bleakly realizes that she has lost him to the Cambridge world of male bonding which effectively excludes women, despite their notional presence in the university:

> Farewell to Cambridge, to whom she was less than nothing. She had been deluded into imagining that it bore her some affection. Under its politeness, it had disliked and distrusted her and all other females; and now it ignored her. It took its mists about it, folding within them Roddy and Tony and all the other young men; and let her go. (p. 302)

At the end of *Dusty Answer* Judith is left alone. She tells herself that she is cured of her weakness, of 'the futile obsession of dependence on other people'. However, Lehmann's text offers no alternative way forward, no other path through life, and the concluding imagery suggests that, one cycle of dependency having been completed for Judith, another will begin.

A rather similar pattern emerges in *The Weather in the Streets* (1936), which chronicles the love affair between Olivia Curtis (the central character of the earlier novel *Invitation to the Waltz*, 1932) and Rollo Spencer. Like Judith Earle, Olivia is an intelligent and well-educated woman, who has passed her Oxford exams 'with flying colours'.[12] Olivia, however, does not use her talents by pursuing a career, but works part-time as an assistant to a friend who is a photographer. When the novel opens, she is twenty-seven years old, has a failed marriage behind her, and lives rather aimlessly, existing on the fringes of the artistic, Bohemian world. Returning to her family home to visit her sick father, she meets Rollo Spencer, the son of the Curtis's aristocratic neighbours, and falls under his spell just as she did as a seventeen year-old in *Invitation to the Waltz*. Rollo is now married, but this does not prevent him from starting an affair with Olivia. The couple meet in secret in London, and have occasional weekends together, and the affair reaches its high point when they have a holiday together in Austria. Olivia then realizes that she is pregnant, and undergoes an abortion, not knowing that Rollo's wife is also now expecting a child. She finally decides to end the affair, but her resolve is weakened as soon as she sees Rollo again. The novel ends uncertainly: we are not sure whether or not Olivia will yield once more to Rollo's charm and 'soft persistence' (p. 352).

Like Roddy in *Dusty Answer*, Rollo belongs to a family that seems the epitome of all that is glamorous and desirable. Olivia and her sister felt 'romantic' about the whole family when they were younger, but it was Rollo who was 'fairly drenched in glamour' (p.14). Rollo, in short, is another godlike figure. A kiss from him is compared to a visitation from the Holy Ghost (p. 123), and Olivia dedicates herself to loving him as she would dedicate herself to a religion. She describes the love affair as existing on a different plane from ordinary life. As it is presented to us, especially through the first-person narrative of Part 2, it seems to take place in a different world, a sealed, magic space of warm interiors and soft colours. Olivia describes herself as enclosed in a 'glass casing' (p. 134). When the external world does break in, as landscape for example, it takes Olivia to a pitch of feeling and intensity which she has not experienced since childhood:

> One night we drove late, up in the mountains. No moon, but starlight made a muffled incandescence ... When I was a child, I had more sense of infinity, the universe, than I have now. I'd stare at the stars till gradually they began to be worlds to me, spinning immense in space, and under the awe and terror of them I'd sink away, dissolve. Now I don't generally bother to look at them, and when I do they remain points of light in the sky ... But that night the feeling came back. 'Look, *look* at the stars!' They hung enormous over peak and valley. (p. 206)

This moment of transcendence has both positive and negative implications: Olivia feels at one with the universe, but also experiences
a feeling of terror as she dissolves and sinks away.

This moment occurs when Olivia is on holiday with Rollo, involved in a romantic idyll which is then destroyed or cut into by
the facts of female bodily life (when Rollo learns that his wife is
pregnant, and Olivia suspects her own pregnancy). Olivia returns
to London and its dusty summer streets, and at this point Lehmann
extends and explores the metaphor of the 'weather in the streets'
which gives the book its title. The image first appears at the beginning of Part 2 of the novel, as Olivia comments on the discrepancy
between her life inside 'the glass casing' of her love affair and life
outside:

> Beyond the glass casing I was in, was the weather, were the win-
> ter streets in rain, wind, fog, in the fine frosty days and nights,
> the mild, damp grey ones. Pictures of London winter the other
> side of the glass – not reaching the body; no wet ankles, muddy
> stockings, blown hair, cold-aching cheeks, fog-smarting eyes, throat,
> nose . . . not my usual bus-taking London winter. (p. 134)

The description of the impact of the winter weather on the unprotected body powerfully suggests the force and pressure of contingency
and immanency. Rather similarly Olivia's return to the London streets
in Part 3 of the novel functions as an extended metaphor for the
shift in the balance of her concerns from the 'transcendence' of
the love affair to the 'immanence' of pregnancy and sickness. I am
using the term 'immanence' here in the sense in which it is used
by Simone de Beauvoir in *The Second Sex*, as when she writes that
'[e]very time transcendence falls back into immanence, there is a
degradation of existence into the "in-itself," of freedom into facticity.
This downfall is a moral fault if the subject consents to it; if it is
inflicted upon him, it takes the form of frustration and oppression'
(p. 29). In this section of the novel, Lehmann combines description of Olivia's nausea (caused by 'morning' sickness which goes
on all day) with description of the dirt and squalor of the city
streets:

> To be alone, sick, in London in this dry, sterile, burnt-out end of
> summer, was to be abandoned in a pestilence-stricken town; was
> to live in a third-class waiting-room at a disused terminus among

stains and smells, odds and ends of refuse and decay. She sank down and existed, without light, in the waste land. Sluggishly, reluctantly, the days ranged themselves one after the other into a routine. Morning: wake heavy from heavy sleep, get up, one must be sick, go back to bed; nibble a biscuit, doze, half-stupified till midday; force oneself then to dress, each item of the toilet laborious, distasteful, the body a hateful burden. (p. 242)

The allusion to Eliot (and there are further references to *The Waste Land*) only serves to underline the fact that this is a specifically female waste land and a female torment. It is as though Olivia has internalized the values of a phallogocentric culture so thoroughly that she now perceives her own body as a kind of waste or residue, to be transcended if she is to save herself. She revolts from her own embodiment, her imprisonment in immanence. As we have seen, both Simone de Beauvoir and Luce Irigaray have suggested that Western culture is founded on a symbolic division which links the spiritual, ideal and transcendental to the masculine and the material, corporeal and immanent to the feminine. Olivia, like other Lehmann heroines, lives out this division, and the result is what could be called a 'false' experience of transcendence and a 'false' experience of immanence. Her drive towards transcendence through the other is necessarily inauthentic, and her perception of her own immanence is shadowed by feelings of limitation and inadequacy.

In her next novel, *The Ballad and the Source* (1944), Lehmann gives a rather different twist to her exploration of the 'symbolic divisions' which structure culture. The novel is concerned, as the title suggests, with the relationship between art and life. It offers an exploration from a feminine point of view of the antithesis which so preoccupied Henry James, among other precursors. The novel has often been described as Jamesian in its structure and complexities of point of view, but the novel also has intertextual connections with the work of male contemporaries such as T. S. Eliot. It offers, then, a feminine 'take' on the art/life dichotomy. The central figure is Sibyl Jardine, whose name immediately points to her role as oracle or prophetess. When we first meet her, she is already an old woman, preoccupied with her relationship with her grandchildren. The story is presented through the eyes of Rebecca Landon, an imaginative child who (characteristically for a Lehmann protagonist) becomes caught up in the glamorous and sophisticated world of the nearby Jardine family. Through a number of first- and second-hand accounts, Sibyl's story unfolds. A young woman in the Victorian period, she marries when she is very young and has a daughter, Ianthe. The marriage fails to satisfy her sexually, and so she elopes with a worthless young man, leaving her daughter behind. Her husband refuses to let her have any more contact with the daughter, whom she does not meet again until she has grown up. Isolated and embittered, Sibyl has attempted to win her daughter back throughout all these years, watching her from a distance, plotting unsuccessfully to kidnap her. Her quest for her lost daughter is obsessive, but when she finally meets the adult Ianthe, it is to discover that she is 'a most unpleasing girl',[13] who resists and rejects her. Despite all Sibyl's attempts at re-establishing her relationship with her daughter, Ianthe eludes her, retreating first into marriage, then into a convent. Rebecca meets Sibyl at the time when she is attempting to forge a link with the next generation, represented by the grandchildren Rebecca plays with. In the long last section of the novel we learn through Rebecca of further tragic events in the Jardine family, and of the climactic final meeting between Sibyl, Ianthe, and Ianthe's daughter Maisie.

The central motif of the novel is that of thwarted mother–daughter relationships. Sibyl's quest for Ianthe is doomed to failure: when the two finally meet in France, Ianthe recoils from her mother in fear and hated, giving one long, terrible scream before casting herself into the river in a suicide bid. Not having been mothered herself, Ianthe is unable to care for her own children, and when she is reunited with Maisie, the mother–daughter roles are completely reversed, with Maisie undressing the distracted Ianthe and putting her gently to bed. *The Ballad and the Source* thus examines the effects on two generations of the withdrawal of the mother's love in early life. Deprived of maternal nurturing, Ianthe develops an unhealthily close relationship with her father, and grows up (according to Mrs Jardine) to be an unnatural, unstable and self-absorbed young woman. When she in turn rejects her children, the ill effects are felt by both her daughters. The younger, Cherry, is narcissistic and self-absorbed; the elder, Maisie, grows up rejecting any emotional ties which might render her vulnerable in any way. The novel seems to bear out Nancy Chodorow's contention that the mother–daughter bond is crucial for 'normal' female development: Chodorow claims that it is the close tie between mother and daughter in the pre-Oedipal period which forms the basis of a woman's capacity to love and nurture her own children.[14]

In *The Ballad and the Source*, Mrs Jardine, in particular, is pre-sented as a woman whose life turns to tragedy because the springs of maternal love are choked and thwarted. Maternal love is pre-sented as natural, and despite Mrs Jardine's advanced feminist ideas, she is shown to be at the mercy of maternal love experienced as primitive passion. She describes her own predicament (and the re-lated plight of Ianthe and Maisie) in romantic, natural imagery:

> 'The source, Rebecca! The fount of life – the source, the quick spring that rises in illimitable depths of darkness and flows through every living thing from generation to generation. It is what we feel mounting in us when we say: "I know! I love! I *am*!"' . . . 'Sometimes,' she said, 'the source is vitiated, choked. Then people live frail, wavering lives, their roots cut off from what should nourish them. That is what happens to people when love is be-trayed – murdered.' (p. 101)

If maternal love is natural and essential, it is also linked in Lehmann's writings about art with women's artistic creativity. As Sydney Janet Kaplan has pointed out, Lehmann's aesthetic theory rarely strays from the analogy between sexuality and maternity, on the one hand, and artistic creativity on the other. Lehmann writes, for example, of the way in which novels grow out of images in the author's unconscious. 'When the moment comes (it cannot be predicted, but can be helped on by the right kind of passivity) these images will start to become pregnant, to illuminate one another, to con-dense and form hitherto unsuspected relationships'.[15] Lehmann's writings on art thus suggest that there is a natural and easy con-nection between women's maternal and artistic creativity. This sense of an easy alliance is not, however, borne out in *The Ballad and the Source*, in which Sibyl Jardine's suffering appears to stem, more than anything else, from the incompatibility between artistic talent and motherhood.

Sibyl Jardine has been a very talented as well as a very beautiful young woman. She has early 'brilliance', and when she leaves her husband, it is for an artistic life with a penniless young painter. After her lover leaves her, she begins to write, and publishes three novels which will, she thinks, last. She tells Rebecca, with charac-teristic confidence and self-belief, that 'my books are forgotten for the moment – but they will be read again' (p. 102). Nonetheless, in leaving her staid husband she loses her daughter, and the implication of the novel is that she suffers an inevitable punishment from society because she has dared to demand not only maternal but self-fulfilment. She has attempted to combine her maternal and artistic roles, ahead of her time. She fails in her attempt, but looks forward to a different future for the younger generation. She tells Rebecca that when *she* is a woman, 'living, as I hope and believe you will live, a life in which all your functions and capacities are used and *none* frustrated', she must spare a thought for forerunners like herself.

Despite Sibyl's hopes, the sense of a split between different aspects of the feminine self is repeated in the stories of Ianthe and Maisie, representatives of the next two generations. Ianthe, in particular, seems to have an almost schizophrenic character. When Maisie shows Rebecca a portrait of her, she is described as being like 'Mrs Darling . . . She was every child's dream of a beautiful mother' (p. 52). ('Mrs Darling' is the ideal mother in J. M. Barrie's *Peter Pan*.) She seems the perfect embodiment of a decorative, soft and nurturing femininity. Yet she has had other aspirations: she has attended Girton College, where she has performed brilliantly, taking a double first in her examinations. During her time at Cambridge, she does not play the part of the feminine beauty, but looks entirely different – 'rather drab and plain' according to Mrs Jardine, who also observes that during this period of her life 'something about her gave me the notion of a person deliberately suppressing three-quarters of her personality' (pp. 173–4). Ianthe, gifted with beauty and brains, seems to alternate between them, and to have difficulty in reconciling the different aspects of her identity. After Cambridge, she goes out to India, marries and has children, embracing the 'feminine' role again – but she is unable to sustain it, and breaks down, because 'she couldn't stand married life, you see, and being a mother' (p. 313). Just before her final collapse, she explains that she wants to return to an academic life, work being 'the only real salvation' for her (p. 298).

Just as Sibyl Jardine experienced a conflict between her talents and maternity, so Ianthe finds her intellect and her femininity, her academic aspirations and her maternal role, to be at odds with one another. Her daughter Maisie attempts to avoid such conflicts by flatly rejecting the feminine role. As a young girl she is a tomboy, and as a young woman she tells Rebecca that she is going to have a different life from other people, because she is never going to fall in love. She is going to become a woman doctor: as she points out, she comes 'from a line of professional women on the maternal side', her mother and grandmother both having brains and talent even if they were not fully expressed. What Maisie seems to have learnt from her mother and grandmother is that it is impossible to contest the 'symbolic divisions' which structure patriarchal society: unlike them, she will not even try. (However, in *A Sea-Grape Tree* (1976), which continues the stories of Rebecca and Maisie, we learn that Maisie has had a daughter, Tarni, and has thus attempted to combine a profession and motherhood.)

Mrs Jardine towers over everything in *The Ballad and the Source*, and it is her image we are left with as the novel closes, as Rebecca dreams of Mrs Jardine in a blue cape, 'faceless, motionless, watching me' (p. 318). Earlier, we have been told that Rebecca's own mother represents for Maisie 'a satisfactory embodiment of that abstract Good Mother figure of which her life was deprived' (p. 97). Lehmann makes direct reference here to the work of Melanie Klein, whose work on the 'good' and 'bad' mother figure emphasizes the ambivalence of the early relationship between mother and child, and explores its destructive as well as its loving aspects.[16] If, in the novel, Mrs Landon represents the internalized 'good mother', Mrs Jardine surely represents the 'bad mother' who has forfeited her claims to reciprocal love because of her arrogance, her imperiousness and her refusal to subordinate her own needs to those of her child. She retains her hold over the other female characters in the novel (and over the reader) precisely because she thus represents all that women must repress in a patriarchal society which denies them their activity and their desire.

In *The Echoing Grove* (1953), Lehmann returns to the subject of romance. The novel, as complex in structure as *The Ballad and the Source*, explores a variation on the theme of the eternal triangle. At the centre of the text is Rickie Masters, who is married to Madeleine, but becomes involved in a long affair with her sister Dinah. Through a series of flashbacks, we piece together the story of Rickie's early marriage, the beginning of the affair with Dinah, the stillborn child that they have together. Soon after the still birth, Madeleine finds out about the affair and Dinah tries to commit suicide. Rickie is torn between the two women, but eventually, under several forms of pressure, agrees to patch up his marriage and continue with family life. He sees Dinah just once more, after several years have passed. Some time after this, the Second World War breaks out. Rickie works loyally for the Admiralty, before dying relatively young from a duodenal ulcer. At the present time of the narrative, the sisters are meeting again after their mother's death, which has been the cause of their belated reconciliation.

The novel is very much of its time, and explores what Lehmann perceived as a crisis in the relations between the sexes in the aftermath of the Great War. In this period, the heroic code of masculinity came under a good deal of pressure. It was to a certain extent implicated in the disastrous carnage of the war, and seemed both out of reach and inappropriate for the more self-conscious generation growing up in the war's shadow. Rickie is characteristic of this generation in many respects. His father died a hero's death in 1914, but left no real clues to behaviour for the son who had to take his place. Rickie tells Madeleine about the effect of his father's death:

> 'I was twelve,' he said. 'My last year at my private. I told her I'd look after her. She told me I was her little son who was going to be a man now for Father's sake. With my head on her shoulder I told her yes, that was how it would be, for Father's sake. I went and lay on my bed face down, and told myself yes, now that Father was dead I must be a man. But the more I went on insisting on it the less I' – he paused – 'the less I seemed to know what to do about it. I *had* to be one, I'd promised, but I couldn't think what it was that I – what responsibilities went with the title.'[17]

Rickie is further handicapped, according to Dinah, because he is profoundly affected by the revolution in class attitudes and working patterns of the years following the First World War. Dinah sees him as 'a romantic orphan boy, irrevocably out of the top drawer. He was never at home in his situation, was he? – I mean the contemporary one, the crack-up' (p. 160). Because of the 'contemporary situation', Rickie has to sell up his estates and go into business, and thus moves away from his patriarchal heritage as a member of the landed gentry – complete with tenants and retainers – and into the tamer and more emasculated world of business (he goes to work for his wife's uncles). This move is characteristic of a period in which, Alison Light has argued, there was a marked 'feminisation' of culture, with more men moving to indoor and office jobs, and an increased emphasis on the pleasures of domestic life.[18]

Light argues that the First World War and its aftermath 'struck at the very basis of masculinity and ... shook to the core former

definitions of sexual difference' (p. 8). So Rickie, in a key 'confes-
sional' scene, tells his lover that:

> I've got it in me – this something, which is nothing, in the
> centre. You don't understand do you? – you're a woman. So much
> the better for you. I'm simply telling you for the tenth time I'm
> no good to you. *Sometimes I think a new thing is happening: men
> aren't any good to women any more.* (p. 245, my italics)

In this period, a general uncertainty over the heroic code of masculinity created a situation in which men were less able to look
outwards to the public and social world for a sense of identity. The
literature of the period would suggest that, instead, they turned for
fulfilment to personal relationships, with the result that such relationships were placed under an unprecedented strain. To return for
a moment to the terms of Simone de Beauvoir's analysis of romantic love in *The Second Sex*, in such a situation both men and women
seek transcendence through love, but, she argues, such an antiso-
cial project is doomed to fail. She writes that '[w]oman preserves
her transcendence by transferring it to [the man]; but he must bring
it to bear upon the whole world. If two lovers sink together in the
absolute of passion, all their liberty is degraded into immanence;
death is the only solution' (p. 668). In Beauvoir's terms, a man like
Rickie is 'no good' to Dinah because he is no longer a subject,
with a project that reaches beyond the self. He has become femi-
nized, and is now what she calls an 'inessential creature'.

Beauvoir's claim that 'death is the only solution' to this predicament may seem overstated, but in *The Echoing Grove* death *is* the
(re)solution that solves the crisis created by Rickie and Dinah's illicit love. The world of the body and of death, which they have
wanted to deny, returns to claim them initially through the death
of their child. Dinah has wanted this child, but characteristically
fails to make adequate arrangements for the birth. The child is
delivered by a friend, in snowbound conditions: it is stillborn, and
Dinah also nearly dies. The dead, illegitimate son of the doomed
relationship is deliberately contrasted with the healthy daughter
born of Rickie and Madeleine's reconciliation: she is 'so firmly planted
in the earth, so squared for the attack that she seemed from her
first hour a laughing-matter, a child of fortune' (p. 89). Death comes
more slowly to claim Rickie. His duodenal ulcer first makes its presence
felt just after he has told Madeleine that he is going to leave her.

He haemorrhages, is taken into a nursing home, and the result of his extreme physical weakness combined with the strength of his wife and mother-in-law is that the whole idea of his leaving Madeleine is dropped. From this time onwards Rickie's health is not good, and his early death seems a foregone conclusion.

Rickie reflects that it is '[s]trange how repeatedly the rhythm of this business had swung to physical disasters, the failure of the body: Dinah's, her father's, Dinah's again, then his' (p. 151). The failure of the body sabotages Rickie and Dinah's relationship, whereas the body underwrites and supports Rickie and Madeleine's relationship. What the novel seems to suggest is that the affair between Rickie and Dinah cannot thrive, because (unlike Rickie and Madeleine's daughter Clarissa) it is not 'firmly planted in the earth'. The difference in character between the two sisters is significant here. Echoing the division which characterized earlier Lehmann heroines, Dinah here represents the intellectual and Madeleine the 'feminine' aspects of the self. Dinah is intelligent and articulate: she writes a novel, involves herself in contemporary left politics, and lives on the bohemian fringes of society. She is, on the whole, analytic and self-contained. Madeleine is equally intelligent, but has never had Dinah's enthusiasm for abstractions or the arts. She lives a far more conventional life, devoting herself to her three children. While the novel focuses more on Dinah than Madeleine, it could be argued that the final balance of narrative sympathy is on Madeleine's side. At one point, for example, Rickie thinks of the sisters in the following terms:

> He was grateful, touched; grateful – oh God! – to both of them, but just at this moment touched, heartwrung, by one alone. The other [Dinah] was strong, clear, stoical, disinterested, an alarming, elevating influence; this one [Madeleine] petty, proud, yielding, generous, sensible, silly, open, dishonest, kindly, cruel . . . everything. Shamelessly human, natural. Yes, she was pretty awful taking it by and large, but somehow it seemed more *natural*. (p. 110)

Here Lehmann seems to articulate very plainly the division which structures much of her fiction. On the one hand is the single-minded character seeking transcendence: she is 'alarming', as well as 'elevating'. On the other, is the character who is content to rest in immanence/femininity: 'open, dishonest, kindly, cruel . . . everything'. Lehmann's fiction works repeatedly with such oppositions, between the intellect and femininity, transcendence and immanence. In the world of her fiction, it is taken for granted that transcendence can only be attained through love: the novels affirm the characters' need for romantic love and desire while at the same time disclosing its limits. Lehmann's fiction, then, is centrally concerned with the tension between her characters' 'craving for the absolute' (p. 271), and the contingent facts of their lives. Her fiction perhaps points ultimately to an ideal meeting of the absolute and the contingent, the transcendent and the immanent. This ideal horizon of her fiction could be linked with Luce Irigaray's concept of the 'sensible transcendental' – which she also calls the 'immanent efflorescence of the divine' – as a state of being which takes us beyond the divisions of the existing symbolic order.[19] Such a state of balance is imaged in *The Echoing Grove* through the metaphor of Rickie's cuff-links, which is threaded through the text. The cuff-links move between the two sisters, symbolizing the complexity of the links between the three central characters. In the very last lines of the novel, they appear again, oddly foregrounded, and described in terms which suggest precisely a balance between the abstract and the solid, the weightless and the weighty:

> She closed her fingers over them, letting them slide into the hollow of her palm, feeling them nudge lightly, settle there; anonymous abstraction: questionable solid; cold, almost weightless weight. (p. 320)

In *A Sea-Grape Tree* (1976), Lehmann extends and deepens this sense of an ideal horizon beyond the divisions of the symbolic order. This novel, published after a gap of over twenty years, has often been considered something of an afterthought and even something of an embarrassment in Lehmann's *oeuvre*. In 1958, Lehmann's beloved daughter, Sally, died suddenly. This was, as Janet Watts puts it, 'the most appalling catastrophe of her mother's life'.[20] It ended the life Lehmann had led until then, although it led slowly to a new beginning. Before her daughter's death Lehmann had shared the atheism of her generation. After it, she came to accept the existence of other worlds and of dimensions beyond mortal and material existence. As Watts points out, this change cost Lehmann a great deal. Her acceptance of the spiritual dimension of life, and of life after death, was to some extent an unwilling acceptance, and it certainly cost her the sympathy of many readers. As Lehmann notes in her postscript to the Virago edition of the novel, *A Sea-Grape Tree*, fully reflecting these new interests, 'courted irritation, head-shaking, even mockery from a few critics ever willing and never afraid to wound' (p. 162). Judy Simons also notes the difficulty many recent critics have had with the 'mystic dimension' of Lehmann's later work. She suggests that they find it 'difficult to reconcile what is perceived as an eccentric, if not utterly cranky, view of life with the hard-hitting cynicism of a book such as *The Weather in the Streets*'.[21]

I want to argue that Lehmann's spiritualism in *A Sea-Grape Tree* is far from being a weakness, and that, on the contrary, her experience leads her to offer in this novel a more profound insight into the nature and possibilities of love. I would suggest that in *A Sea-Grape Tree*, Lehmann offers a critique of 'romance' and 'love' as they have been presented in her earlier novels, and that this critique can be juxtaposed illuminatingly with Luce Irigaray's analysis of 'love' in a phallocentric culture. In *A Sea-Grape Tree*, Lehmann spiritualizes the love relationship which has been so central to her work, and thus resolves the conflict between male transcendence and female immanence which has marked her earlier fiction.

An Irigarayan reading of *A Sea-Grape Tree* is encouraged by the emphasis in the novel on mother–daughter relationships. The novel is itself a daughter-text of *The Ballad and the Source*, taking up the lives of the characters of the earlier novel after a gap of sixteen years. Rebecca Landon, now a woman, has been deserted by her un-named married lover, and travels alone to what Lehmann herself describes as a 'magical' Carribean island. There she meets and has an affair with Johnny, a former air pilot who has been paralysed from the waist down in the First World War. Johnny tells Rebecca that Mrs Jardine is buried on the island, and it gradually becomes apparent that he has been, in Lehmann's words, Mrs Jardine's 'last, adored protégé' – she had followed him out to the island, determined to nurse him and make him well. While Rebecca is staying on the island she has a long, telepathic conversation with Mrs Jardine, who continues to instruct her in the mysteries of life (and now death), and who also battles with her over possession of Johnny. Johnny is able to tell her what has happened to Mrs Jardine's grand-daughter, Maisie, who has become the head of a gynaecological department, and who also has an illegitimate child, Tarni, named for Tanya, the shadowy young wife of Gil in *The Ballad and the Source*. Through her relationship with Johnny and with the other inhabitants of this 'Prospero-type isle', Rebecca finally comes to terms with the vibrant spirit of Mrs Jardine, and as Lehmann expresses it, '[h]er sinister shadow is finally lifted' (p. 162).

In *The Ballad and the Source*, Mrs Jardine's relationship to Rebecca is that of a Demeter figure, as is suggested by the fact that they first meet after Rebecca and Jess have been gathering baskets of primroses on Mrs Jardine's hill. The effect is intensified by Mrs Jardine's appearance on this occasion, 'dressed in a long gown of pale blue with wide sleeves embroidered thickly with blue, rose and violet flowers' (p. 10). As Kaplan has shown, Lehmann repeatedly invokes the myth of Demeter and Persephone in this novel, in which mother–daughter relationships are so crucial. However, as Irigaray has pointed out, classical mythology is inadequate to articulate the needs and desires of the present. Our task, in her view, is to create new myths, to 'invent a divine for our own times'.[22] The problem with the Demeter and Persephone myth is that it can be said to acquiesce in rather than to challenge patriarchy. In *A Sea-Grape Tree*, Lehmann moves towards the inscription of 'new' mother–daughter and woman-to-woman relationships. Irigaray has argued that an authentic feminine identity can only be discovered in such relationships, where contact between women is unmediated by patriarchy. So she writes that we must 'try to discover the singularity of our love for other women . . . This love is necessary if we are not to remain the servants of the phallic cult, objects to be used by and exchanged between men'.[23] She also stresses the importance of a 'maternal genealogy' in sustaining female identity:

> A woman celebrating the eucharist with her mother, sharing with her the fruits of the earth she/they have blessed, could be delivered of all hatred or ingratitude towards her maternal genealogy, could be consecrated in her identity and her female genealogy.[24]

A Sea-Grape Tree abounds in positive representations of the mother–daughter relationship. Among the minor characters, both Ellie and Miss Stay 'think back through their mothers', remembering the closeness of the relationship – 'we were all in all to one another', as Ellie puts it (p. 20). In keeping with the novel's emphasis on the bonds between the living and the dead, Ellie claims that she is still watched over by her mother – 'She's gone a long way on now, I expect, but we're never really out of touch. She'd know if I was in for trouble before I knew it myself' (p.148). And one of the most important developments in the novel is the way in which Mrs Jardine/ Sibyl Anstey modifies her relationship to Rebecca, ceasing to struggle with her over Johnny. In letting Johnny go, Sibyl frees herself from a dependent relationship with a man, and makes way for a different kind of relationship between Rebecca and Johnny. She thus becomes a productive and regenerative mother, making new possibilities rather than subordinating herself and Rebecca to the existing phallic law. And she finally establishes the maternal genealogy which she has been pursuing since she lost her daughter Ianthe – Maisie, whose profession as a gynaecologist (a healer of women) is surely not accidental, gives her in Tarni both her 'last joy' and a 'true flesh and blood descendent' (p. 60).

A Sea-Grape Tree thus seems to focus on regenerative mother–daughter relationships, and also moves the discussion of love on to newly fertile ground. In Lehmann's earlier fiction, as we have seen, the structure of the love relationship between men and women is asymmetrical. Putting it in Simone de Beauvoir's terms, man is seen as an essential and absolute creature whose drive to transcendence leads him to 'extend his grasp on the world': woman is doomed to immanence and can only dream of 'transcending her being towards one of these superior beings'. In such a structure, authentic love is impossible. Irigaray's analysis of love in patriarchal society reveals a rather similar pattern. For Irigaray, the love relationship is inauthentic because it has not been spiritualized. She argues that because of the division of functions between the sexes (man being equated with the mind, woman with the body), it is only relations between men, and not between men and women, which have been spiritualized. A change can only occur with the advent of the 'sensible transcendental'. Margaret Whitford glosses this idea as follows:

> Hence the concept of the sensible transcendental – apparently a contradiction in terms – but in fact a recognition that the body should be recognized and symbolized in such a way that women are no longer sole guardians of the corporeal, so that men *can incorporate their own corporeality into their sublimations, so that women can sublimate as women*.[25] (my italics)

Irigaray's insights are extremely illuminating in relation to *A Sea-Grape Tree*. She suggests that love can only be authentic when men and women *each* have their own spiritual as well as corporeal morphology. In Whitford's words, each sex can then '[assume] its own "I" and [address] its "you" to a transcendent other'.[26]

In *A Sea-Grape Tree* the male lover, Johnny, is compelled to 'incorporate his own corporeality into [his] sublimations' because he is literally grounded and 'trapped' in his body – because of his injuries he cannot escape his embodied nature. (He forms an interesting comparison with Rickie in *The Echoing Grove*, by far the most sympathetic of Lehmann's earlier heroes and similarly 'trapped' in an ailing body.) Both Johnny and Rebecca accept their corporeality, but also move to transcendence through each other. I would like to juxtapose here a passage from Irigaray describing the 'amorous encounter', and a passage from *A Sea-Grape Tree*. First Irigaray, arguing with Levinas's conception of love:

> This autistic, egological, solitary love does not correspond to the shared outpouring, to the loss of boundaries which takes place for both lovers when they cross the boundary of the skin into the mucous membranes of the body, leaving the circle which encloses my solitude to meet in a shared space, a shared breath, abandoning the relatively dry and precise outlines of each body's solid exterior to enter a fluid universe where the perception of being two persons [*de la dualité*] becomes indistinct.[27]

Irigaray goes on to write of 'that ecstasy which is our child, prior to any child': this is an embrace which is *fertile*.

Now *A Sea-Grape Tree*:

> Presently they were lying on his bed. Rain rustled and chattered in the sea-grape tree, poured with a voice like a waterfall from the steep-angled roof, driving his house of shells down, down as if into some subaqueous chamber made of echoes, whispers, gleams and shadows, where, clasped together, plunged into one another's being, they were swept again and again through drowning surges; to be thrown up at last into the fertile shallows of a spent flood tide. (p. 105)

Lehmann uses the same imagery as Irigaray to suggest a reciprocity of desire in a 'shared' and 'fluid' space in which each lover is open to the being of the other. Each accepts what Irigaray calls the 'wonder' of the other, and, crucially, in acceding to love each accedes too to a fuller understanding of life, death and the horizon beyond death. *A Sea-Grape Tree* is full of intimations of mortality, but for both Rebecca and Johnny the experience of love makes possible an under-standing of death as, in Irigaray's words, 'the other face of life'.[28] We can see this particularly clearly in one exchange, when Rebecca asks Johnny if they will be together for the rest of their lives:

'For the rest of our lives?' He makes it almost a question, then says, after a pause: 'We can but try.' A strange thing to say: as if he were facing a mystifying problem; some sort of grave opera-tion whose outcome is uncertain. Yet his face remains serene; as if, on some other level, the solution is discerned. (p. 154)

In *A Sea-Grape Tree*, Lehmann offers an image of love which comes very close to Irigaray's ideal of a spiritualized relation between the sexes. This brief and haunting novel thus offers a crucial reworking of the themes of Lehmann's earlier work and constitutes a major intervention in twentieth-century writing about 'women in love'.

2
Elizabeth Bowen: 'Becoming-Woman'

Elizabeth Bowen's exploration of female embodiment differs significantly from that of Lehmann. While Lehmann moves towards a reworking of the relationship between mind and body and towards a valorization of the body and the 'feminine', Bowen takes a different path, away from gender specificity. I want to follow this move 'beyond' gender by making reference to the work of Gilles Deleuze and Felix Guattari, which may illuminate aspects of Bowen's work which have been particularly resistant to analysis. It should be made clear at the outset that Bowen's fiction is always written from the point of view of the woman. Often, her novels contrast an older woman (middle-class, educated, perhaps with a professional job) with a girl who may be as young as sixteen, unformed and not yet defined by the codes of patriarchy. This recurrent pattern, this hesitation between the viewpoint of the girl and that of the woman, recalls the suggestive analysis of femininity in Deleuze and Guattari's *A Thousand Plateaus*.[1] In the central section of this book, Deleuze and Guattari distinguish between dispersed libidinal energies ('molecular' energies) and those which strive to aggregate into totalities ('molar' energies). Femininity (in the conventional sense) is linked with molar energies, with the attempt to form and stabilize identities through divisions of classes, races and sexes. 'Becoming-woman', on the other hand, is linked with molecular energies, which, in the words of Elizabeth Grosz, 'traverse, create a path, destabilize, enable energy seepage within and through these molar unities'.[2] For Deleuze and Guattari, the adult woman exists as a molar entity, she is 'the woman as defined by her form, endowed with organs and functions, and assigned as a subject' (p. 275). By contrast, the girl is the privileged site of 'becoming-woman': they write that 'she is defined by a relation of movement and rest, speed and slowness, by a combination of atoms, an emission of particles: haecceity . . . She is an abstract line, or a line of flight' (pp. 276–7). 'The girl' is, of course, a metaphor: 'she' can appear at any stage in life – 'girls do not belong to an age group, sex, order or kingdom: they slip in everywhere, between orders, acts, ages, sexes: they produce *n* molecular sexes' (p. 277). But the state of the (actual, historical) girl before the acquisition of 'molar' femininity is most likely to produce that activity and energy which Deleuze and Guattari associate with 'becoming-woman', with the release of the energy of '[s]exuality, any sexuality', or desire, before it becomes locked into the binary constructions of molar sexual identities.

Deleuze and Guattari's distinctive emphasis on desire as generative and productive suggests a connection with Luce Irigaray. While Irigaray has distanced herself from some aspects of their work, she shares their hostility to the dominant Freudo-Lacanian psychoanalytic narrative which seeks to define 'woman' as the embodiment of man's lack. In wider terms, Deleuze and Guattari's attempt to rethink the body has other connections with feminist thought, especially with that of Judith Butler. For Deleuze and Guattari, the body is seen not as the locus for a conscious subject nor as an organically determined object; rather, it is assessed in terms of what it can do, the things it can perform, the linkages it can establish. In this connection, Elizabeth Grosz quotes this passage from Deleuze and Parnet's *Dialogues* which offers, she suggests, 'a rare, affirmative understanding' of the body:

> Spinoza's question: *what is a body capable of?* What affects is it capable of? Affects are becomings: sometimes they weaken us to the extent they diminish our strength of action and decompose our relations (sadness), sometimes they make us stronger through augmenting our force, and making us enter into a vaster and higher individual (joy). Spinoza never ceases to be astonished at the body: not having a body, but at what the body is capable of. Bodies are not defined by their genus and species, nor by their organs and functions, but by what they can do, the affects they are capable of, in passion as in action.[3]

Such an understanding of the body is liberating because it points to the existence of a material potential which exceeds both human subjectivity and our conception of the body-as-organism. Important, too, is its emphasis on the linkage of the human body with other bodies, both human and nonhuman, animate and inanimate. Organs, flows and bodily processes are linked with atmospheres and material objects: Deleuze and Guattari assume, in Grosz's words, 'the vast and necessary interrelation and mutual affectivity and effectivity of all beings on all others'.[4] In this respect, too, their experimental thought is illuminating for a consideration of Elizabeth Bowen's fiction, with its particular intensities and instabilities and its idiosyncratic treatment of the relationship between consciousness and the external world.

This chapter will explore Bowen's experimental working-out of organs, processes and flows with particular reference to her female characters. I want to open the discussion with Bowen's third novel, *To the North*, which was first published in 1932. The novel follows the lives of two young women over one summer. Cecilia Summers, a 29-year-old widow whose husband has been killed in the Great War, lives with her sister-in-law, Emmeline, who runs a travel agency. The two live quietly and amicably together, until a chance meeting leads to Emmeline's beginning a love affair with a young lawyer, Markie Linkwater. At the same time, Cecilia gradually becomes more deeply involved with the man she will ultimately marry, the solid and reliable Julian Tower. The two women drift apart, and the novel ends with their shockingly different fates. Cecilia is last seen at home cosily ensconced with Julian, while Emmeline, the love affair having foundered, drives off in desperation, killing Markie and herself in a car crash.

One of the most immediately striking aspects of this novel, and of Bowen's work in general, is its presentation of individual identity. For her characters, identity is both intermittent and discontinuous: as Cecilia wryly remarks, one so seldom is oneself. Cecilia in particular is frequently assailed by the feeling that she exists only by virtue of the reflections cast back by others. Alone, she feels her life to be transparent, almost non-existent. At such moments, even the stylized accoutrements of her femininity seem emptied and null:

> Her life became visible in the hour like water poured into a glass; momentarily no one cast a shadow, momentarily not a bell rang. Slipping off her rings one by one, she heard each clink on the table-top. The glass-topped table, flounced like a shepherdess, with tapering stoppered bottles, attendants to vanity, and Venetian

powder bowl, was in itself pretty: she exclaimed in thought: Mine, but nothing replied: Cecilia. In the cupboards her dresses hung bosom to bosom coldly, as though they had never been worn. She ran down like a clock whose hands falter and point for too long at one hour and minute: the clock stops dead.[5]

As soon as the phone rings, however, Cecilia is restored to her sense of self, or rather to the personality she has concocted over the years and which is guaranteed by characters such as her over-bearing aunt, Lady Waters, who blithely, and blindly, affirms that '[n]o one can be *more* herself than Cecilia: she is touchingly open-hearted' (p. 217).

Lady Waters can be seen as a figure of 'molar' femininity, one in a triptych of figures representing stages in its formation. The first of these figures is Pauline, Julian Tower's niece. It is made clear from our first encounter with her that Pauline is acting the part of the little girl, in preparation for the more difficult role of the woman: '[s]he was diligently little-girlish ... [s]he alternated between the romp and the dream-child, occasionally attempting the mouse' (p. 41). For his part, Julian is mortified by glimpses of 'the woman so drearily nascent in her immaturity' (p. 42). When Cecilia and Julian visit her at school, she and her friend Dorothea speculate on the possibility of an engagement, and when this duly transpires Pauline writes to congratulate Cecilia in arch and conventional tones. She is wholly caught up in the conventional narrative of femininity, as is suggested by her being engrossed in reading *The Woman Thou Gavest Me* when she stays for the weekend with Cecilia and Lady Waters. Cecilia, the middle figure in the triptych, is a more com-plex character. At the outset of the novel, the narrator tells us that neither she nor Markie have 'nice' characters, and she herself re-flects, looking at Markie, that in an afterworld she might deserve just such a companion as he – 'too close, glancing at her ... without sympathy, with just such a cold material knowingness' (p. 8). There are indications that Cecilia has been capable of love and of an expansion of the spirit, but has been shocked into contraction and retreat by her husband's death. Now she too acts the part of femi-ninity, and mimes love: '[s]he enjoyed the repose of small intimacies, susceptibility she could command, reflections of passion momen-tarily commanded her' (p. 115). It is only towards the end of the novel that we glimpse her profound sense of failure. Emmeline con-gratulates her on the way in which her engagement has turned out:

'Yes,' Cecilia said, 'things do arrange themselves, don't they. All the same, I naturally feel – '

She broke off. Emmeline said, curious: 'What do you naturally feel?'

' – A poor thing,' said her sister-in-law, with a complete change of tone and surprising bitterness. 'Not very much of a life. I have flopped all ways; I hang on looking pretty about it, like one of those wretched creepers. First Henry, then you, now Julian. I don't think you know how I've leaned on you – and so dishonestly, too.' (pp. 246–7)

In referring to herself as a creeper or parasite, Cecilia suggests her inauthenticity, her inability to function on any level deeper than that of the socially constructed self. Lady Waters, the final figure in the triptych, shares this inability to move beyond the social and conventional. Throughout the novel she is represented as massive, monumental, awe-inspiring: near the end, as she scolds Cecilia for not taking more care over Emmeline's reputation, we see how a cultivated mystique has veiled her merely prudential and expedient nature – 'The fumes subsided, off went the Delphic trappings: here spoke sheer Aunt, empowered by plain good sense. That voice went back through the school-room and to the cradle' (p. 255).

Against these figures stands Emmeline, the character who can be aligned most closely with Deleuze and Guattari's 'girl' and with 'becoming-woman'. Emmeline is described on her first appearance as looking 'very young, or perhaps rather ageless'. Bowen adds that '[t]he spring of her hair, the arch of her eyebrows, her air between serenity and preoccupation made her look rather like an angel' (p. 16). Emmeline's openness to experience, her potential to move into new relations with the bodies and minds she encounters, is brilliantly suggested through her work as a travel agent. For Emmeline, her job is 'an affair of passion'. As she explains to Julian, the agency has been set up because 'what everyone feels is that life, even travel, is losing its element of uncertainty: we try to supply that'. Emmeline's work, then, is all about uncertainty, the provisional and the potential: even the agency's slogan, 'Move dangerously', suggests a willingness to take risks in the interests of new experience. In this respect, Emmeline closely resembles the 'girl' invoked by Deleuze and Guattari in *A Thousand Plateaus*:

Trost, a mysterious author, painted a portrait of the girl, to whom he linked the fate of the revolution: her speed, her freely machinic body, her intensities, her abstract line or line of flight, her molecular production . . . (p. 277)

The risk that Emmeline takes is that of falling in love with Markie; specifically, Bowen writes that '[s]he might be said to be drawn, with a force of which she was hardly aware, by what existed in Markie in spite of himself' (p. 82). In other words, Emmeline is drawn to the potential which there is in Markie for 'becoming', for participating in the world in ways which exceed the constraints of one's 'personality'. Extending the travel/flight metaphor, the first climax of the love affair comes when Emmeline and Markie fly to Paris together (Emmeline, significantly, is going to Paris to define the terms of an 'inter-play' with another travel agency). Emmeline is transported by the experience of flight: she is 'wrapt' and 'enchanted', while Markie remains resistant and disgruntled. In love, too, she is ready to travel to an extent and at a speed which he is not, leaving him baffled and stupefied:

[H]e had been oppressed since last night by sensations of having been overshot, of having, in some final soaring flight of her exaltation, been outdistanced: as though a bird whose heart one moment one could feel beating has escaped from between the hands. The passionless entirety of her surrender, the volition of her entire wish to be his had sent her a good way past him. (p. 164)

The striking metaphor of the trapped bird (one which will recur in Bowen's work) emphasizes Markie's will to contain the relationship, to keep it within the bounds of the already known. As the relationship continues, Markie is increasingly appalled by Emmeline's risk-taking, by 'this wildness, this flood, this impetus that he could not arrest' (p. 214). Markie cuts off the possibility of a reciprocity of desire(s), for 'he was unwilling ever to love her too much. In his nature some final displacement was still impossible' (p. 211). With cool clearness, Markie sees that Emmeline has stepped:

clear of the every-day, of conduct with its guarantees and necessities, into the region of the immoderate, where we are more than ourselves. Here are no guarantees. Tragedy is the precedent: Tragedy confounding life with its masterful disproportion. Here figures cast unknown shadows; passion knows no crime, only its own movement; steel and the cord go with the kiss. (pp. 213–14)

Deleuze's concept of 'becoming-woman' (which is seen by him as the prototype of all 'becomings') is particularly helpful in unlocking Bowen's text here. We could say that following the 'line of flight' of her passion for Markie, Emmeline has entered the space of becoming, of being released into connections and linkages with other beings which are beyond the reach of the socially constructed self. Yet Bowen predicts 'tragedy' because of the disparity between Emmeline and Markie in this respect. Using Deleuze as a resource once more, one could argue that the tragedy which ends the novel has, however, positive as well as negative implications. When Markie breaks off the affair, Emmeline has nowhere to go: she becomes an aimless wanderer in the city, 'walking the streets blindly'. Meeting Markie again at Cecilia's insistence, her decision to drive Markie 'to the north' can be seen as a necessary reversal of the previous flight south to Paris. The parallel between the two journeys is underscored in the text. As they are driving, Markie says 'I wish we were still flying', and Emmeline replies with an irrepressible smile, 'I wish it were still that day'. A few minutes later Markie thinks that Emmeline's speed has 'the startled wildness of flight' (p. 281). It could be argued that what Emmeline does, as she drives in intent despair, telling Markie that there is nowhere left for them to go, is to make a move to negate a negation, to react against the dullness and deadness which have become the inescapable coordinates of the relation between herself and Markie. Such a flight can be seen as a kind of 'active destruction', to use a phrase which Deleuze borrows from Nietzsche. In destroying the nullity of their lost connection, Emmeline remains true to her own fine sense of freedom:

An immense idea of departure – expresses getting steam up and crashing from termini, liners clearing the docks, the shadows of planes rising, caravans winding out into the first dip of the desert – possessed her spirit, now launched like the long arrow. The traveller solitary with his uncertainties, with apprehensions he cannot communicate, seeing the strands of the known snap like paper ribbons, is sustained and more than himself on a great impetus: the faint pain of parting sets free the heart. (pp. 282–3)

The renewed emphasis here on the uncertain and the unknown suggests a reorientation towards the future, though it may not be a personal future: as Deleuze puts it '[a]ctive negation or active destruction is the state of strong spirits which destroy the reactive in themselves'.[6]

Implicit in this discussion of *To the North* has been the view that Deleuze's categories of 'molar' and 'molecular' femininities can be usefully aligned with the interpretive categories used in Chapter 1. Roughly speaking, 'molar' formations can be linked with the destructive experience of immanence of many of Lehmann's protagonists: in both cases, there is an emphasis on rigidity and sedimentation, and a sense of entrapment within the body as coded by patriarchy. Deleuze's molecular formations, on the other hand ('becoming-woman') can be aligned with the 'sensible transcendental' as it has been outlined in discussion of *A Sea-Grape Tree*. For Deleuze the 'thousand sexes' which are 'so many uncontrollable becomings' exist on a plane of immanence: like Irigaray, he is suspicious of the (phallocentric) idealist tradition in Western philosophy. Aurelia Armstrong has emphasized this point in her discussion of the relationship between Deleuze and Spinoza. She writes that:

> [A] becoming has nothing to do with imitation or analogy between two previously conceived identities, that is, bodies conceived under an order of 'molar' categorization which identifies them according to their type and place in an order of oppositions. Spinoza himself would call such categories inadequate ideas to the extent that they do not express the *relation* which defines the body and the *affects* of which it is capable, but rest on gross resemblances and imaginary universals.[7]

Deleuzian becomings represent instead the discovery, on the plane of immanence and through action, of 'ideas of composition of relations'. These actions-ideas evade the organizing plane of molar definitions, producing new powers and affects which may enable us to resist and undermine the various organized limits to our powers.

Bowen's *The House in Paris* (1935) is pre-eminently concerned with such resistances. Like *To the North*, this novel can be considered a modified tragedy, preoccupied with the constraining power of restrictive social codes and practices. 'Molar' femininity is represented in this novel by Mrs Michaelis and Mme Fisher, and to a lesser extent by Henrietta's grandmother Mrs Arbuthnot. All three are older women past middle-age who attempt to bind girls and young women into restrictive notions of feminine subjectivity. Henrietta's grandmother is a 'wicked' manipulator of her granddaughters' lives; Mrs Michaelis is a more formidable custodian of social and gender codes. When she refuses to confront her daughter over a lie, Karen thinks that 'when mother does not speak it is not pity or kindness; it is *worldliness beginning so deep down that it seems to be the heart . . .* She will hold me inside the lie till she makes me lose the power I felt I had'[8] (my italics). As Karen realizes, her mother is incapable of love, which is 'obtuse and reckless': prudence and expediency govern every word and action. If Mrs Michaelis is formidable, Mme Fisher is the most sinister of these older women. She presides over a house in which young English and American girls can stay for a year in Paris, attending the Sorbonne or studying music and painting. Mme Fisher offers her girls 'freedom inside the bounds of propriety': the whole point of their stay is that they should internalize the codes and values of 'molar' femininity while being under the illusion that they are free – 'She asked no questions, but knew: she knew where you went, why, with whom, and whether it happened twice' (p. 94). Mme Fisher is a latter-day version of Mme Beck in Charlotte Brontë's *Villette* (1853): like Mme Beck, she lives by the normative codes of feminine behaviour and makes her living by enforcing them.

Among the young girls in the novel, the youngest, Henrietta, puts up the least resistance to 'molar' femininity. When Leopold first meets her, her manner strikes him with its 'touch of clearsighted, over-riding good sense' – '[s]he might marvel, but nothing, thought Leopold, would ever really happen to her' (p. 18). Naomi Fisher is a little more successful in her resistance, but it is Karen Michaelis on whom the novel focuses most intensively. Karen comes from a 'nice' and 'charming' family, and when she first appears in the novel is about to marry a cousin's cousin, thus remaining safe within the orbit of the world she knows. What startles her out of this is a visit to her Aunt Violet in which she first encounters death. Her uncle tells her that her aunt is to have an operation:

'Oh – . Is it – is it as bad as that?
Up there in the drawing-room Aunt Violet began playing Schubert: notes came stepping lightly on to the moment in which Karen realised she was going to die. Phrases of music formed

and hung in the garden, where violently green young branches flamed in the spring dusk. A hurt earthy smell rose from the piteous roots of the daisies and those small wounds in the turf that her uncle, not speaking, kept pressing at with his toe. (p. 71)

In this complex passage, pronominal ambiguity enforces our sense of Karen's strong identification with Aunt Violet (the 'she' who is going to die might be Aunt Violet, or Karen, or both). What is also suggested is a contrast between Aunt Violet's light and uncomplaining music, and the raw violence of the spring scene (branches 'flame' and are 'violently green'; the earth is 'hurt' and wounded). What appals Karen most about Aunt Violet's death is its quiet and unresisting manner, the way in which it conforms with the rest of her life. Having lived according to a code of femininity which has sealed in and closed down her energies and desires, Aunt Violet is now dying in a similarly attenuated and decorous fashion. She speaks belatedly to Karen of her wish that she had done more in life, selfishly, for herself, and Karen sees that:

[t]o something proud and restless – the spirit, perhaps – that looked out from inside her, nothing must make death more humbling than the idea of its ease: death should have a harder victory. *This* was stepping through still one more door held courteously open for her. Better be rooted out hurt, bleeding, alive, like the daisies from the turf, than blow faintly away across the lawn like a straw. (pp. 74–5)

Karen wonders whether 'having been so much a woman all through her own life', Aunt Violet hopes that she, Karen, will be 'something more'. It is in response to this implicit challenge, and to all that this visit makes her see (the potential smallness of life, the need to move beyond prescribed identities, to enter into new relations with other bodies) that Karen embarks on a love affair with the 'French-English-Jewish' Max Ebhert.

This relationship with Max cracks the mould of Karen's life, involving a complete rejection of all that her mother has brought her up to be. Early on in her relation with Max, she thinks of her mother's crisp, dismissive analysis of Max's character. Acknowledging its force, Karen nonetheless rejects outright the claims of a 'truth' based on received ideas and generalizations, on 'gross resemblances and imaginary universals', to borrow Aurelia Armstrong's phrase. The potential in Max can only be discovered by abandoning preconceptions, placing oneself in a position of risk, ignorance and desire:

> All the same, [Mrs Michaelis's] well-lit explanations of people were like photographs taken when the camera could not lie; they stunned your imagination by *being* exact. Would those unmysterious views in a railway carriage make you visit a place, even in dreams? You could not fall in love with the subject of an Edwardian camera-portrait . . .
>
> Blurs and important wrong shapes, ridgy lights, crater darkness making a face inhuman as a map of the moon, Mrs Michaelis, like the camera of her day, denied. She saw what she knew was there. Like the classic camera, *she was blind to those accidents that make a face that face, a scene that scene, and float the object, alive, in your desire and ignorance.* (p. 110, my italics)

Karen and Max have nothing in common, not even a language. They share no social or personal history, and as Bowen puts it, '[t]heir worlds were so much unlike that no experience had the same value for both of them' (p. 135). But it is precisely because they are unknown to each other and because they come together without social or linguistic preconceptions that their relationship is productive and generative in all kinds of unexpected ways – so, looking at Max, Karen feels a shock of tenderness and of 'life opening' (p. 157).

It is the child of the relationship, Leopold, who most obviously images its life-giving and productive elements. The illegitimate child is a recurring figure in Bowen's work, also appearing in *The Death of the Heart* (1938), *The Heat of the Day* (1949) and *A World of Love* (1955).[9] In very literal and obvious ways, the existence of such a child is accidental and unpremeditated: he or she is the outcome of what Karen calls 'a leap in the dark'. These children also exist outside conventional social structures and live outside the dominant narrative of 'family life' whereby we acquire our normative identity. Living in exile in Italy with his adopted uncle and aunt, Leopold has been deprived of the personal history and personal ties which would enable him to develop an appropriate subjectivity. In an important sense, he lives outside ideology, outside the aggregations of molar/social formations of sex and class.

In this novel, it is the male child Leopold who comes closest to 'becoming woman' in the free play of his attachments. His position in relation to his parents is vividly sketched in by Mme Fisher – '[t]o find oneself like a young tree inside a tomb is to discover the power to crack the tomb and grow up to any height' (p. 193). (The metaphor of the tree is a Deleuzian one, a point to which I will return). Max and Karen each in their way give up on their relationship and on its potential. Max commits suicide when he feels his life seized by Mme Fisher, when he feels himself stripped of autonomy and creative power. Karen, having had her child, and had him adopted, marries Ray Forrestier and reverts to the 'femininity' of her mother – '[f]everishly, she simulated the married peace women seemed to inherit, wanting most of all to live like her mother' (p. 208). Left in a tomb to the extent that his mother has denied his existence, Leopold discovers his power to annul this annulment of his being. He moves and responds to those around him, desiring in the present without forethought or calculation. He is met in this openness by Ray Forrestier, who comes to rescue him at the close of the novel. Ray moves freely towards Leopold (the word free is repeated five times in this context) and takes him up like a figure in a fairy tale – he strides off with Leopold 'like a robber with one babe through a wood'. The text ends in a magical suspension, with Ray and Leopold gazing out over Paris as they wait for a taxi. Everything is about to begin: Leopold shivers like 'someone drawing a first breath'. The text ends on a note of pure expectation, pointing to a future, or a line of flight, which is, perhaps, unrepresentable within the novel as domestic realism:

> Egotism and panic, knowing mistrust of what was to be, died in Ray as he waited beside Leopold for their taxi to come: the child commanded tonight. I have acted on his scale . . .
> . . . The copper-dark night sky went glassy over the city crowned with signs and starting alight with windows, the wet square like a lake at the foot of the station ramp. (p. 229)

In *The Death of the Heart* (1938), becoming woman is expressed and explored through the figure of a girl, the 16-year-old Portia Quayne. Like Leopold, Portia is in the position of the illegitimate child, being conceived outside marriage although she is technically legitimate. She is the product of an adulterous relationship between a retired businessman, Mr Quayne, and Irene, 'a scrap of a widow . . .

with damp little hands, a husky voice and defective tear-ducts that
gave her eyes always rather a swimmy look'.[10] When she hears that
Irene exists, and is pregnant, Mr Quayne's wife forces him to divorce her and marry Irene, then to spend the rest of his life abroad,
moving from one cheap hotel to another. When first Mr Quayne
and then Irene dies, Portia is sent to have a taste of *'normal, cheerful* family life' (Bowen's italics) with her half-brother Thomas and
his wife Anna. The novel charts the first few months of this stay,
and focuses on Portia's relations with Thomas, Anna, the housekeeper Matchett and a young man, Eddie, who is something of a
protégé of Anna. Portia's relationship with Eddie proves to be the
most important for her, and it dominates her mind until she gets
hold of the (mistaken) idea that Eddie has betrayed her confidence
by telling Anna about the diary that she has been keeping. Distraught, Portia flees the Quayne's comfortable house in Regents Park,
and throws herself on the mercy of an acquaintance of theirs who
is eking out a miserable life in the Karachi Hotel, Kensington. The
novel ends with Anna and Thomas sending Matchett to bring Portia
home, though neither they nor the reader knows whether this is
the 'right' thing to do in the circumstances.

As with Leopold, Portia lives in a kind of suspended state, outside the dominant social order. Anna characterizes her very existence
as a kind of mistake or error – 'What is she, after all? The child of
an aberration, the child of a panic, the child of an old chap's piti-
ful sexuality' (p. 296). Brought up in exile in hotels and flats on
the Riviera, Portia knows nothing of 'normal, cheerful' family life
nor of wider (middle-class) social mores. After her father's death,
she and Irene cling together in a willed return to the Kristevan
semiotic, avoiding social structures and contact:

> Untaught, they had walked arm-in-arm along city pavements,
> and at nights had pulled their beds close together or slept in
> the same bed – overcoming, as far as might be, the separation
> of birth. Seldom had they faced up to society – when they did,
> Irene did the wrong thing, then cried. (p. 69)

At the time when the novel opens, Portia is divided between her
'untaught', unconscious, bodily life, and the demands of the social
world. As she moves in the Windsor Terrace drawing-room, scruti-
nized by Anna and her friend St Quentin, we learn that 'each
movement had a touch of exaggeration, as though some secret power

kept springing out. At the same time she looked cautious, aware of the world in which she had to live' (p. 36).

As in Bowen's earlier books, the potential of 'the young girl' contrasts sharply with the molar femininities of the older women in the novel. The elder Mrs Quayne (the one who 'sacks' Mr Quayne and condemns him to a life of exile) is particularly fixed and rigid in her ideas and behaviour – Anna describes her as 'one of those implacably nice women whose niceness you can't get past, and whose understanding gets into every crack of your temperament' (p. 20). When she finds out about Irene, her response is 'quite ecstatic', and when she has decided what should be done, her idealism 'spread[s] around the house like flu' (p. 25). What she cares about is 'the look of the thing' and that she should seem to be 'a living saint' (Mr Quayne's phrase). When she dies, Anna inherits her furniture, and seems to have other qualities in common with her. The furniture is foregrounded by Bowen, representing tradition and something to be worked at (by Matchett, of course, not by the Quaynes). Matchett sees the furniture as lovely and valuable, but it could also be seen as simply dead wood, representing the rigid and sedimented social codes from which Portia must escape.

At the time when Portia comes to stay with her, Anna Quayne has already had a failed love affair and a failed career, and has been unable to have children with Thomas. These failures have made her melancholy and closed-in. She and her friends have 'no spontaneous wish for each other', but compensate for this 'lack of *goût*' (appetite, desire) by getting on, making allowances for each other, saving each other's faces. In other words, living as a stylish married woman, Anna is nonetheless completely cut off from desire in the Deleuzian sense, desire as 'immanent, as positive and productive, a fundamental, full, and creative relation'.[11] It is this which Portia *unconsciously* makes her see, or feel:

> The *idea* of her never leaves me quiet, and by coming into this room she drives me onto the ice. Everything she does to me is unconscious: if it were conscious it would not hurt. She makes me feel like a tap that won't turn on. (p. 296)

Anna ought to act as Portia's mentor, but instead cuts her off and diminishes her. At one point, after looking at a drawing of Anna at the age of twelve, Portia dreams that she is sharing a book with Anna as a little girl. They are in a situation of danger, but also of possibility – there is a wood, or a forest, under the window. To return here to the metaphor of the tree/wood: while Deleuze and Guattari specifically argue against 'aborescent' structures of thought in *A Thousand Plateaus*, the tree as a (recurrent) motif in Bowen's work can, nonetheless, fruitfully be read in the light of their wider argument. In Bowen's fiction, I would suggest, the metaphor repeatedly functions to signal the distinction between sedimented social forms and practices (wood) and new material growth and its potential disruption of such forms (tree). If the Windsor Terrace furniture can be called dead wood, then living wood functions in the novel as the space of desire and dream (as in fairy stories). As Portia reads with Anna, the crucial point is that the forest is being *varnished* all over, leaving no way of escape. The varnish represents the social polish which is both Anna's protection and her downfall.

Portia, untaught, experiences life in untaught ways. She has a heightened awareness of the body and of its forces and energies, and, for example, when Anna is uncomfortable because her ex-lover is being discussed, Portia 'tunes in' to her agitation through a kind of bodily exchange:

> Anna, on the sofa in a Récamier attitude, had acted, among all she had had to act, a hardy imperviousness to [Portia's gaze]. Had the agitation she felt throughout her body sent out an aura with a quivering edge, Portia's eyes might be said to explore this line of quiver, round and along Anna's reclining form. (p. 60)

Portia is also repeatedly likened to a cat or a kitten, so that she might be said to move along the path of 'becoming animal' as well as the path of 'becoming woman'. In *A Thousand Plateaus* Deleuze and Guattari write that in 'becoming animal' we do not imitate an animal, or conceive of our likeness to it, but rather enter into a relation with its otherness via a mediating third term – '[d]o not imitate a dog, but make your organism enter into composition with *something else* in such a way that the particles emitted from the aggregate thus composed will be canine . . .' (p. 274). Major Brutt is likened repeatedly to a dog, and various other characters are compared with animals. The effect of this in Bowen's text is not to suggest homologies between humans and animals, but to conjure up some of the more unexpected 'paths of becoming' which are open to us.

The most important path of becoming which lies open to Portia is through her love for Eddie. In her relation with Eddie, the very qualities which have made her a potential victim are turned right round:

> The force of Eddie's behaviour whirled her free of a hundred puzzling humiliations, of her hundred failures to take the ordinary cue. She could meet the demands he made with the natural genius of the friend and lover. The impetus under which he seemed to move made life fall, round him and round her, into a new poetic order at once. Any kind of policy in the region of feeling would have been fatal in any lover of his – you had to yield to the wind. Portia's unpreparedness, her lack of policy – which had made Windsor Terrace, for her, the court of an incomprehensible law – with Eddie stood her in good stead. She had no point to stick to, nothing to unlearn ... By making herself so much his open piano that she felt her lips smile by reflex, as though they were his lips, she felt herself learn and gain him: this was Eddie. (p. 128)

Having nothing to unlearn, Portia is free to enter into relation with the effeminate Eddie (who is equally, in many respects, a pre-social being), making her naivety the bridge (or third term) between them which enables each to 'become other'. Her relation with Eddie depends on their both accessing what Deleuze and Guattari call the 'Body without Organs' (BwO) – a tendency, a plane of consistence which is not identical with 'a' body, with its presumed conscious subject and organic determination, but which constitutes rather a pre-personal, pre-organic plane. As Deleuze writes, 'It seemed to us that desire was a process and that it unrolled a *plane of consistence*, a field of immanence, a "body without organs", as Artaud put it, criss-crossed by particles and fluxes ...'.[12] Portia seems to figure just such a plane or body to herself as she lies on the verge of sleep. She imagines a landscape which is like a sea containing smaller ripples, just as, for Deleuze and Guattari, the plane of immanence is a single wave which rolls up and unrolls the multiple waves of its concepts:

> Safe for the minute, sealed down under her eyelids, Portia lay and saw herself with Eddie. She saw a continent in the late sunset, in rolls and ridges of shadow like the sea. Light that was

dark yellow lay on trees, and penetrated their dark hearts. Like a
struck glass, the continent rang with silence. The country, with
its slow tense dusk-drowned ripple, rose to their feet where they
sat . . . (p. 104)

Portia and Eddie's love falters, nonetheless, because each forms a
partially idealized image of the other – to this extent, they are
unable to escape conventional forms and determinations. Portia wants
Eddie to be 'faithful', and cannot bear his holding hands with Daphne
Heccomb at the cinema: Eddie wants Portia to rise above such petty
considerations. Their love seems to fall to pieces, only to reassert
itself on a physical plane which has nothing to do with their conscious concerns and connections. As they walk up through the spring
trees (again, the same metaphor), smelling the gummy smell of the
leaves in bud, '[i]n spirit, the two of them rose to the top of life
like bubbles' (p. 262). This alternation between an optimistic and a
pessimistic inflection persists until the close of the novel, which
ends, like *The House in Paris*, on a threshold moment – literally in
this case, as Matchett puts her hand on the door of the Karachi
Hotel. The text is (susp)ended in an undecidable moment of an-
ticipation. Bowen writes of 'a sort of joy' which will 'open in all
hearts' as summer comes with roses burning in the dusk – and yet
the final action in the novel is that of the repressive Matchett, and
the last word of the novel is 'authority'. The text ends on a note
of alternation, oscillation, and instability which is one of the hall-
marks of Bowen's fiction.

The Heat of the Day (1949) is also structured around the interplay
between the implacability of custom and the unpredictability and
potential of individual bodies. The novel has (at least) a double
structure. The main protagonist, a forty-ish divorcee, Stella Rodney,
is living in London two years after the Blitz and two years into a
love affair with Robert Kelway, who works, like her, in intelligence.
At the beginning of the novel a stranger, Harrison, approaches Stella
and tells her that Kelway is a spy who has been passing information to the enemy. Stella refuses to believe this at first, and hesitates
to confront Robert with what she has been told. To gain time, she
travels to Ireland, to visit a run-down estate which her son has
inherited. On her return, Robert asks her to marry him, and then
confesses that all Harrison has told her is true. The novel ends
with Kelway's (probable) suicide and Stella's engagement to 'a cousin
of a cousin', a brigadier.

The double significance of the novel lies in the parallel which Bowen makes explicit between the particular story of Stella and Robert and a wider 'story' about the relations between the sexes. The relationship between Stella and Robert is presented as particular and contingent, bound by and moving in time:

> But they were not alone, nor had they been from the start, from the start of love. Their time sat in the third place at their table. They were the creatures of history, whose coming together was of a nature possible in no other day – the day was inherent in the nature. Which must have been always true of lovers, if it had taken till now to be seen. The relation of people to one another is subject to the relation of each to time, to what is happening.[13]

Yet in her uncertainty over whether Robert is telling her the truth, Stella is like hundreds of other women, 'suspecting what they refuse to prove' about their husbands and lovers. This memorable phrase occurs in the middle of a densely written excursus in the section of the novel dealing with Stella's visit to Ireland. Stella goes into the drawing-room at Mount Morris, and carries the lamp over so that she can see her own reflection in a mirror. For a moment, she looks like 'a lady of the house', but it is an appearance only, for she has quite 'lost the secret' of being such a lady. She thinks back, however, to the women who lived at Mount Morris in the past and who 'had been pressed back, hour by hour, by the hours themselves, into cloudland. Ladies had gone not quite mad, not quite even that, from in vain listening for meaning in the loudening ticking of the clock' (p. 166). Bowen writes of these women:

> Everything spoke to them – the design in and out of which they drew their needles; the bird with its little claws drawn to its piteously smooth breast, dead; away in the woods the quickening strokes of the axes, then the fall of the tree; or the child upstairs crying out terrified in its sleep. No, knowledge was not to be kept from them; it sifted through to them, stole up behind them, reached them by intimations – they suspected what they refused to prove. That had been their decision. So, there had been the cases of the enactment of ignorance having become too much, insupportable inside those sheltered heads. (p. 167)

These women have gone 'not quite mad' because they have been asked to represent something rather than to be something, to present a flawless image of 'feminine' serenity and peace. They have been expected to deny the violence of the world, and perhaps more importantly the violence within them, in order to conform to the standards of 'molar' femininity. Nonetheless, they see destruction and death everywhere – 'the little bird lying big with death on the path', as Bowen puts it in a striking image of reverse pregnancy.

Bowen is writing at this point of earlier generations, and she makes this historical specificity quite clear. The most recent 'lady of the house' has been Cousin Nettie, who acts as a transitional figure, moving between the women of the past and women like Stella Rodney. Cousin Nettie, having married her cousin Frank, finds herself unable to act the part of his wife. She tries 'this, that and the other', until she falls into 'a terrible melancholy'. Unlike earlier generations of women, however, she rebels against her false position by accepting and exploiting the idea of her madness or 'oddness'. This enables her to live apart from Francis and Mount Morris in the seclusion of the English countryside. When Roderick, Stella's son, goes to visit her we discover that she is, of course, far from mad. Indeed, she is presented as a kind of visionary or seer:

All Cousin Nettie's life it must have been impossible for her to look at the surface only, to see nothing more than she should. These were the eyes of an often-rebuked clairvoyante, wide once more with the fear of once more divining what should remain hidden. (p. 199)

One of the things that Cousin Nettie sees is the structural difference in men and women's relation to power and to 'becoming'. As Deleuze and Guattari explain in *A Thousand Plateaus*, masculinity is always molar:

There is no becoming-man because man is the molar entity par excellence, whereas becomings are molecular . . . man constitutes the majority, or rather the standard upon which the majority is based: white, male, adult, 'rational,' etc., in short the average European, the subject of enunciation. (p. 292)

Robert Kelway's betrayal of his country and of Stella can be seen as the result of an over-investment in masculine standards and values, an over-identification with 'the standard upon which the majority is based'. As Stella looks at his photograph, just before he finally leaves her, she notices his appearance of '[t]wisted inspiration' and 'romanticism'. He has betrayed his country not because he *rejects* its code of heroic masculinity (as a conscientious objector might, for example), but because he finds it more fully articulated and developed in the rhetoric of the enemy.

Bowen's text thus suggests that identification with masculine, majoritarian identities is inseparable from the exercise of power and domination. The characterization of Robert Kelway offers a complex analysis of the way in which such identifications feed into oppressive and exclusionary structures, as is suggested by the following exchange between him and Stella. Robert asks:

> '*You* think, in me this was simply wanting to get my hand on the controls?
> 'I don't think I think.'
> 'Well, it's not: it's not a question of that. Who wants to monkey about? To feel control is enough. It's a very much bigger thing to be under orders.'
> 'We are all under orders; what is there new in that?'
> 'Yes, can you wonder they love war. But I don't mean orders, I mean order.' (p. 264)

Here, everyone apart from Robert (including, presumably, Stella) is dismissively lumped together as the 'they' who love war – elsewhere he speaks of them as 'your mass of "free" suckers, your democracy – kidded along from the cradle to the grave' (p. 259). For Robert, democratic freedom is an illusion: he commits himself, rather to abstract conceptions of 'law', 'order' or 'strength' which have chilling implications in the context of Fascism.

As in her other texts, however, Bowen suggests that femininity can be inflected towards a molar or a molecular formation. Some characters, such as Mrs Kelway, Robert's mother, are associated with an oppressively 'fixed' femininity and sense of superiority – she is described as 'relentlessly' and 'dauntingly' distinct in her feminine beauty, sitting in the dead centre of 'a bewitched wood' (p. 104). Others, like Stella, and the character who functions as her uneducated double, Louie, offer a different kind of potential. This is where an ethical dimension makes itself felt in the novel, in the emphasis on the ability of these characters to 'become woman', moving outside or beyond the fixity of conventional subjectivity. In one of the most remarkable passages in the novel, the narrative follows Stella at Mount Morris, walking in the woods:

> Still, though, this was the early morning of a unique day: the very day in which – who knew? – something might intervene to save her. She was at the foot of the most advancing promontory of the Mount Morris woods, at the point where, borne forward on inside rock, they most nearly approached the river. A rapture of strength could be felt in the rising tree trunks rooted gripping the slope, and in the stretch of the boughs; and there travelled through the layered, lit, shaded, thinning and crossing foliage, and was deflected downward on to the laurels, a breathless glory. In the hush the dead could be imagined returning from all the wars; and, turning the eyes from arch to arch of boughs, from ray to ray of light, one knew some expectant sense to be tuned in to an unfinished symphony of love. (p. 170)

The text emphasizes the particularity, the specificity of this scene. Stella is out at a particular point in the early morning, her senses tuned to the stretch and grip of the rising tree trunks. She participates in the 'becoming' of these trees through the mediating third term of the light which strikes indifferently on the trees and on herself. In this moment of energy and release of being, her thoughts turn to the dead, 'expectantly'. It is this complete readiness and expectancy, here linked with those who seem most *un*-expectant and beyond recall, which marks Stella's openness to unfathomable 'becomings' and exchanges of being. It is she who is tuned in to 'an unfinished symphony of love' (Bowen is particularly fond of metaphors of wavelengths and magnetism in such contexts). Louie shares Stella's openness, and so it is not surprising that towards the end of the novel she should, however reluctantly, 'become' Stella, tuning in to a different mode of being:

> Louie felt herself entered by what was foreign. She exclaimed in thought, 'Oh no, I wouldn't be *her*!' at the moment when she most nearly was. Think, now, what the air was charged with night and day – ununderstandable languages, music you did not care for, sickness, germs! You did not know what you might not be tuning in to, you could not say what you might not be picking up; affected, infected you were at every turn. (pp. 239–40)

Louie's capacity to yield to others eventually bears literal fruit: after an unplanned pregnancy, the novel ends with the birth of her child. The child's father is not her husband, and so Bowen once again (as in *The House in Paris* and *The Death of the Heart*) ends a novel with the whole weight of the future seeming to rest on a child con-ceived outside marriage, outside the fundamental structure of patriarchy. Bowen's repeated use of this motif suggests the degree of her investment in that which lies outside majoritarian and con-servative structures: it is only from a position outside these structures that growth and movement can come.

A World of Love (1955) might be said to intensify the subjects and themes of *The Heat of the Day*. As Bennett and Royle have pointed out, the title of the earlier book is woven into the first sentence of *A World of Love*,[14] and the setting of *A World of Love* seems to repeat (though with a difference) the Mount Morris scenes of *The Heat of the Day*, opening out, as it were, Stella's apprehen-sion of 'an unfinished symphony of love'. The plot of the novel is very simple. A young girl, Jane Danby, living on a run-down estate in southern Ireland, discovers a packet of old love letters up in the attic. They have been written by a young man who was killed in the First World War, the former owner of the estate and former fiancé of her mother. His name is 'Guy'. It is not clear who the letters were written to, but their discovery sets up a strong current of feeling in Jane, her mother Lilia and her adopted aunt, Antonia. Lilia and Antonia are brought to meditate on the past and on their relationship with each other, while Jane 'falls in love' with the writer of the letters and in a scene of extraordinary intensity in-vokes his name at a dinner-party at a neighbouring castle. The novel ends when the chatelaine, Lady Latterly, asks Jane to go to the airport to meet a cast-off lover of hers. No sooner has Richard Priam stepped off the plane than his eyes meet Jane's: the novel ends with the sentence 'They no sooner looked but they loved'.[15]

Given this plot, the 'world of love' of the title could be inter-preted as the world of romantic love. If this is the case, then romantic love is presented at an ironic distance. The love the three women feel for Guy, fluttering round the flame of his letters 'like butter-flies', as one reviewer put it,[16] is shown to be a fantasy grounded in mistaken ideas about the transcendent power of love. Lilia, in particular, requires such fantasies in order to sustain her sense of being. Lilia is unequivocally presented in terms of molar feminin-ity. She is strongly identified with the social/bodily construction of femininity, and relies on her hairdresser to sustain what Bowen calls 'the life-illusion'. Miss Francie's salon is a place of refuge where Lilia can renew her sense of feminine glamour, climbing up 'pink-linoed stairs', smelling a breath of 'perfumed singeing', then sitting enclosed in 'triple net blinds' looking at magazines on a 'gilded wicker table'. Bowen foregrounds Lilia's dependence on the social construction of femininity – at one point, at the hairdresser's, when she asks Jane for a magazine, 'Jane supplied her with *Woman*. But after all, Lilia did nothing more than contemplate, with her head aslant, prototype Woman on the cover' (p. 134). Lilia needs the prototype, and needs the illusions of the past and the present. She needs to believe that she was Guy's only love, and although she knows that there may have been another lover at the time when he left for the Front, she pushes this to the back of her mind, because 'if not the Beloved, what was Lilia? Nothing. Nothing was left to be' (p. 143). Lilia believes that her only authentic existence is as the object of Guy's transmuting and transforming love: she is only able to transcend herself by virtue of his love.

One of the questions the novel does not answer is whether Jane and Richard's love will be grounded in a similarly distorting and damaging asymmetry. The fact that this love is promoted by Lady Latterly does not augur well. The very name Vesta Latterly suggests a belated fanning of a questionable flame, and Lady Latterly is, like Lilia, strongly linked with molar femininity. Before the dinner-party, Jane sits in Vesta's bedroom, comparing it with the disorder and chaos of Antonia's room at Montefort:

> *Here*, it was true, the scene was differently set – no smears, no ash, no feathers on the floor; instead, whole areas of undinted satin, no trace of anything having been touched or used. Here and there only, footprints like tracks in dew disturbed the bloom of the silver carpet. Here, supposed Jane, courteously looking round, must be a replica, priceless these days, of a Mayfair *décor* back in the 1930s – apparently still lived in without a tremor . . . The necessity, the fragility and perhaps the pathos of all this as a carapace did not strike the young girl. (pp. 81–2)

The untouched, and perhaps untouchable, *mise en scène* of femininity links up with the chiffon and varnish which make Lady Latterly 'seem to be made of plastic' – just as Lilia is later described as one who has 'seceded from life and become marble' (p. 143). These women are as though transfixed and immobilized by social and cultural pressures, incapable of original or spontaneous action.

Lady Latterly is not, however, the only cause of Jane's love for Richard. Guy, the writer of the letters, whose name suggests that he stands in for any man/guy, is more deeply implicated in this. Guy can be seen as a betrayer-figure and thus linked with Robert Kelway in *The Heat of the Day*. He seems to stand for the doubleness of twentieth-century masculinity and patriarchy: he has position and power as a landowner, but loses this through his involvement in the catastrophe of the First World War. He tempts all the women in the novel, reversing the convention of the woman as temptress, seducing them by the power of his address. Each imagines herself as the only object of desire: so Jane, *belatedly* reading a line from the letters, instates herself as the object of love:

> '*I thought*,' he wrote, '*if only YOU had been here!*'
> A thread lay dropped on the grass, for Jane to pick up. 'But here I am. Oh, here I *am*!' she protested. (p. 69)

She *is*, she imagines, because she is loved: she is authenticated by being the object of male desire, the 'beloved'. It is the script which Guy has left which prepares her for the 'romantic' encounter with Richard.

If *A World of Love* presents romantic love from a critical distance, it also, however, and more importantly, endorses a different and far more idiosyncratic vision of 'a world of love'. This might be described as a world of desire, in the Deleuzian sense. Deleuze and Guattari's concept of the 'haecceity' is particularly helpful here, throwing into relief a quality which is always present in Bowen's writing but which is especially marked in this novel. In *A Thousand Plateaus* Deleuze and Guattari define a haecceity in the following way:

> There is a mode of individuation very different from that of a person, subject, thing, or substance. We reserve the name *haecceity* for it. A season, a winter, a summer, an hour, a date have a perfect individuality lacking nothing, even though this individuality is different from that of a thing or subject. They are haecceities in the sense that they consist entirely of relations of movement and rest between molecules and particles, capacities to affect and be affected. (p. 261)

We have seen how Bowen's fiction dramatizes 'becoming woman' and 'becoming other', but perhaps the most striking aspect of her work is the way in which it presents 'haecceities' as Deleuze and Guattari describe them. Bowen's work focuses intensively on seasons and hours and on their 'perfect individuality'. In *The Heat of the Day*, this is one of the issues which most divides Robert and Stella. When Robert denies that there is any such thing as a country, Stella feels that 'his denials of everything instinctive seemed now to seal up love at the source'. She protests that there *is* a country, but that it is made out of place and time and consists, precisely, of innumerable individuations. Such an individuation, 'different from that of a thing or subject', is disclosed in her early-morning walk at Mount Morris. *A World of Love* opens with a similar scene:

> The sun rose on a landscape still pale with the heat of the day before. There was no haze, but a sort of coppery burnish out of the air lit on flowing fields, rocks, the face of the one house and the cliff of limestone overhanging the river. The river gorge cut deep through the uplands. This light at this hour, so unfamiliar, brought into being a new world – painted, expectant, empty, intense. The month was June, of a summer almost unknown; for this was a country accustomed to late wakenings, to daybreaks humid and overcast. At all times open and great with distance, the land this morning seemed to enlarge again, throwing the mountains back almost out of view in the south of Ireland's amazement at being cloudless. (p. 9)

In a haecceity, heterogeneous bodies are yoked together on a plane of consistence and connected together to form a new ensemble, a new individuation. So in this passage, the rocks and fields, the implied human subject/observer, and the heat, the stillness and the light are brought into relation and made to form a new and singular 'event'. The novel as a whole can be said to consist of a stringing together of such events: the text passes through them like one of Deleuze and Guattari's 'lines of flight'.

A World of Love is a novel which is, above all, productive and generative, insisting on and articulating new connections and flows of energy, new modes of feeling. It explores the relations between bodies, minds, landscapes and weathers, charting/expressing 'events' of desire on a plane of immanence. It is a radical novel, and it is also one of Bowen's most optimistic. Although the text seems to end with Jane on the brink of a romance taken straight out of Lilia's *Woman*, we feel, at the same time, her capacity for 'the desire of some Great Thing' as the novel's epigraph puts it, her potential for a love of a different kind from romantic love. Bowen's interest in such a 'line of flight' might not please all feminist readers, but it represents her distinctive response to the problem of entrapment within the patriarchally coded adult female body.

3
Elizabeth Taylor's Speaking Bodies

In Chapter 1, the work of Luce Irigaray was invoked in order to shed light on Rosamond Lehmann's understanding of female immanence. Irigaray's work seems even more pertinent to the explorations of female embodiment in Elizabeth Taylor's fiction. The core of Irigaray's critique of phallogocentrism can be found in her first major work, *Speculum of the Other Woman*.[1] Here, Irigaray argues that the Western metaphysical tradition is founded on an elision of the feminine. Woman, or the maternal-feminine, provides the unsymbolized basis of the masculine theoretical constructions which shape our world. In *Speculum*, she analyses the works of the 'master-thinkers' from Plato to Freud, and argues that they have (wrongly) theorized human subjectivity in terms of a transcendental rationality. Rationality, or reason, is the light by means of which the male subject sees himself as transcendent, self-identical. As Rosi Braidotti puts it, 'This specular game essentially functions at the expense of the woman's body; material body, matrix of being, it is repudiated and devalued by the self-affirmation of the masculine logos.'[2] A metaphor which Irigaray concentrates on in this respect is that of the mirror. The woman's body functions as a mirror within which man sees himself. When man looks in the mirror, all he sees is himself: what is being elided and disavowed is the physical material of the mirror, the glass and its silver backing.

Irigaray suggests, then, that meaning and identity as they have been constructed in Western metaphysics are illusions resting on a disavowal of the woman's body, of matter and of the corporeal roots of the human intellect. Throughout her work, Irigaray explores the consequences of such a denial both for philosophy and culture. As Margaret Whitford has stressed, for Irigaray there is a crucial link between the philosophical and the social/political spheres. As Whitford puts it, 'there is a connection between the status of women in western thought and the status of women in western society; the two domains share the same imaginary, so the difference between the metaphorical and the social reality becomes . . . blurred'.[3] In the philosophical imaginary, truth and its co-ordinates of unity, teleology, linearity and self-identity are inextricably bound up with the morphology of the male body, whereas the female body represents the 'outside' of truth, a 'hole' or unsymbolized residue. This philosophical imaginary extends into the social imaginary with damaging consequences for women, who find themselves in a state of *déréliction*, cast out of the symbolic order.

Elizabeth Taylor's fiction, so often thought of as gentle ('feminine') social comedy, tackles these issues head on. Her fiction is centrally concerned with 'male' and 'female' worlds (in both the philosophical and social senses), and with their intersection and interrelation. Her third novel, *Palladian*, published in 1946, has been praised for its intertextuality and for its 'penetrating analysis of the interface between romance and the Gothic'.[4] Patsy Stoneman argues that the novel offers a twentieth-century rereading of *Jane Eyre* and *Wuthering Heights*. The orphaned heroine, Cassandra Dashwood, goes to Cropthorne Manor to act as governess to Sophy, the daughter of Marion Vanbrugh. Cassandra falls in love with her employer, as does Jane in *Jane Eyre*, but, confusingly, Marion is a rather effeminate figure modelled on Edgar Linton from *Wuthering Heights*, while Marion's cousin, Tom, acts as 'a sort of glowering Heathcliff'.[5] Complicating matters further, Taylor also invokes the theme and some of the atmosphere of Daphne du Maurier's *Rebecca*, which was published in 1939. Marion's dead wife, Violet, who was also Tom's mistress, is presented to Cassandra as an image of perfection, a beautiful and brilliant woman whom she can never equal: '[s]he guessed that the dead one was an undisputed barrier between [Marion] and life, a barrier he would never challenge, a fixed standard by which all else would inevitably fail' (p. 51). As Stoneman points out, Cassandra follows the path of the heroine of *Jane Eyre* rather than that of the heroine of *Wuthering Heights*: she does not die tragically, but accepts marriage with a hero who has by the end of the novel come to seem a rather diminished figure. This is, of course, also the fate of the unnamed heroine of *Rebecca*.

While Stoneman concentrates on Taylor's critique of romance in her reading of *Palladian*, I would like to focus on a different and arguably more important critique which is also embedded in the novel. As the title suggests, the novel is concerned not only with romance but also with the classical tradition, reaching back in architectural terms from Inigo Jones in the eighteenth century via Palladio in the sixteenth century to the large-scale public architecture of ancient Greece and Rome. Cropthorne Manor is a neo-classical building which has fallen into a state of decay, largely because of Marion Vanbrugh's inward-looking, narcissistic temperament. When Cassandra first arrives, the house makes a gloomy impression on her:

> Cassandra . . . received an impression of the facade and, as well as the rows of sashed windows and not quite central pediment, smaller details were snatched at and relinquished again by her commentating eye; pieces of dismembered statuary, of dark grey stucco fallen from the walls and a wrought-iron lamp at the head of the steps with its greenish glass cracked. (p. 20)

The house functions in a complex manner, figuring on the one hand the decaying classical tradition and on the other the abandoned and neglected body/material substance of life which is ignored by Marion. This neglect has fatal consequences: Marion's daughter Sophy is killed by the falling statue of a goddess, either Flora or Pomona.

The classical tradition is strongly connected with Marion. He hires Cassandra to teach Sophy Latin, and supervises the teaching; later he offers to teach Cassandra Greek. As he watches Cassandra copying out Greek letters, he feels 'his gift to her [to be] the most precious he could bestow. He sat still, the book drooping in his hand, and watched her pen shaping the unfamiliar and beautiful letters' (p. 98). Yet Taylor explicitly condemns his classicism on the grounds of its abstract and cerebral bias, its derogation of the reality of the body. At one point, Marion takes Cassandra's hand, and then drops it again. Taylor writes:

> For the first and only time she imagined what it might have been like to have been Violet, [the dead first wife] and pitied her; saw with clarity, for what it was, the titillation of Greek lessons, the cerebral intimacy, the impersonal taking up and dropping of hands. (p. 82)

After Sophy's funeral, Cassandra picks up her copy of *The Classical Tradition*, given to her by its author, her old headmistress. '*The Classical Tradition*, she thought, taking the little book from a drawer. What in heaven's name was it all about?' (p. 154)

One answer might come from Irigaray. In 'Plato's *Hystera*', the third section of *Speculum*, she offers a reading of Book VII of *The Republic* in which Plato presents the allegory of the cave. Plato suggests that the relation between the world of matter (the apparent world) and the world of ideas (the invisible, divine world) is analogous to that between the world of a dark cave and the world outside the cave, lit by the light of the sun. Psychoanalysing Plato, Irigaray argues that his analogy gives away the game of Western metaphysics. Plato's cave is, in psychoanalytic terms, a womb (*hystera*), and the analogy brings back into view that which metaphysics wishes to disavow. For Irigaray, the abstractions of metaphysics depend on the disavowal of the female body and of the sensible, material conditions of life: '[e]clipse of the mother, of the place (of) becoming, whose non-representation or even disavowal upholds the absolute being attributed to the father' (p. 307).

In *Palladian*, Taylor brings the materiality of the female body back into representation, moving into an area which was (and perhaps still is) generally taboo. Taylor's fiction is unusual in its representation of the pregnant female body, present here in Margaret, Tom's sister and Marion's cousin. Throughout the time-scale of the novel, Cassandra's classical education is paralleled by the stealthy growth of the child in Margaret's womb, born at the end of the novel. The male characters find the thought of pregnancy repellent. Tom remembers Violet's death in childbirth and her animal screams which 'had frozen the world with terror' (p. 66). Now he withdraws from the pregnant female body, anatomizing it in beautiful but cruel drawings:

> This one which he did so painstakingly was like an engraving in some ancient medical book – the Rubens ripeness of the woman, the large belly laid open to show a child curled in the womb, the four lappets of flesh furled back like leaves. It was a beautiful and complicated drawing, but done on a scrap of torn paper, not clean. He placed a rose in the woman's hand, drew in the veins along one arm and the coarse hair starting from the armpit, then, looking pleased, he cleaned his pen-nib carefully and finished dressing. (p. 40)

Margaret is not an entirely pleasant character, being sarcastic and high-handed in her dealings with inferiors such as Cassandra and the servants. Nonetheless, her pregnancy and a complex of images of the productive female body act as a necessary counterpart in the novel to the fetid and decadent (classical) world which Marion inhabits. In *Palladian,* Taylor opposes the *hystera* to the world of Marion's classical learning, mocking the illusions of male transcendence shared by Tom and Marion. The *hystera*'s role as 'the place (of) becoming', as the necessary precondition of being, is emphasized and foregrounded. Part of the comedy but also part of the seriousness of the book lies in the fact that Taylor does not shrink from what are usually seen as the gross aspects of pregnancy. Lasciviously, for example, Margaret eats:

> She cut a thick slice of wholemeal bread, covered it with butter, then with the cheese, began to eat greedily, dealing craftily with the crumbs, turning the pages of the cinema paper. When she had finished, she was still hungry. She cut another slice and spread it as before. The thought of all this good, wholesome food going into her was pleasing. (pp. 53–4)

And 'the Anglo-Saxon language of the old wives' (Nanny and Mrs Adams, in the kitchen) brings other tabooed aspects of pregnancy back into discourse:

> "With Madam she carried the boys right under the bust, it was much remarked upon, but Miss Violet she carried so low that she could never as much as go up the stairs without sitting down half-way for a rest, that's when we began having the chair on the half-landing. Then trouble with her water. 'I've been in and out of bed all night, Nanny,' she used to say. Pressing on the bladder, you see." (p. 112)

Palladian thus offers a witty critique of 'the classical tradition' and of a Platonic metaphysics which disavows the feminine/the body as ground and precondition of being. Taylor re-presents the feminine not only in the figure of Margaret, but also in the cleaner Mrs Adams and her baby which 'though female, though such a trouble with wind, was real to her and tugged her homewards' (p. 70). Mrs Veal, Tom's despised mistress, is also given her due by Taylor – 'Mrs Veal, stepping out of her bath, had a Rubens magnificence. Her little rosy knees looked lost under the great massing thighs. One curve of flesh ran into another' (p. 144).

Bringing the feminine back into representation, into the symbolic, Taylor nevertheless presents a world in which the male *logos* and female *physis* are far apart from each other, simply not in relation. It is this lack of relation, of exchange and mutuality, which is potentially so destructive for all the characters in the novel, but especially for Cassandra. She seems reserved for some dreadful sacrifice: in the last line of the novel, as she walks into the hall of the house with Marion, we're told that 'the dark shadows of indoors fell coldly . . . like a knife'. Her first name, of course, carries overtones of doom which override the happier Austenian associations of 'Dashwood'.

Just as Taylor's novel suggests the need to bring masculine and feminine, *logos* and *physis* into relation, so it suggests the need to relate the spheres of 'high' and 'low' culture. As the novel makes clear, the opposition between high and low culture is connected with the opposition between masculine and feminine: it is a *gendered* opposition. Referring back to the work of Hilary Radner on the woman's novel, we might say that 'high' culture, with its discourse of mastery, its obsessional drive towards interpretation, is gendered as masculine, whereas 'low' culture, with its hysterical (from the Greek *hystera*) pleasure in feeling and sensation is feminine.[6] As a woman's novelist, Taylor recognizes and incorporates *both* discourses. As Radner suggests, the woman's novel is like a gestalt picture, facing both ways, combining two discourses which are usually considered to be mutually exclusive.

A good example of this deconstructive tactic occurs in a scene in *Palladian* which explores Sophy's feelings after she has been to see the Hollywood film of *Pride and Prejudice* – presumably the 1940 version starring Laurence Olivier as Darcy and Greer Garson as Elizabeth Bennet.[7] Needless to say, the outing to the cinema is looked on with scorn and derision by Tom and Marion. Tom is opposed to it on the grounds that 'no films are suitable' (p. 46); Marion takes the opportunity to prevent Cassandra from going, offering her a Greek lesson instead. Sophy therefore goes to see the film with Nanny, whose intention to consume the film is signalled by her taking a large bag of food with her, just in case she should feel faint during the second feature. The opposition between high and low culture, the Greek and the popular, could hardly be made clearer. Yet when Sophy returns, Taylor shows us the importance of the popular text and its centrality in the construction of women's subjectivity, in particular. Both Nanny and Sophy are in thrall (via a series of displacements on Nanny's part) to the idea of the woman as privileged object of the male gaze:

> "That Elizabeth Bennet was beautiful." Sophy took the lump of sugar from its frilled paper case and put it in her cheek.
> "Yes. She's good. That's a lovely place she's got up in Beverley Hills, swimming pool and one of those Loggias. Some of the old-fashioned stories make up into a nice film."
> "Such lovely dresses," said Sophy. "When I'm eighteen I should like a long dress. It must feel wonderful to walk in." (She sat down, the skirt spread all around her, she laced her fingers in her lap, leaned forward a little and smiled.) (p. 55)

As Laura Mulvey has argued, mid-century Hollywood cinema was predicated on the relationship between a male viewer/voyeur and a female object of the gaze: Angela Carter has also argued for the importance of the cinema in the construction of sex and gender identities in the twentieth-century.[8] In *Palladian*, Taylor presents Sophy's developing gender identity as primarily constructed through such cultural scripts as Hollywood films, in the absence of other models either in life (her mother is dead) or in art (The Lord's Prayer is the only text offered to her in her Latin lessons).

Including such aspects of Sophie's experience, rather than ignoring them, *Palladian* thus offers a critique of the high/low cultural divide as well as of 'the classical tradition', and is in both respects a self-reflexive text, defining its own terms of reference as a 'woman's novel'. Taylor's next book, *A Wreath of Roses* (1949) takes the issue of the place and function of her art further, in a sophisticated, self-referential text which offers a critique of the High Modernist novels which were its immediate precursors. The epigraph of *A Wreath of Roses* comes from Woolf's *The Waves* (1931):

> So terrible was life that I held up shade after shade. Look at life through this, look at life through that; let there be rose leaves, let there be vine leaves – I covered the whole street, Oxford Street, Picadilly Circus, with the blaze and ripple of my mind, with vine leaves and rose leaves.[9]

Woolf's work haunts Taylor, and part of the purpose of *A Wreath of Roses* is to make a (painful) distinction between Woolf's 'great' art and Taylor's different aims and achievements. The debate about art is focused in the novel through the character of the elderly painter, Frances Rutherford, who has come to have doubts about the meaning and validity of her life's work. She has come to feel that her paintings have been too 'feminine', failing to explore the violence which, she now feels, is at the heart of life. In this mood, she thinks of her work with jaundiced despair:

> Trying to check life itself, she thought, to make some of the hurrying everyday things immortal, to paint the everyday things with tenderness and intimacy – the dirty café with its pock-marked mirrors as if they had been shot at, its curly hat-stands, its stained marble under the yellow light; wet pavements; an old woman yawning. With tenderness and intimacy. With sentimentality, too, she wondered. For was I not guilty of making ugliness charming? An English sadness like a veil over all I painted, until it became ladylike and nostalgic, governessy, utterly lacking in ferocity, brutality, violence. Whereas in the centre of the earth, in the heart of life, in the core of even everyday things is there not violence, with flames wheeling, turmoil, pain, chaos?[10]

The description of Frances's paintings could readily be applied to Taylor's own writing, which certainly depicts 'the everyday things with tenderness and intimacy', and the passage could thus be read as auto-critique. If we link the metaphor of the veil with Rhoda's 'shade after shade' (as in the epigraph quoted above) we might take Taylor to suggest that Frances's paintings/her own art act merely as decorative screens, protecting the viewer from the harsh realities of life. Yet Frances's sense of the inadequacy of her art is strongly challenged in the novel. Morland Beddoes, a successful film director, has collected Frances's paintings for many years, supporting and cherishing her work. In fact, it is Frances's paintings which have made his own career possible, inspiring him with a particular kind of vision. The first time he saw one of her paintings, of a girl sitting on a sofa, the direction of his life changed:

> There are great paintings which are for everybody, and then there are lesser pictures which will reflect light only here and there, rather capriciously, to individuals. Life itself shifts round a little, and what we had thought all whiteness, or all darkness, flashes suddenly, from this new angle, with violet and green and

vermilion. So that old picture of Liz sitting on the sofa, seen through the rain-washed window, turned life a little under his very eyes, put beauty over the people in the streets, the dwarf, and a woman with dyed hair standing in a doorway. (pp. 130–1)

The crucial point about Frances's work, the text makes clear, is that it is *inclusive*. Her paintings accept and represent the world of the body as well as the mind: to use Irigaray's terms again, they do not privilege abstract and transcendent ideals, but try to place such ideals in the context of the material world. Frances's art thus approaches the ideal horizon of the 'sensible transcendental', expressing, as Irigaray puts it 'the *immanent* efflorescence of the divine'[11] (my italics). So for Morland Beddoes, Frances's paintings 'put beauty over' imperfection and corruption, over the dwarf and the 'woman with the dyed hair standing in a doorway' (presumably a prostitute).

Frances's negative view of her art is thus strongly challenged by the text. It is made clear that it stems from a despair which is almost suicidal: as she contemplates her last, unfinished canvas, she compares herself to the distracted Ophelia handing out flowers – '"The last terrible gesture but one"' (p. 241). Moreover, the epigraph from *The Waves* comes from the 'speech' of Rhoda, the character who also eventually commits suicide. What Taylor's text suggests is that, *pace* Frances and Rhoda, 'everyday things' and the art which depicts them cannot be dismissed as shades and illusions: they are/ they represent the stuff of life, which must always be lived in and through its contingency and materiality. This is an argument, then, for an art of inclusion, an art which accepts the immanence and contingency of life. It is an argument for an art which differs from that of Woolf in its commitment to the mundane.

It is significant, too, that Frances's art is linked with mass-consumption through her connection with Morland Beddoes. Her art translates without difficulty into cinematic terms:

He became a director; and then millions of eyes began to see through his the faces beyond the rain-washed pane (a favourite symbol), the landlady, the stained bath, the dwarf, the cat, the cripple, and Mrs Betterton sniffing into her crumpled handkerchief. (p. 131)

In this self-reflexive text, Taylor thus links her own art with the cinema specifically as a *popular* form ('millions of eyes'). It is also a form which is by its very nature time-bound and contingent – as Angela Carter puts it in describing an old film:

> The film stock was old and scratched, as if the desolating passage of time were made visible in the rain upon the screen, audible in the worn stutterings of the sound track, yet these erosions of temporality only enhanced your luminous presence since they made it all the more forlorn, the more precarious your specious triumph over time.[12]

Carter stresses the fact that film will not endure for ever, and emphasizes the fact that this literally undoes the notion of art as transcendent. Taylor's attention to film is part of a feminist-realist aesthetic far removed from High Modernist illusions of transcendence.

A Wreath of Roses is not, of course, solely and self-reflexively concerned with its own meaning and status as art but is, like all Taylor's texts, a study of the intersections between male and female worlds. The world of masculinity is represented in the novel not by Beddoes, who lacks all the obvious signs of male authority, but by Richard Elton, a character who turns out to be extremely dangerous, indeed a murderer on the run: the novel ends with his suicide. Elton is a type rather than an individualized character, but that is very much Taylor's point: through Elton she is attacking some of the myths of masculinity purveyed by the popular media. Such stereotypes and myths feed into what Taylor calls 'the world of violence, of people in newspapers' (p. 253). The feminine world is represented by the women in Frances's household: Frances herself, Camilla, a spinsterish school secretary, and Liz, a young mother. Frances has an ambivalent relationship to femininity, while Camilla has been damaged by her childhood in a male-centred Cambridge household – she tells Elton '"I accepted it all, their voices, the cerebral atmosphere; though I was being choked by it"'. Camilla has been cut off from the positive aspects of femininity in this 'man's world' (p. 93). Liz, on the other hand, embodies these positive aspects. Liz is the girl in the painting Morland Beddoes first saw, and so she has a curious status in the novel, doubling as subject (character) and object (girl painted). This unsettling of the subject/object opposition is explored further through the representation of Liz as a breastfeeding mother. If Margaret's baby is the subtext of *Palladian*, then Liz feeding her baby is the subtext of *A Wreath of Roses*, the one subtext leading into the other.

In relation to pregnancy, Julia Kristeva has argued that it is 'a dramatic ordeal: a splitting of the body, the division and coexistence of self and other, of nature and awareness, of physiology and speech'.[13] She argues that it thus constitutes a 'fundamental challenge to identity'. Because neither mother nor foetus is a unified subject, the site of pregnancy is the place of a different articulation of identity, one not founded on the transcendental claims of the subject. Pregnancy thus becomes a privileged site, a site with particular ethical implications. I would argue that Taylor foregrounds pregnancy precisely for these reasons, because it represents a destabilization of conventional subjectivity (a point to which I will return in discussion of her other novels). But Kristeva also argues that the exchange between mother and child *after* birth continues to complicate questions of subjectivity and identity, and, moreover, also provides the foundations of language acquisition. As Kelly Oliver puts it, 'Before the paternal law is in place, the infant is subject to maternal regulations, what Kristeva calls "the law before the law"'.[14] After birth, there are exchanges between the maternal body and the infant, with the mother monitoring and regulating what goes into and comes out of the infant's body. Kristeva is arguing here for the importance of a primary maternal function which is downplayed in conventional psychoanalytic theory – Lacan, of course, argued that language stemmed from the paternal function, the 'law of the father'. Both Kristeva and Irigaray can be described as practising a strategic essentialism in this respect, instating (an illusory) feminine origin and identity in order to challenge (an illusory) masculine origin and identity which is taken to be the ground of meaning and truth.

In *A Wreath of Roses*, Liz's relationship with her baby anticipates some of the emphases of Kristeva. Liz's identity is destabilized by the relationship, and the anxiety which attends it, but it also opens up a different dimension which is envied by Camilla:

> Behind her, back in the shadows of the room, Liz sat on a low chair and fed the baby, who, full and contented, turned from her breast and flung out an arm, his eyes wandering, milky dribble running from a corner of his mouth...
> ... "Surely he has had too much," Camilla suggested. (p. 37)

Liz's relationship with her baby is bound up with her capacity for intersubjectivity and relationship with the other. *She* is the figure of hope in the novel, and her ready responsiveness is seen as re-demptive. Frances celebrates this quality in her:

> "Life persists in the vulnerable, the sensitive," she said. "*They* carry it on. The invulnerable, the too-heavily armoured perish. Fearful, ill-adapted, cumbersome, impersonal. Dinosaurs and men in tanks. But the stream of life flows differently, through the unarmed, the emotional, the highly personal . . ." (p. 80)

Later in the same conversation, Frances urges Camilla to be more open to life, more inclusive. She tells her in almost Irigarayan terms that '"there is room in [life] for everything. Like light, it contains all the colours. You are too fastidious"' (p. 81).

A Game of Hide and Seek (1951), Taylor's best-known book, develops many of the themes of *Palladian* and *A Wreath of Roses*. The novel charts the love between Harriet Claridge and Vesey Macmillan, first when they are together at the age of eighteen, then when they meet again twenty years later, Harriet being now married with a daughter of fifteen. The binary oppositions between immanence and transcendence, mind and body, high and low culture dominate the novel from the outset. These themes are first signalled by a reference to 'the story of Mrs Rossetti's exhumation' which is told by Vesey to Harriet, who listens 'chin in hand'.[15] This is the story of Lizzie Siddal, Rossetti's model and then his wife, whose likeness appears most famously in the painting *Beata Beatrix* (1863). Rossetti loved Lizzie's physical beauty, but felt guilty about his own sexual desire for her: like many Victorian men, he found it difficult to accept that women had both a soul and a sensual body. This conflict between the spiritual and the sensual in his relationship with Lizzie was in a sense resolved by his dramatic gesture when Lizzie died – he buried his manuscript book of poems with her body, bringing soul (poetry) and body together. Seven years later, however, Rossetti instructed a friend to exhume the body and re-trieve the poems, which he now wished to publish. Soul and body were thus – grotesquely – parted again. The significance of the story for Taylor lies in the difficulty Rossetti had in reconciling his feelings for Lizzie as a divine soul and his sexual desire for her. The exhu-mation also suggests the unsettling of the boundary between life and death, as Taylor makes clear when she refers to the story for the second time, near the end of the novel. This time, it is Betsy, Harriet's daughter who has been writing a 'morbid' essay on Rossetti:

I wrote about him digging up his wife's body to get at the poems
he'd buried with her ... nice and gruesome ... her hair came
away with the poems ... (p. 239)

Lizzie Siddal's story blends in with another intertext of the novel.
One of the most famous legends about Lizzie is of her posing in a
bath for Millais's painting *Ophelia* (1851–2), and *Hamlet* is one of
the other key texts for *A Game of Hide and Seek*. This is the play in
which Vesey is acting when he meets Harriet after a gap of twenty
years. Though a professional actor, he is not a very successful one,
and is only playing Laertes when Harriet sees him. Nonetheless,
there are clearly parallels we are intended to draw between Vesey
and Hamlet, as also between Harriet and Ophelia. Hamlet is famous
for his indecision, but of more significance to Taylor is his attitude
towards women. Jacqueline Rose has suggested that in *Hamlet* the
'image of femininity' cannot be fixed, but oscillates uncontrollably
between degradation and idealization.[16] Such an oscillation or
instability seems to appear in Vesey's response to Harriet, for it is
as though he cannot connect the love which he feels with sexual
desire for her. (Vesey has also, like Hamlet, had to confront the
unsettling evidence of his middle-aged mother's active sexuality.)
Harriet is placed in the Ophelia position because of her vulnerability
to Vesey's unpredictable shifts of behaviour, and because the codes
of feminine behaviour make it almost impossible for her to take
any active part in the relationship.

Through the allusions to Rossetti and to *Hamlet*, Taylor thus foregrounds a common difficulty in Western culture. It is as though, unable
to consign women wholly to the negative category of the body/nature,
yet unable to integrate their sense of a woman's soul with their sense
of her body, (some) men veer unstably from one point of view to the
other, torn between 'degradation and idealization'. Taylor makes a
similar point through her use of a popular intertext, David Lean's
1945 film *Brief Encounter*. This is the ultimate text of renunciation,
in which the noble doctor-hero, Alec, urges the more impetuous
Laura to keep their love pure, not to commit adultery:

Alec. Everything's against us – all the circumstances of our lives
– those have got to go on unaltered. We're nice people, you and
I, and we've got to go on being nice. Let's enclose this love of
ours with real strength, and let that strength be that no one is
hurt by it except ourselves.[17]

Alec can only think of Laura in idealized, almost chivalric terms, and forces her to conform to his expectations of her. He ends the affair by going abroad, out of reach of temptation. Similarly, at the end of *A Game of Hide and Seek*, Vesey tells Harriet he is leaving for South Africa. Taylor's references to the film (Harriet's mother-in-law mentions it with specific reference to her suspicions that Harriet is having an affair) broaden out the novel, pointing to the fact that the same symbolic divisions structure both 'high' and popular cultural texts.

In *A Game of Hide and Seek*, as in Taylor's earlier novels, the worlds of men and women do not really intersect. At the gown shop where Harriet works before her marriage, for example, we are shown an all-female community in which the shop assistants band together against their manager and the (male) world. They spend their time on beauty tips and their appearance, helping each other to put on as good a face as possible in their struggle to get a man. There is a clear sense of war or battle between the sexes, and of a woman's vulnerability without male protection. (Years later, Harriet tells Vesey of the suicide of one of the girls, in the aftermath of an affair.) Most of the male characters, on the other hand, inhabit a sealed-off world of business deals and clubs, treating their wives and mothers with condescension and even dislike. The relationship between Harriet and Vesey is almost the only one in which there is real communication between the sexes. Their closeness to each other may stem from their having known each other from early childhood, before strict gender divisions were in force: it is also true that both Vesey and Harriet cross gender boundaries in their young adult characters. Vesey is effete and effeminate:

> In his mother's room one day he put on her jewellery, sniffed at her scent, varnished his nails, read a book on birth-control, took six aspirins, then lay down like Chatterton on the window-seat, his hand drooping to the floor. (p. 7)

Harriet, on the other hand, wears no make-up and has 'boyish and practical' clothes. She is also, as Vesey sees, 'brave and candid', both characteristics which are more usually associated with men and boys.

The love between Harriet and Vesey founders in the earlier part of the book largely because of their inexperience and timidity, but when they meet again, more complex factors are in play. There is a sense that their love cannot be consummated because it has missed its moment, become something which has more to do with loss and retrospection than with desire. When Harriet thinks of the 'place' of her love for Vesey, for example, she thinks more of the past than the present:

> "His climate!" Harriet thought, staring down at the fire until her eyes smarted. The word expressed something of her feelings at being with him: how she had loved, when she was young, merely to stand close to him. When he had drawn away, he took something miraculous from her. (p. 165)

At the very end of the novel, Harriet feels that her love is let down, or misrepresented, by her middle-aged body:

> She saw so clearly that her youth was gone. Her body had bloomed and had faded. She brought to Vesey all the signs of middle-age, the blurred outlines and the dullness of the flesh. She thought of undressing at night, her waist pinched, her sides creased and reddened from her corset; the brightness of girlhood softened, dimmed. (p. 229)

A Game of Hide and Seek is such a resonant text because it suggests the difficulty of heterosexual love in a patriarchal society dominated by the symbolic oppositions of man/woman, soul/body, transcendence/immanence. Only momentarily does love flower in the novel, at the point when Harriet and Vesey dance a tango together. Technically, this dance brings the two parts of the book together (it is a dance deferred for twenty years): thematically, it brings together man/woman, soul/body, transcendence/immanence:

> They were suspended in some magic which caught up also, meaninglessly, gilt baskets of azaleas, some paper streamers and a great chandelier like a shower of grubby acid-drops. Remotely, the figures of other people drifted at the perimeter of their enchanted space of floor. They dictated their own music. (p. 107)

From this point on, the relationship declines into doubts, scruples and uncertainties, and it ends with Vesey dying (of pneumonia) in Harriet's arms.

However, *A Game of Hide and Seek* is not a negative text, a point which can be confirmed by making a comparison which Taylor invites us to make. At the beginning of the novel, Vesey comments that Virginia Woolf has brought the novel 'to the edge of ruin':

> The novel – headstrong parvenu – seemed headed for destruction. No one could stay its downward course and, obviously, it did not deserve that Vesey should try. Virginia Woolf with one graceful touch after another (the latest was *Mrs Dalloway*) was sending it trundling downhill. (p. 12)

As in *A Wreath of Roses*, Taylor alludes to Woolf only to distance herself from her. Woolf wrote in 'Professions for Women' that she did not think that she had solved the problem of 'telling the truth about [her] own experiences as a body'.[18] Writing a realist text in the period immediately after Modernism, Taylor does exactly that, showing us the depredations of time on Harriet's body, but also celebrating aspects of female bodily experience, as in her evocation of the inter-subjectivity of Harriet's friend Kitty's pregnancy. This kind of feminist realism brings a number of aspects of 'the feminine' back into discourse and culture.

Taylor's next novel, *The Sleeping Beauty* (1953), is a dark modern version of the fairy tale, shot through with bleakness. If the original story tells of a young girl magically protected from predators until she is awakened by a true lover, Taylor's novel is far more ambivalent about the gifts which its lover/prince is able to bring. Vinny Tumulty, the lover/prince figure in *The Sleeping Beauty*, is characterized by a subtle egotism which is expressed through compassion. At the very beginning of the novel, we are told of the way in which he gravitates towards the bereaved, moving 'with sympathy professional in its skill; yet adept, exquisite'.[19] For him, compassion is a form of self-expression and ultimately of self-love: hence the danger which he poses to the women who catch his attention. During the course of the novel, he misleads the friend whom he has come to comfort after the death of her husband, and falls in love with another, younger woman whom he marries – bigamously, it turns out. Vinny's sympathy and understanding are there not for the objects of his compassion, but for himself, for the purpose of self-affirmation – 'self-affirmation of the masculine logos', as Braidotti puts it.[20] Vinny, then, is a well-disguised version of the transcendent male subject, subtly denying subjectivity and autonomy to the objects of his pity.

The novel charts his relationships with three women, each of whom can be said to be in some sense a 'sleeping beauty'. The central figure is Emily, first glimpsed by Vinny as she crosses a deserted beach with her niece, the two of them making 'a most beautiful picture... mysterious, romantic' as they move along in the dusk. Vinny decides that Emily must be beautiful even though it is too dark to see her face, thus from the very beginning appropriating her for a love story of his own devising. But as it turns out, Emily has already been appropriated and turned into the embodiment of male desire in the most literal manner possible. As a young girl, she was terribly injured in a car accident, her face ruined. Her fiancé left her because of this, and she then spent many months in hospital having her face reconstructed by a plastic surgeon, months in which 'she must not move or speak or cry'. She left hospital looking 'very beautiful in a way, but not in the way in which she had been beautiful before' (p. 46). In place of her face, Emily is given a perfection of *blank* beauty which is the projection of the male surgeon's desire, so that the new Emily is a literal embodiment of the 'masquerade' as Luce Irigaray describes it in *This Sex Which Is Not One*:

> Or rather, [women] find themselves there, proverbially, *in masquerades*. Psychoanalysts say that masquerading corresponds to woman's desire. That seems wrong to me. I think the masquerade has to be understood as what women do in order to recuperate some element of desire, to participate in man's desire, but at the price of renouncing their own. In the masquerade, they submit to the dominant economy of desire in an attempt to remain "on the market" in spite of everything. But they are there as objects for sexual enjoyment, not as those who enjoy.[21]

Irigaray writes of woman's entry into a system of values that is not hers, in which she can appear and circulate only when 'enveloped in the needs/desires/fantasies of others, namely, men'. After her accident, Emily appears in just such a way, as what Irigaray would term a *fetish*, covering over and standing in for (supposed) female lack.

With her mask-like face, her abstract and unreal 'femininity', Emily is perfect for Vinny, who picks up, as it were, where the surgeon has left off. If the surgeon has created Emily's appearance, Vinny takes over the (re)construction of her personality, as Emily herself suggests towards the end of the novel:

"Oh, I am nothing without you," she said. "I should not know what to be. I feel as if you had invented me. I watch you inventing me, week after week." (p. 187)

In the circumstances, it is impossible to see Vinny as a true lover: instead, we become increasingly aware of his possessiveness and uneasy about Emily's future with him. In leaving the twilit life she has led with her sister to marry Vinny, Emily seems merely to be exchanging one sort of imprisonment for another.

The parallels between women are important in this novel, especially that between Emily and Vinny's old friend Isabella. The most important relationship in Isabella's life is not, in fact, with Vinny, nor even with her son Laurence, but with Evalie Hobson, with whom she has a friendship which is at once superficial and precious. The two women need and support one another in their battle against middle-age. For, if Emily's imprisonment in the masquerade is destructive, so too is the loss of the ability to 'perform' the masquerade and remain, as Irigaray puts it, 'on the market'. Isabella and Evalie fight together 'all the petty but grievous insults of greying hair, crowsfeet, and the loathed encumbrances of unwanted flesh'. Taylor lightly charts their battles with bodies which refuse to conform to the contours of the masquerade:

> They laughed a great deal over their experiments: one week they bent and stretched with such fury that Evalie broke a blood vein in her eye; the next week they drank nothing after luncheon; another time ate only grapes all day long. They counted up calories, brought new corsets and tried new face-creams; cut paragraphs out of magazines for one another and went together to the Turkish baths. (p. 33)

Astutely, Taylor foregrounds their predicament as middle-aged women who can no longer conform to the masquerade (what Irigaray calls a 'being-for-men') but who resist the adoption of a post-menopausal 'masculinity' like that of those 'American women [who] go to all those lectures when they reach the change of life' (p. 34). Isabella and Evalie want neither the masquerade nor masculinity, but rather a feminine identity which would challenge the categories of the existing symbolic order. Such an identity is/might be bound up with their middle-aged bodies, which constitute a crucial site of resistance in this novel. To argue this is not to endorse a crude biological determinism, but to suggest that if middle-aged women's bodies are bodies that *do not matter* (to use Judith Butler's phrase), then it is from this invisible/outsider position that resistance to the dominant symbolic order might develop. Within that order, Isabella and Evalie do not matter, do not signify, because they can no longer reproduce (men). Yet through the characters' ironic and courageous response to their predicament, Taylor suggests the posssibility of a *re*-signification of those bodies. Middle-aged female embodiment might be seen as *the* paradigm for a feminine identity 'for itself', existing without reference to the needs of men. As narrator, Taylor certainly moves towards a celebration rather than a derogation of such embodiment:

> In the hot-room they sat down in deck-chairs. Slim girls with brown narrow backs and neatly-painted toenails guarded their beauty jealously, with towels carefully tucked up under their armpits. They sipped lemon-juice and knitted, glancing in a bored way at newcomers. An enormous woman in a pink plastic cap slowly stirred and stood up. Her dimpled thighs were like beaten pewter. In the next room, Henry Moore figures were being slapped rosy on marble slabs. (p. 78)

Notwithstanding such possibilities, Isabella's fate in the novel is not a happy one. Vinny allows Isabella to believe that he is in love with her, and leads her to expect that he will propose marriage. She looks forward to a decorous but romantic relationship, with the proposal being renewed and refused every year: to have such a reliable but non-threatening suitor would give her standing and importance in the community. When Vinny's mother tells her of his love for Emily, Isabella is dismayed. Her innocent plans for the future collapse, leaving the fear of loneliness and isolation. Vinny brings misery to his wife, Rita, too, when he asks her for a divorce. This threatens her way of life as a supposed widow, bringing the possibility of scandal and intensifying *her* sense of age and isolation. So despite the fact that Taylor points to the possibilities of a different, positive identity for her middle-aged women characters, in practice their prospects seem bleak. In relation to this issue, there is an interesting anecdote in Robert Liddell's memoir of Elizabeth Taylor and Ivy Compton-Burnett, *Elizabeth and Ivy*. Liddell quotes from a letter in which Taylor describes going to see Beckett's *Happy Days* with Ivy Compton-Burnett. Taylor writes:

The play – just the middle-aged woman buried in a mound – was to me quite unexpectedly wonderful – I went for Ivy, and found myself forgetting her ... It is really devastating, and as much as one can bear – a middle-aged woman's gallantry (I see so much of it) signifying the human tragedy – the terrifying attempts at optimism and the Molly Bloom nostalgia – heart-rendering. ['Rendering', Liddell explains, was a word of his servant][22]

This is a fascinating comment in that it supports a reading of *The Sleeping Beauty* as containing bleak and even tragic elements. It is also interesting, however, in that Taylor here credits Beckett – and indeed Joyce – with making the move which she makes in all her fiction, that of making the *feminine* the norm, making the feminine representative of 'the human', of the human condition. As Christine Battersby argues in *The Phenomenal Woman*, this is a profoundly radical move, with a wealth of possible implications. Describing her project, Battersby writes:

I am attempting to construct a new subject-position that makes *women* typical. In effect, this means dispensing with the (Kantian) notion that the 'I' gives form to reality by imposing a grid of spacio-temporal relationships upon otherwise unformed 'matter'. Focusing on the female subject involves treating humans as non-autonomous, and instead thinking relationships of dependence (childhood/weaning/rearing) through which one attains selfhood. It also involves thinking the process of birthing as neither monstrous nor abnormal.[23]

Earlier in this chapter, I have noted Taylor's foregrounding of women's 'relationships of dependence' such as those involved in pregnancy and breast-feeding. I want to explore further her treatment of what Battersby calls 'natality' (the normality of the body that can birth) in a consideration of the *The Wedding Group* (1968).

The Wedding Group explores the exploitation of a young girl first by the dominant male order and then by a manipulative older woman. Cressida MacPhail has grown up under a fairly extreme version of patriarchy. Her grandfather, the painter Harry Bretton, has founded a community in which he paints while his wife, daughters and granddaughters grow food, bake bread, weave and scrub. The family, who have all converted to Catholicism and have their own resident chaplain, form a self-sufficient unit largely removed from contact with the outside world. Harry, known as 'the Master' to his family, has an ambivalent relation to women. In theory he reveres them, but in practice he exploits and derogates them. He tells his family that 'it's our women who have the wisdom', and continues sanctimoniously:

> "For all our precious ideals, our inventiveness, it's the essential, instinctive mother-wife we crave at last. We return, after our escapades or great deeds, to *her*, for forgiveness and healing and approval."[24]

Cressida rebels against this. Bravely, she tells her grandfather that 'It's one-way traffic' (p. 50), meaning that in such a relationship as he describes, women are expected to give endlessly without gaining anything in return. Recklessly – and truthfully – she tells him 'You think nothing of women. You won't even let us vote at elections' (p. 51). Later in the novel, we learn that Harry has a great deal of pornographic material locked away for his own use, and when one of his granddaughters becomes pregnant, Cressy briefly suspects Harry of incest. Harry alternates, then, between a sentimental idealization of women and a sexualization which degrades them: he is unable to reconcile the feminine soul with the feminine body.

However, Quayne is not just a patriarchal community: it is also and crucially an artistic community. Here Taylor returns to one of the themes of *A Wreath of Roses*, exploring again the question of (male) transcendence in art. Harry Bretton is a type of the male artist who sees his own work as transcending the limitations of place, time and gender. He is modelled on the religious painter Stanley Spencer (1891–1959), and also, John Crompton has convincingly argued, on the artist and craftsman Eric Gill (1882–1940), who lived for a while in a self-contained Catholic community which has many similarities with Quayne.[25] Harry's art, like that of Spencer and Gill, is wholly bound up with the Christian mythology which divides women into the two categories of virgin and whore. Yet more disquieting is the fact that in his preoccupation with painting the Virgin Mary, Harry endorses and perpetuates the Christian myth which would sever sexuality from natality. Through the metaphor of the virgin birth, the Christian religion separates woman's sexuality and her desire from the possibility and process of giving birth, appropriating a (sanitized) version of the birthing body for patriarchal religious purposes. In *The Wedding Group*, Taylor thus shows Harry transmuting his pregnant granddaughter Pet into the sanctified images of first the Virgin Mary and then her cousin Elizabeth, mother of John the Baptist:

> As far as [Harry] was concerned, her plight had come at the right time. Before her pregnancy showed, he had painted her as the Virgin Mary entering the house of Zacharias. She stood in the doorway, wearing a homespun skirt and a fairisle sweater, her hair falling to her shoulders. Her head was haloed. These days, she was posing for the other half of the picture – the pregnant Elizabeth, just risen from a chair in greeting, one hand on the table, the other on her belly, some knitting fallen from her lap to the floor. (p. 165)

Such a move 'paints out' a different story about woman's sexuality and natality, a story which would link together woman's desire, woman's sexuality and her capacity for giving birth.

Cressy rebels against Quayne and against her grandfather's denial of the female body which in fact subtends his life and work. She leaves Quayne to work in an antique shop, meets the journalist David Little, is taken up by him and by his mother, and eventually marries him. She seems to have escaped the constraints of Quayne without losing her openness to new experiences: when David takes her out to coffee bars with juke-boxes and to cinema cafés he is touched by seeing her 'falling in love with the present time' (p. 101). Her pregnancy also seems to suggest a potential for growth, as the boundaries between her body and the outside world loosen and change. As in other novels by Taylor, pregnancy sets up new connections between the body and the world, and the body and itself. Again, Christine Battersby outlines the implications *for feminist metaphysics* of an acknowledgement of such experiences:

> Recognizing natality – the *conceptual* link between the paradigm 'woman' and the body that births – does not imply that all women either can or 'should' give birth. Instead, an emphasis on natality as an abstract category of embodied (female) selves means that we need to rethink identity. The 'self' is not a fixed, permanent or pre-given 'thing' or 'substance' that undergoes metamorphosis, but that nevertheless remains always unaltered through change. Instead, we need to think of identity as emerging out of

a play of relationships and force-fields that together constitute the horizons of a (shared) space-time. We need a metaphysics of fluidity and mobile relationships; not a metaphysics of fixity, or even of flexibility.[26]

Taylor does not suggest that Cressy's pregnancy can transform her situation in 'the real world'. In practice, what happens is that, as Harry puts it, in leaving Quayne she simply gets 'out of one rut and into another' (p. 211). For David's mother is terrified that Cressy and her son will leave the countryside for London, and so schemes and manipulates to keep them near her. She stages a burglary in order to stress her vulnerability as a woman living alone, and after the baby is born makes herself indispensable on a practical level to the uncertain young mother. In effect, she appropriates Cressy's son Tim to herself, resting all her hopes for the future on the expectation that she will continue to be closely involved in his upbringing. Midge, then, is shown to be as manipulative as Harry and perhaps more successfully so. At the end of the novel, however, the fraud of the burglary is exposed, and David begins to see his mother in a more negative light. He vows to move to London with Cressy, and on the strength of this Cressy begins to feel optimistic about the future again. The novel has an open ending, with Cressy feeling 'happy and confident' about her future with David in London, but Midge equally confident that she will keep her son, daughter-in-law and grandchild with her in the country. Like all Taylor's novels, *The Wedding Group* explores female embodiment at various stages of women's lives, registering the responses of the protagonists to the cultural scripts imposed on/open to them, but offering no straightforward blueprint for the future. In a letter to Taylor, Elizabeth Bowen acknowledges the openness and depth of the novel's ending. She writes, 'For one thing, though I speak of "the last page", the novel seems to have no arbitrary or snipped-off end. I mean, it continues. It is to be gone deeper into the more one thinks about it, and think about it I do.'[27]

4
Margaret Drabble: Natality, Labour, Work and Action

In the previous chapter, the fiction of Elizabeth Taylor was read through the philosophy of Luce Irigaray, whose work provides a recurrent point of reference for this study. In this chapter, I want to connect the novels of Margaret Drabble to some extent with Irigaray, but more particularly with the profound and controversial philosophy of Hannah Arendt (1906–75). Seyla Benhabib has described Arendt as the thinker who has 'countered Western philosophy's love affair with death' with her concept of natality,[1] and I would suggest that there are several aspects of Arendt's work which can powerfully illuminate the concerns of Drabble's fiction. Arendt is referred to in *The Gates of Ivory* (1991), and this reference would seem to confirm, not a determining influence from Arendt, but a congruence between her concerns and those of Drabble.[2]

There are three aspects of Arendt's work which are particularly relevant for a consideration of Drabble. The concept of natality was mentioned in the previous chapter with reference to Christine Battersby's appropriation of the term, but I wish here to distinguish between Battersby's emphasis and Arendt's original discussion. Defining natality as 'the *conceptual* link between the paradigm "woman" and the body that births',[3] Battersby's focus is very much on female subjectivity and the development of a feminist metaphysics, whereas Arendt does not focus on one sex/gender but sees natality as 'inherent in all human activities'.[4] In *The Human Condition* (1958), she defines natality in the following way:

> The miracle that saves the world, the realm of human affairs, from its normal, "natural" ruin is ultimately the fact of natality, in which the faculty of action is ontologically rooted. It is, in

other words, the birth of new men and the new beginning, the action they are capable of by virtue of being born. Only the full experience of this capacity can bestow upon human affairs faith and hope, those two essential characteristics of human existence which Greek antiquity ignored altogether. (p. 247)

Natality for Arendt represents the human capacity to generate the new and the unforeseen, the innovative and the astonishing, *in this world*. As the sardonic reference to the Greeks suggests, Arendt dissents from Platonic (or any other) 'two-world' metaphysics which seeks to understand the human condition in the light of a principle which grounds or precedes the world of appearance. In her view, to be human is to act and speak with others *within* the world of appearance: to be is to be present to others. Hence her emphasis on 'the new beginning inherent in birth', which marks the possibility of development and change within the human world of plurality. This plural world of interaction with others is the only one in which we can intervene or create, the initiative aspect of birth being echoed or repeated through the initiation of action in later life.

As noted above, Arendt does not foreground gender in her discussion of natality, but as Benhabib and others have pointed out, there is a profound gender subtext in her work: it is surely no coincidence that the philosopher of natality should be a woman. This gender subtext is still more evident in the distinctions she makes in *The Human Condition* between the categories of labour, work and action. These categories each correspond to 'one of the basic conditions under which life on earth has been given to man' (p. 7). Labour is the activity necessitated by the biological processes of the human body, the life of which must be renewed, sustained and nurtured. As Benhabib puts it, 'procuring daily nourishment, cleaning and grooming the body and the space that humans inhabit, tending to the wear and tear of the everyday things around one, of the world of objects that humans need, all belong under the category of labor'.[5] Work corresponds to the 'unnaturalness' of human existence, and provides an artificial world of things distinct from our natural surroundings. Through work, we create a world of objects which have a certain permanence, 'housing' us but also outlasting us and leaving a record of our existence. Action is the category most highly valued by Arendt: it is, she writes in *The Human Condition*, 'the only activity that goes on directly between men without the intermediary of things or matter' and it corresponds to the human condition of plurality, to the fact that 'men, not Man, live on the earth and inhabit the world' (p. 7). Both labour and work can be imagined outside the society of man, but '[a]ction alone is the exclusive prerogative of man; neither a beast nor a god is capable of it, and only action is entirely dependent on the constant presence of others' (pp. 22–3).

Again, Arendt does not note the gendered nature of the distinctions which she makes, although this must have been obvious to her. At the time when she was writing, labour was the human activity assigned almost exclusively to women, whereas work and action – the more highly valued activities – were generally assigned to men. However, despite Arendt's lack of explicit attention to gender, what is valuable in her analysis for the contemporary feminist critic is her lucid exposition of a deeply engrained cultural hierarchy of human activity. Using her terms of reference, one could argue that the difficulty for the middle-class woman in the second half of the twentieth century has been how to move from the sphere of labour into those of work and action (action is the only sphere Arendt links with politics). I want to suggest that it is precisely such a progression which is explored in Drabble's fiction, and that what is distinctive about this progression is its effort to be cumulative and inclusive. In other words, Drabble's female protagonists do not seek to *exchange* one sphere for another, but to link labour, work and action.

Benhabib has argued that the distinctions which Arendt makes tend to collapse when we bring gender into the discussion. She argues that if we link labour with the domestic sphere, it is clear that such labour involves not only housework but also child rearing. This in turn involves qualities which are normally associated by Arendt with work and action, as we transmit our sense of the world and our values to the child. I want to make a slightly different suggestion, which is that there is an ethics deriving specifically from labour which can profitably be drawn into the spheres of work and action. And I would suggest that one of the dominant themes of Drabble's fiction is the effort to link such a traditionally private ethics with the public, political world.

Just as Arendt maintains the distinctions between labour, work and action, so she maintains a distinction (which is, indeed, central to her work) between the private and the public sphere. Again, this distinction remains useful for contemporary feminist analysis.

Despite her overall privileging of the public sphere of social action, Arendt writes evocatively about the need for privacy if the self is to maintain depth and authenticity:

> A life spent entirely in public, in the presence of others, becomes, as we would say, shallow. While it retains its visibility, it loses the quality of rising into sight from some darker ground which must remain hidden if it is not to lose its depth in a very real, non-subjective sense. (p. 71)

The metaphor of the ground, shadowed by the image of a plant growing, suggests a connection between Arendt's understanding of the hidden, private sphere and Irigaray's analysis of the hidden or occluded aspects of 'the feminine'. This connection becomes clearer in another passage from *The Human Condition* in which Arendt discusses the significance of the private sphere in ancient times:

> The sacredness of this privacy was like the sacredness of the hidden, namely, of birth and death, the beginning and end of the mortals who, like all living creatures, grow out of and return to the darkness of an underworld. The non-privative trait of the household realm originally lay in its being the realm of birth and death which must be hidden from the public realm because it harbors the things hidden from human eyes and impenetrable to human knowledge. (pp. 62–3)

Arendt's description focuses on those same issues of birth, death and embodiment which, Irigaray argues, are culturally linked with 'the feminine'. Just as with the category of labour, I would suggest that a major component of Drabble's fiction is her focus on an ethics deriving from the private sphere as described by Arendt, and her effort to bring such an ethics into the sphere of public/social action.

Arendt's categories of natality, labour and privacy can clearly be connected with the categories of immanence and female embodiment explored in previous chapters via the work of Beauvoir, Irigaray, Deleuze and Guattari. The connection with Beauvoir seems especially strong. For example, Beauvoir explicitly connects the sphere of labour with female immanence in a passage in *The Second Sex* which anticipates with uncanny accuracy the distinctions which Arendt makes. Beauvoir writes that:

Since the husband is the productive worker, he is the one who goes beyond family interest to that of society, opening up a future for himself through co-operation in the building of the collective future; he incarnates transcendence. Woman is doomed to the continuation of the species and the care of the home – that is to say, to immanence.[6]

It is, however, Arendt's refusal to consider private experience in isolation from social matters which makes her a particularly suggestive figure in relation to Drabble. I would like to begin the discussion of Drabble's fiction with her fifth book, *The Waterfall* (1969), at first sight the *least* socially directed of her novels. It opens with a birth, and seems to celebrate natality in Battersby's sense, exploring a fluidity of feminine identity which is directly linked to the experience/potential of giving birth. Irigarayan metaphors of water, liquid, milk and blood add to the sense of a revaluation of the derogated maternal body – blood, in particular, being associated here with warmth and generation rather than death:

The snow fell outside the uncurtained window, and she could feel the blood flowing from her into the white moist sheets. There was newspaper under the sheets, but it too was warm now from the heat of her body: warm and sodden, having lost the dry hard edges and crackling noises that it had made at first, as she moved and stirred in labour.[7]

In this respect, the novel may be compared with *The Millstone*, Drabble's third novel, which was discussed briefly in the introduction. Like Rosamund Stacey of *The Millstone*, Jane Gray at the opening of the novel is a woman who finds physical fulfilment in motherhood but is unable to connect her bodily life with the life of the mind (she has been a published poet). In other words, she suffers from the 'mind–body problem' discussed in the introduction, from the conflict between the intellect and femininity which also structures Rosamond Lehmann's fiction. Jane analyses this divided state:

[M]y ability to kiss and care for and feed and amuse a small child merely reinforced my sense of division – I felt split between the anxious intelligent woman and the healthy and efficient mother – or perhaps less split than divided. I felt that I lived on two levels, simultaneously, and that there was no contact, no interaction between them. (pp. 103–4)

In *The Waterfall*, mind and body are reconciled, as they are not in *The Millstone*, through Jane's love affair with her cousin's husband James, which in some respects resembles the affair between Rebecca and Johnny in Rosamond Lehmann's *A Sea-Grape Tree*. It is a relationship founded on mutuality and reciprocity, made possible because James is an atypical masculine figure. He is drawn to Jane because she has just given birth (though not to his child), and his desire is to participate in the warmth and creativity of that event. He thinks that 'it's like heaven' in the room where the baby has been born, and that he will die if he is not allowed into the warmth of Jane's bed. Much later, Jane notes that 'the baby thing attracted him as much as it repels most men: he liked having babies around, he liked the idea of taking them on clandestine holidays, and why else did he choose such a point in time to get into my bed?' (p. 207). James is attracted to the mutual, shifting relation of dependency between a child and its mother/carer, and it is such a relation which characterizes and shapes his affair with Jane, too, in complex ways. In the first phase of this affair, it is primarily James who is cast in the role of parent and protector, bringing a corpse-like Jane back to life, feeding her and cherishing her, whereas after their trip north and a serious car accident, it is Jane who is cast in the role of protector and restorer to life as James lies injured in hospital. At this point, Jane comments on the significance of dependency in their relationship, underscoring the symmetry between their isolation in James's sickroom, and in the bedroom where the novel begins:

> We were happy, in that hospital. Such imprisonment suited our natures. Dialogues in a sick room, in claustrophobic proximity. Dependence, confinement, solicitude. (p. 223)

In many ways, the love affair is presented as an idyll, restorative for both participants. Jane's first orgasm, for example, is described as a 'deliverance' bringing about a mutual rebirth, suggesting Arendt's positive conception of natality as part of the 'human condition' for both sexes:

> How could it not be serious, this matter? How could it be taken so lightly, and so dismissed? It was like death, like birth: an

event of the same order. Her cry was the cry of a woman in labour: it broke from her and her body gathered round it with the violence of a final pang . . . A woman delivered. She was his offspring, as he, lying there between her legs, had been hers. (pp. 150–1)

However, a significant feature of the novel is that the narrative is split between first and third person, and it is notable that the lyrical presentation of Jane's deliverance occurs only in the third person sections of the text when Jane is seen at a distance. The use of the first person, in contrast, brings with it questions of ethics and of responsibility for one's actions, and it is in the first person sections that the ethical implications of the affair come into view. The most striking of these is that it involves the betrayal of Lucy. Jane's betrayal of her husband is less significant, for he has, after all, first left her and been unfaithful. The question of Lucy is a far more complex one. It is significant that Lucy is Jane's cousin: all the relationships in the novel are family or kinship relationships, thus belonging in Arendt's terms to the private sphere. For Arendt, family relationships are imposed on us by the needs of biological life, and are driven by necessity, not freedom, but Drabble's novel shows very clearly that freedom and responsibility exist within this sphere. Jane persuades herself that her sophisticated cousin, so like herself in many respects, must know all about her affair with James and must delicately condone it. When it transpires that she does not, Jane is amazed by Lucy's coarse and violent response, at her tone 'of such venom, force and feeling that I could hardly believe my ears' (p. 210). Although Lucy quickly recovers her normal manner, Jane is forced to recognize the extent to which she has hurt Lucy, and has to recognize, too, her own predatory behaviour.

The novel thus suggests an ambivalent response to the love affair between Jane and James. On the one hand, the relationship has been grounded in what we might call an 'ethics of labour', of the preservation of bodily life, and the nurture and sustenance of weak and fragile life (a point which will come up again in relation to Drabble's later novels). On the other hand, it has led to the cultivation of a privacy and mutual solipsism so extreme as to be damaging to others. Because it shatters this private world, the car accident can be seen as a positive catalyst of change. After James has recovered from it, he goes back to live with Lucy who now *knowingly* chooses to share him with Jane. More importantly, the accident propels Jane back into the world of work from which she has been excluded for so long. While James is in hospital, she writes a sequence of poems, and afterwards discovers 'new-found desires to see my poems in print' (p. 232). She even acquires an au pair girl to look after the children, so that she can have time to write. She thus combines the sphere of labour and that of work. While Arendt does not consider work as a properly public activity, she places the making of a work of art as the highest activity of *homo faber*, and celebrates poetry as the highest form of art. In *The Human Condition* she describes poetry in this way:

> Of all things of thought, poetry is closest to thought, and a poem is less a thing than any other work of art; yet even a poem, no matter how long it existed as a living spoken word in the recollection of the bard and those who listened to him, will eventually be "made," that is, written down and transformed into a tangible thing among things, because remembrance and the gift of recollection ... need tangible things to remind them. (p. 170)

Jane's poetry, as 'written speech' in this sense, is far removed from the claustrophobic privacy of her earlier relationship with James, and marks a welcome return to wider horizons and connections.

The Waterfall explores what we might call a private ethics, founded on an unspoken contract of care between beings who are unequal in status and capacity, and it also opens up for consideration the relationship between such an ethics and the wider world. In Drabble's next novel, *The Needle's Eye* (1972), she undertakes a fuller exploration of the relationship between private and public worlds. The novel charts the friendship between Rose Vassiliou, an heiress who has given up her fortune to live with her children in a shabby house in North London, and Simon Camish, whose social trajectory has been in the opposite direction, from an impoverished childhood in the North East to a successful career as a Hampstead barrister. Through these two characters Drabble explores the complex connections between labour, work and action, and between private and public spheres.

Rose comes from a dysfunctional family, the only child of a boorish, self-made millionaire and his egotistical and unresponsive wife. She is redeemed from the wasteland of her childhood and adolescence when she meets and marries (against parental opposition) Christopher

Vassiliou. The relationship with Christopher deteriorates quite rapidly, but Rose's love for her three children continues to ground and illuminate her life. The relationship between parent and child, founded as it is in inequality yet often involving the tenderest mutual recognition, is valued by Drabble as offering the potential for the highest form of human feeling. Such a view is powerfully communicated in the novel through Rose's insight into the relationship between a particular mother and child, seen on a bus and never forgotten:

> ... a little boy with a huge birth mark all over his face, and cheap glasses and short hair, sitting with his mother in silence – a cross, dumpy woman, the mother was ... and Rose had thought to herself poor boy, poor boy, and then the boy had got off at the bus stop outside the Hospital for the Enfants Malades, leaving his mother on the bus, and he had kissed her goodbye, and she had kissed him so tenderly, and he had run off, waving, smiling, radiant, illumined, his mother waving with a tender pride, the boy gawky thin and sparrow-like and marked, the mother no longer cross but smiling quietly to herself, reflectively, and Rose had remembered that sudden change of countenance, that sudden transformation of what she had understood to be a grim relation, and could never think of it without a lifting of the spirit.[8]

Separated from Christopher at the point when the novel begins, Rose creates in her home a female space of privacy and labour. It is shabby and impoverished, but full of the signs of warmth and nurture. Simon is enchanted when he first sees it, and entirely distracted from Rose's legal documents:

> He could hardly concentrate on these latter objects, so taken was he with everything else about him, with Rose herself sitting in a rocking-chair with a mangy cat upon her knee, with the flowered walls and litter of teddy bears and unwashed cups, with the crocheted tea-cosy on the teapot, with the peculiar objects upon the mantlepiece. (p. 44)

It takes Simon some time to work out why this scene is on some hidden level familiar to him: he finally realizes that Rose's home reminds him of his grandmother's house. This is a motif which is

picked up in Drabble's next novel, *The Realms of Gold*: in both
novels the approving references to grand-maternal homes seem to
point to the importance of a maternal genealogy and also to the
need for a home to incorporate the traditions and traces of past
generations.

The specifically female nature of Rose's space, with its tea-cosy
and bundle of knitting, is emphasized, as is the fact that Rose is
supported in her life by a network of relationships with other women
without whom she could not have survived. The most important
of these is with Emily, whom she has known since they were at
school. There is enormous tonal approval in the novel for their
friendship, which has seen them through their combined experiences of marriage, children, betrayal, abuse and poverty. This warmth
and support extend into other crucial relationships: for example,
in an encounter in the local sweet shop between Rose and one of
her children's teachers, Miss Lindley, mutual support is expressed
through apparently trivial comments on packets of fags and sherbet
fountains. As they part, the narrator comments, lightly foregrounding
some of the key terms of the novel, 'And thus, doing each other
rightly more than justice (because it was not a question of justice
but of goodwill and faith) they diverged' (p. 159).

In contrast to Rose Simon inhabits, almost exclusively, the male
spheres of work and action. His home is uncomfortable, his marriage unhappy, and he has little real contact with his three children,
whose welfare he leaves almost entirely to his wife. His professional
field of interest, however, connects interestingly with Rose's private life and principles. Simon's expertise is in Union Law, and
this is a field to which he has been drawn by private experience:
when he was a child his father, a shop steward, was disabled by a
workplace accident and left dependent and wheelchair-bound with
very meagre compensation. The law is in the widest sense the necessary precondition for political activity. Arendt notes in relation to
the Greek *polis* that:

> Before men began to act, a definite space had to be secured and
> a structure built where all subsequent actions could take place,
> the space being the public realm of the *polis* and its structure
> the law. (pp. 194–5)

Simon argues eloquently for the importance of the law in conversation with Rose, but his particular view of the function of the law

is instructive. Whereas Arendt sees the law as establishing the basis for a political sphere of action in which men (*sic*) are equal though distinct individuals, Simon emphasizes the fact that in the public just as in the private sphere human beings can never be considered equal. Simon's position is rather like that of Benhabib, who criticizes Arendt's vision of the public sphere as a rarefied idealization. And for Simon, it is the law which must operate not only to enable action in the public sphere, but also to curtail it. While for Arendt freedom is an absolute requirement for a public/political sphere in which men can reveal themselves in speech and action, Simon's view is that freedom must be limited in the name of a more inclusive ethics. Freedom cannot escape being balanced by necessity, in the form of one's obligation to the weak or enfeebled. Simon thus speaks of:

> the way in which democracy had to assume that all are equal, in degree of responsibility, whereas in reality some are wicked and some are gullible, some exploiters and some exploited, and mediation must take place between the two. "The law as an institution," he ended up saying, "as an institution, is admirable, they've got it all wrong, it's the uses to which it is put that are wrong." (p. 268)

The discussion then moves on to a consideration of which is more important, the letter of the law or the spirit, with Simon defending the letter and Rose the spirit.

Simon's professional work, as in the 'closed shop' case on which he has been working at the time of this conversation, is founded on his passionate belief in a more inclusive public ethics. He has an 'unfashionable' belief in public service, and it could be argued that he and others like him are able to introduce some of the principles on which Rose operates in her private sphere into public/political life. The irony is that Simon's own private life suffers in part because of his devotion to his work.

Rose's relation to the public world is more complex. Her decision to give her money away when she comes into some of her inheritance at the age of twenty-four can be seen as a public 'action' in the emphatic Arendtian sense, as when Arendt writes that in acting and speaking, 'men show who they are, reveal actively their unique personal identities and thus make their appearance in the human world' (p. 179). As Arendt points out, action, in this definition, has unforeseeable consequences, and in this case they are tragic. Rose's twenty thousand pounds, donated for the construction of a school in Central Africa, literally goes up in smoke as the school is obliterated in an outbreak of civil war and the children are killed. Rose is not in any way responsible for their deaths, but the text points to the ambivalence of her gift. On the one hand, it was an action carried out in good faith, if one accepts, as Rose does, the distinction between faith and works: it was an action carried out in the right 'spirit', to recall the terms of Rose and Simon's discussion about the law. On the other, it might be seen as evidence of *hubris*, of setting the self and its spiritual development above other considerations.

This question of the relationship between the letter and the spirit (or between justice and faith, to pick up the terms that the narrator uses in relation to Rose and Miss Lindley), comes up again in connection with the most painful aspect of the novel, Rose's decision to allow Christopher to return to live with her and the children. Rose makes this decision simply because 'she could not bear to keep the children from him': it is an act of pure charity, of recognizing the rights of others. In many respects, it is the exact obverse of her earlier act of generosity in giving away her money. Here, Christopher and the children benefit (as the African children did not), whereas Rose suffers, spiritually. She becomes irritable, petty and resentful, and feels that she has given up her soul for Christopher and the children. She describes her fall to herself in this way:

> She had sold for them her own soul . . . the price she had to pay was the price of her own living death, her own conscious dying, her own lapsing, surely, slowly, from grace, as heaven (where only those with souls may enter) was taken slowly from her, as its bright gleams faded. (p. 395)

From Rose's point of view, her life without Christopher, existing peacefully with her children and supported by her (mostly female) friends was a life of grace, and so it seemed to Simon too. And yet from another point of view, it could be seen as self-indulgent, as Rose herself reflects: 'she knew it had been narrow, her conception of grace, it had been solitary' (p. 395). And so she chooses justice over faith, and does her duty, for others, 'in the dry light of arid generosity'. This complex novel is thus concerned, among other things, with the difficulties of balancing justice and faith, the letter and the spirit, action and labour. Unfairly, it seems that Simon gets this balance right more easily than Rose, because he is able to pursue his career not just out of an abstract concern for justice but also, as Rose points out, out of love.

The heroine of Drabble's next novel, Frances Wingate of *The Realms of Gold* (1975), is given many more opportunities than Rose – perhaps in reaction to the bleakness of *The Needle's Eye*. Frances is a successful archaeologist, divorced and bringing up four children on her own. Because of her professional success and the fact that her ex-husband is rich, she has many freedoms which Rose lacks. She can seem ambitious and predatory: at one point her lover Karel lists what he sees as her bad points, including 'the way she kept leaving her children to go off to foreign parts', 'her excessive interest in her work', 'her predatory instincts about people – her liking to be liked'.[9] Nonetheless, her energy and life-force also make her very appealing: her nephew Stephen, for example, admires her energy, her talent for survival, her 'splendid carelessness' in not worrying overmuch about her children. The children flourish, too:

> They were an excitable, assertive, healthy, resolute, daring bunch, her children, constantly milling and seething with an excess of energy, conditioned by herself, perhaps, into an irregular way of life, all stops and starts, departures and homecomings, presents and dramas and disasters. (p. 60)

Beneath the surface level of what she is doing – looking after her children, lecturing, travelling, first losing and then finding her lover again – Frances is searching for a way to fit her life into a pattern, to relate it to those of others. As a 'career woman' she seems to be a new kind of woman, without precedent for her behaviour, but during the course of the novel it becomes clear that this is of course not so. As an archaeologist, her academic interests have taken her away from classical archaeology, from the Greeks and the Romans and 'the praise of Western thought' (p. 123). Instead, her most important work has consisted of the rediscovery of a city/emporium from a much earlier Saharan civilization. The society which she reconstructs from the buried remains of this city matters immensely to her:

> She had made them live again, and she had loved them, her traders, her merchants, her agents, she had loved and defended

them, with their caravans and their date palms, their peaceful negotiations. Men of peace, not war, they had been exchanging useful commodities and works of art. (p. 34)

Like Cassandra in Elizabeth Taylor's *Palladian*, Frances thus rejects the Western classical tradition, with its emphasis on agonistic action and transcendence, in favour of an earlier society in which she finds some echo of her own desires. She reflects on the fact that through interpretation, archaeologists and historians create the past which they need: thus in her peaceful Saharan tribe, she finds an image of 'a possible if not an ideal society' (p. 124).

Frances's professional archaeological activities are paralleled by her search for her family history, and especially for a female genealogy: it is significant that at the beginning of the novel she is reading Woolf's *The Years*, which also traces a family history, focusing on three generations of Pargiter women. Frances has an unmotherly mother, an enthusiastic campaigner for birth control and the wider availability of abortion – hence, Frances thinks, her own defiant fruitfulness and love of children. When Frances falls ill with a lump in her breast (which turns out to be benign), she turns to her family for support, but receives little from her mother. Nonetheless, her visit home suggests a journey back to her dead grandmother's cottage. When she discovers, against her expectations, that this cottage is still standing, she feels intense relief that it has been 'reprieved':

She wasn't sure what she wanted, or why she had come, but her heart was quick, the shape of the roof and the windows and the big tree, so long unseen, so often imagined in her inward eye was calling up some corresponding pattern in her mind, its lines were the lines of memory, a shorthand carving, like the graph of her heart or brain. (p. 116)

What Frances rediscovers in this visceral way is her relationship with her grandmother, and she is also searching for something that she can learn from their joint past. When she is called back to the area by the bizarre incident of her great aunt Con's death from starvation and visits Aunt Con's cottage, Frances discovers that Aunt Con was the more important forerunner. Con, who has lived in isolation and been considered mad or a witch, had an illegitimate child in 1914. It seems that she did not have her daughter adopted, although the child died only eighteen months later. She was in effect a single parent who kept her child in the face of public opinion and lived a life of integrity. Frances resembles her as she looks in an old photograph 'upright, unsmiling, stern, beautiful... savage and predatory, grim and determined' (p. 284). Frances also reminds her brother of Boadicea as she appeared in a picture book of their childhood. Through images like these, the novel thus maps out a line of inheritance for Frances, a history of forebears who make her seem not a freak in her role as career woman/single mother but part of a long tradition.

In likening Frances to Boadicea, who resisted the Roman invasion of Britain, Drabble reinforces the point that Frances stands in opposition to the classical tradition and to various dominant strands in Western culture. This opposition is more fully explored through the relationship between Frances and her nephew, Stephen. In a central scene in the novel, Frances and Stephen discuss Freud's *Beyond the Pleasure Principle* and his idea of the death wish, the belief that all living creatures desire to return to an earlier, inorganic state of being. They discuss too Freud's suggestion that 'the extraordinarily violent instincts of sex arose by accident', and that 'to seek life was some silly new idea, the chance result of a Darwinian accident' (pp. 194–5). Stephen is clearly much affected by these ideas, and goes on to raise the subject of Empedocles, the philosopher who flung himself into the boiling volcanic crater of Etna. Various interpretations of this act are put forward: was it in order to prove he was a god or was it the result of an overwhelming death wish? Arnold's dramatic poem 'Empedocles on Etna' is mentioned, and a reference found in Milton. The discussion alerts us to Stephen's sense of the futility of life (a sense of which Frances is uneasily aware), and also suggests a connection between the classical drive to transcendence and a morbid fear of death.

Stephen, who has an anorexic wife and a young baby, subsequently kills himself and his daughter in the light of the revelation that comes to him 'like a light from heaven' that it was 'better to be dead than alive'. Following Empedocles, he reasons that 'if one leapt now, unsubdued, into the flames, one would be freed, one would have conquered flesh and death, one would have departed whole, intact, undestroyed' (p. 349). Frances is appalled and distraught by this, and although she comes to accept the fact of Stephen's death we are aware that she stands absolutely at the other end of the spectrum from him. Frances believes in the potential of human

life, and like Arendt, and unlike Stephen, she celebrates life precisely *because* it is a miraculous accident. Arendt writes in *The Human
Condition* that 'the origin of life from inorganic matter is an infinite
improbability . . . The new always happens against the overwhelming odds of statistical laws . . . the new therefore always appears in
the guise of a miracle' (p. 178). Frances embodies and endorses the
human condition of natality in Arendt's sense. She believes in the
unexpected, the unforeseen, in the power and potential of new
lives and new beginnings: she thus has the 'faith and hope . . . which
Greek antiquity ignored altogether'. More selfish than Rose Vassiliou,
she nonetheless is able to combine natality, labour and work productively. She optimistically nurtures her children and in her work
uncovers and preserves evidence of a civilization offering some
alternative to the denigration of this world which marks/mars Western
classical thought. So, as Drabble has herself suggested, while Frances
is selfish she is also 'in many ways admirable', successfully bringing qualities associated with the private sphere into the sphere of
work and potentially into the sphere of action.[10]

All Drabble's novels are double-voiced in that they combine literary and popular references and elements (in *The Realms of Gold*,
for example, Frances quotes Shakespeare, Keats, Milton, Horace and
Virgil to take her mind off her toothache). Elizabeth Fox-Genovese
has complained of what she sees as this disjunction in Drabble's
work, but this is to miss the political point.[11] Drabble cites canoni-
cal literary texts in order to critique them, to contest their founding
assumptions through a more readerly form and a more woman-
centred content. *The Middle Ground* (1980) represents her engagement
with Woolf, a writer who seems to haunt the imagination of the
'woman's novelist'. Drabble's book is a reprise and critique of *Mrs
Dalloway* (1925), resembling Woolf's text in its loose structure, its
dependence on retrospective narrative and focus on apparently trivial
domestic incidents and encounters. The two central characters mirror those in *Mrs Dalloway* and enable Drabble, like Woolf, to explore
the apparent gulf between the sexes. Woolf links Clarissa Dalloway
with the party-going spirit, with the need to connect with other
people and to find correspondences. Both Septimus Warren Smith
and Peter Walsh, on the other hand are alienated and self-divided,
linked with war and imperialism. Rather similarly, Drabble links
her middle-aged heroine, Kate, with her maternal role, whereas Hugo
(the equivalent of Septimus/Peter), a foreign correspondent with a
weakness for the 'hot spots' of the world, is linked with a desire to

evade personal responsibilities through his involvement with international conflicts, particularly in the Middle East. Kate and Hugo's
differing responses to the 'Middle Eastern question' are, as we shall
see, revealing.

Kate is a journalist who 'started to write new-wave women's pieces
some time before they became fashionable' and made her name by
'sharing her pregnancies and exhaustions and indignations with a
shocked and enthralled public'.[12] She is now rather tired of all this
and wants to learn more about wider political issues, but she remains a woman-identified woman, haunted (as was Woolf) by the
concept of the 'real woman' whom she has failed to be. Her friend
Evelyn seems to her to be such a woman, just as Evelyn's husband,
Ted, seems to Hugo to be a 'real man'. Curiously, and repeating a
motif from *The Waterfall*, Kate has an affair with Ted, and thus
'shares' him with Evelyn for several years – but this strengthens
the tie between the two women rather than weakening it. They
'collude', they depend on each other, in a reversal of Eve Sedgwick's
'homosocial triangle'.[13] Here, it is a man who is the object of exchange between two women whose primary affiliation is to each
other. Kate and Evelyn have a shared view of the world: both are
deeply committed to what I have called an ethics of labour. Labour
in Arendt's sense refers as we have seen to the care of the body
and of life which must be renewed, sustained and nurtured. It also
necessarily involves relations of inequality and dependency, and it
is this aspect of labour which has, I would suggest, the most profound ethical implications. The experience of mutual and shifting
dependency between carer (almost always the mother or female
relative) and child must surely qualify and modify Enlightenment
assumptions that the self is free, autonomous and self-determined.
As Christine Battersby suggests, it is more appropriate to acknowledge that the self is neither free nor determined, but is always 'scored
by a variety of relationships with "otherness"'.[14] If this is the case,
and if the ideal model of the 'free', 'equal' self on which civic
society is founded is false, then this suggests an urgent need to
revise the legal and political structures of that society. It suggests
the need for a more flexible legal and political system which recognizes an ethical imperative that may need to move beyond the
idealized abstractions of equality and freedom. Morton Schoolman
makes this point in his introduction to Seyla Benhabib's book on
Arendt. He writes that:

When . . . Benhabib finds that Arendt limited the scope of the public sphere and its agenda, and further undermined both with a narrow conception of morality, she also looks to discover in Arendt's theory ways to introduce *inside* this rarefied and fore-shortened universality opportunities for participants to redraw the lines of public space to make it far less exclusive. Here Arendt's notion of "enlarged thinking" or "enlarged mentality," with which Benhabib develops a concept of political judgement, *embraces the full perspectival quality of the political world for the public sphere – the perspectives of concrete others, the particularities of identities and their differences, of the excluded and neglected.*[15]

Such issues preoccupy Kate and Evelyn and inform their opposition to Ted's mechanistic, Darwinian view of society:

How Evelyn disliked Darwin, and Ted himself for arguing that she and her tribe were busy saving the useless at the expense of the useful, thus interfering with the natural wastage of society. How Kate had disliked Darwin, with what spirit in the old days she had tried to reject his suggestion that she herself was a fine specimen of nature's ruthless accidental adaptation. (p. 186)

Kate interferes with the 'natural wastage' of society by acting as proxy mother to a range of people, the most important of whom is the Iraqi refugee Mujid. The text is explicit about the fact that her care of Mujid is an extrapolation from her own experience of labour, in both the literal and the Arendtian sense. Mujid is the fiancé of a girl whose mother Kate got to know when she was in hospital giving birth to her first child: in conventional terms 'a tenuous connection', as the narrator remarks. Nonetheless, thinking of Beatrice, 'a jolly, talkative, wordly woman, full of good advice about babies and breast feeding', and of Beatrice's son, killed in a street battle in Beirut, Kate takes Mujid in to live with her, despite her friends' protestations that she has absolutely no obligation to do this. Juxtaposing Kate's action and Hugo's ineffectual journalistic analysis of Middle Eastern affairs, the novel invites us to see Kate's willingness to meet need beyond the call of duty or 'equality' as a model for a new conception of public as well as private relations. Rather similarly, Evelyn as a social worker attempts to take an ethics of labour into the sphere of state social provision. She, too, works beyond the call of duty, unshaken in her conviction that one must join 'the ranks of the caring' despite the risks this may involve (she is indeed badly injured when visiting one of her clients).

As in *The Realms of Gold*, the novel thus stages a clear opposition between an ethics of labour and an ethics of agonistic action which threatens to tip over into destruction. Ted Stennett, the Darwinian, is a good example of this latter tendency: he is not only stimulated by the idea of the survival of the fittest, but is also 'excited' by the notion of international disaster and of a pandemic which might destroy the world. This conflict of attitudes is brought into painful focus when Kate accidentally conceives Ted's baby and a scan reveals that the child has spina bifida. Kate agonizes over what to do, wrestling with 'fantasies of keeping the baby, however damaged it might be . . . she would devote what was left of her life to the child' (p. 71). In the end, she decides to have an abortion, on the rational grounds that '[s]he had no right to invoke suffering' (that is, the suffering of the child). Nonetheless, the decision haunts her and threatens to destroy her, taking away her 'natural flow of good spirits'. Talking it over with Hugo, she wonders if she would have been 'full of the spirit of life and love and joy and hope if I'd had a wretched baby with no bowel control and a spine split like a kipper and a head like a pumpkin', and concludes that yes, she probably would (p. 79). Drabble here foregrounds the negative flipside of a readiness to care: the danger of dependency on others' need of oneself. Nonetheless, Kate's attitude is seen as preferable to that of Hugo, who has a disabled son whom he has virtually abandoned, leaving his wife to care for him with loving devotion. In this novel Drabble comes close to suggesting that these differing responses to weakness and incapacity are not only gendered but are due to essential as well as cultural differences between the sexes. In her worst moments, Kate takes this view. She never tells Ted about the baby because she feels that he cannot help her, that he would not understand her suffering over 'the violence done'. Towards the end of the novel she reflects on the differences between herself and him:

> Just as she could not, in her heart, understand the jealousy that could lock a woman in a room for months or draw a knife on her for love, so he could not understand the deep drag of her nature, its steady pull towards the lost. They would gaze at one another for ever, good friends perhaps, old allies, old enemies, across this impossible void, trying new voices, new gestures, making

> true efforts to hear, to listen, to understand. But hopelessly,
> hopelessly ... Men and women can never be close. They can
> hardly speak to one another in the same language. (pp. 230–1)

In this novel Drabble explicitly ties an ethics of labour to the
rhythms and experience of women's bodily life and in particular
to maternity. While this emphasis may seem to tend towards a
rather negative essentialism, it is also true that the novel offers a
very positive image of the creative power and force of its heroine.
This power is vividly suggested when Kate, like Mrs Dalloway, goes
to buy flowers for her party. Distressed by the cut blooms, 'so short
of life, so delicately nurtured for this one moment' (an allusion to
Woolf's 'moments of being'?), Kate decides to replace them with
something more lasting, and buys a bay tree which the shop assistant tells her will outlive her, if she looks after it. Despite its sombre
elements, the novel thus ends with an optimistic orientation to a
future which depends on nurturing and sustaining the life of others.

In *The Radiant Way* (1987), Drabble maintains her interest in
bringing together Arendt's natality, labour, work and action. A new
departure, however, is that she invokes psychoanalysis far more
explicitly than in her earlier work as a means of registering and
exploring the imaginary structures which underpin the divisions
between public and private worlds. The novel centres on three middle-
class, middle-aged, educated women – exemplary figures for the
woman's novel. Of the three, Liz and Alix are both twice-married;
Liz has two children and three stepchildren, Alix two children. They
both work, but, significantly, their professional functions are a kind
of extrapolation of their maternal/domestic roles. Liz is a psycho-
therapist, specializing in family relationships, adoption, fostering
and step-parenting; Alix works part-time teaching female offenders
and works also in a Social Policy Unit in this area. Esther Breuer
(named for Freud's first collaborator, flagging the Freudian subtext
of the novel), unmarried and childless, evades social responsibility.
She is an art historian, living in a private world of aesthetic con-
templation. The novel is set in a period of 'unmotherly' politics, in
the Thatcher era: Liz's stepson Alan remarks on 'the novel oddity
of a woman prime minister who was in fact a mother but was not
nevertheless thereby motherly'.[16] This ties in with Kristeva's cel-
ebrated 1977 analysis of women in positions of power in Eastern
Europe:

The women who have been promoted to positions of leadership and who have suddenly obtained economic (as well as narcissistic) advantages that had been refused to them for thousands of years are the same women who become the strongest supporters of the current regimes, the guardians of the status quo, and the most fervent protectors of the established order.[17]

Jacqueline Rose has also written illuminatingly on Thatcher's counter-investment in the symbolic order.[18] Drabble is particularly interested in the idea of 'the state as mother', and suggests in this novel that the undermining of the Welfare State by Thatcher can be seen as a rejection of 'motherly' values (the values of labour, in Arendt's sense, taken into the public sphere). Alan discusses 'the history of those who clung to the state as mother . . . the psychology of those who wished to orphan themselves from the mother' (p. 17).

Liz, Alix and to a lesser extent Esther are opposed to this 'unmotherly' political and social climate, but they are all profoundly affected by it. Despite (or because of) her indifference to social issues, it is Esther who is most vulnerable. She is conducting a long-term affair with Claudio Volpe, an anthropologist, satanist and sick man, subject to obsessions and megalomania. In a revealing dream, Esther associates him with John the Baptist, and thus via the decapitation motif with fear of castration. In a public lecture in which he recounts an encounter with a werewolf, Claudio also self-identifies with Freud's Wolf Man, whose case history is given in Freud's paper 'From the History of an Infantile Neurosis'. Drabble has said that in the figure of Claudio she was exploring the ways in which the irrational erupts into the rational world.[19] If we look closely at the specific nature of the novel's Freudian allusions, it seems that such 'irrationality' is strongly linked with aspects of male sexuality. Freud's Wolf Man suffers from an intense male narcissism which is bound up with fear of castration and with over-valuation of the phallus. Freud writes that:

[The Wolf Man's] last sexual aim, the passive attitude towards his father, succumbed to repression, and fear of his father appeared in its place in the shape of the wolf phobia.

And the driving force of this repression? The circumstances of the case show that it can only have been his narcissistic genital libido, which, in the form of concern for his male organ, was fighting against a satisfaction whose attainment seemed to involve the renunciation of that organ.[20]

Claudio may be a repressed homosexual, as the Wolf Man is in Freud's view, but in the light of Eve Sedgwick's work on homosociality, and Irigaray's analysis of a 'hom(m)o-sexual' economy,[21] it is perhaps more appropriate to suggest that he embodies the connections between phallocentricity and homosociality.

While Esther is conducting her long-term and long-distance affair with Claudio, who lives in Italy, she is living in a flat just off the Harrow Road, a place of topical interest because of the existence of the 'Horror of Harrow Road', a serial killer with a preference for decapitating his female victims. *The Radiant Way* was written a few years after the case of Peter Sutcliffe, the Yorkshire Ripper, who between 1975 and 1981 killed thirteen women, and is in part a reflection on that case. In her brilliant study of the Yorkshire Ripper, *'The Streetcleaner': The Yorkshire Ripper Case on Trial*,[22] Nicole Ward Jouve brings out the connections between Sutcliffe's misogyny and his 'secret love' for his father, and in Drabble's novel the killer's preference for decapitation points again to over-valuation of the phallus, fear of castration and rejection of women. The severed heads of his victims resemble, of course, the Medusa, and in his 1922 note 'Medusa's Head' Freud writes that:

> To decapitate = to castrate. The terror of Medusa is thus a terror of castration that is linked to the sight of something. Numerous analyses have made us familiar with the occasion for this: it occurs when a boy, who has hitherto been unwilling to believe the threat of castration, catches sight of the female genitals, probably those of an adult, surrounded by hair, and essentially those of his mother.[23]

Claudio and the Horror of Harrow Road are linked symbolically through a potted palm which Claudio gives to Esther, a kind of fetish which stands in for him while he is in Italy. The 'silent young man' who lives above Esther only speaks to her once during the thirteen years in which they inhabit the same house, and this is to protest when she puts the palm outside on a cold night. He thus 'identifies' with Claudio: he also turns out to be the Horror of Harrow Road. Esther has been in double jeopardy throughout the novel, at risk from Claudio's psychic aggression and also from the literal, physical aggression of the serial killer.

Exploring the darker side of the construction of masculine identity, the novel suggests that in identifying with masculinity a leader like Thatcher may be endorsing a culture of violence and narcissism rather than of strength. Against such a bleak prospect, Drabble sets the efforts of those who oppose such an 'unmotherly' politics, including Esther's friends Liz and Alix, and also Alix's husband Brian, 'motherliness' in this sense not being tied to one sex/gender. Liz 'saves Esther's life' by listening to her stories about Claudio, and illuminates the murkier areas of her patients' lives, but it is Alix who is most passionate about taking her 'private' values into the public sphere and attempting to transform it. The warden of the institution where she works hopes that the younger women look on her 'as a mother', and Alix herself relates to her students as far more than a teacher. She takes a particular interest in one case, that of Jilly Fox, a drugs offender, for whom she feels a 'slightly dangerous, slightly irregular sympathy' (p. 214). When Jilly is released from Garfield, Alix struggles with the question of how far she should keep in touch with her, and how far she can or should take responsibility for her. Against the advice of her colleagues (and of Liz), she goes to see Jilly in a derelict house off the Harrow Road. Jilly herself says that Alix is 'mad' to come, but also 'wonderful'. Jilly is in a state of despair. To the last, Alix tries to save her, to get her in touch with 'sympathetic' professional help, but to no avail. Inevitably, it seems, Jilly is murdered by the Horror of Harrow Road: in Alix's view, 'Jilly Fox had chosen to meet a violent death' (p. 336). In a novel of substitutions, Jilly seems in some way to have taken Esther's place: she is linked by name with Claudio Volpe (*volpe* = fox) and seems to have become the counterpart and victim of both Claudio and the serial killer.

The novel foregrounds the fact that it has been impossible to help Jilly Fox because there is no 'half-way house' between an institution like Garfield and Alix's home. In other words, there is no bridge between the home and the penal system, the private and the public worlds, and Jilly is the victim of the lack of connection between these spheres. The novel is on the whole pessimistic about the chances of establishing such a link. Alix seems to embody it in her work for Garfield and for the Social Policy Unit, but as her colleague in the latter points out, 'Nobody ever takes up any of our recommendations. Nobody listens, ever' (p. 324). As she also tells Alix, 'At your age, with your talents, with your experience, you ought to be the Governor of Holloway or the Mistress of Girton'. But she is not, and at the end of the novel, with her Garfield classes and the Social Policy Unit shut down because of government cuts, Alix has come to feel that the community 'does not want her, and she does not at the moment much care for the community. There is no hope, in the present social system, of putting anything right' (p. 392). The novel ends on a curious note, with Liz, Alix and Esther in the country, reunited with 'their first presiding deity', a woman called Flora who had invited them to her room on their first visit to college. The name Flora calls up the Demeter and Persephone myth and foregrounds the secure matriarchal/maternal world of the (then) all-female colleges which launched these women in life. The pastoral setting for their reunion is serene and restorative, but there is a strong suggestion here of retreat from the effort of 'putting anything right' in the public sphere.

In a paper based on a talk given at a conference in 1995, Drabble writes of the difficulties which still face women 'because when women have babies they find themselves back to square one, discovering that many of the problems which they thought had been solved by feminist theory are not solved by feminist practice'.[24] The question of feminist *practice* is at the heart of Drabble's work. She focuses directly on the fact which is still absolutely central to most women's lives, which is that they are the primary carers of children and other dependent relatives. Her female characters struggle to bring the knowledge gained from this experience into the public sphere, with varying degrees of success. While there can, of course, be a danger in lauding women's 'caring' experiences in that it may make it more difficult for them to escape being automatically cast in a caring role, it is nonetheless equally dangerous if the lessons learned from such experience are ignored and neglected in the public and political sphere. Drabble constantly returns to this issue, and to the key question raised by Seyla Benhabib in her critique of Arendt: 'How can we both nurture the child and preserve the world?'[25]

5
A. S. Byatt's Gardens

Byatt is on occasion scathing about the 'woman's novel' and has described in her 1991 preface to *The Shadow of the Sun* her early fear of the form 'as an immoral devouring force'. Nonetheless, her fiction is structured around the dilemma which Radner sees as central to the woman's novel, defining it in terms of its content and form. That dilemma is of course the 'mind/body problem', the conflict which the 'educated woman' experiences between the claims of the intellect and the experience of the body, an experience crucially determined by the ways in which the female body is culturally coded. This is the central theme in all Byatt's novels. For example in the best-selling, Booker prize-winning *Possession* (1990) the central issue is the conflict between Christabel's right to be a great writer and her falling in love with Randolph Ash, with all its consequences. As Byatt puts it:

> Christabel gives a cry which I think is my cry throughout the book: you're taking away my autonomy, you're giving me something wonderful that I regard as secondary, my work is what matters: and nevertheless she falls heavily in love because she's a very powerful and passionate woman.[1]

Formally as well as thematically, Byatt's fiction fits exactly Radner's description of the woman's novel, poised ambivalently between high and low culture:

> The woman's novel says, by and large, what it means to say, refusing to reveal its secrets under the scrutiny of the analyst by displaying these last for all to see, literati and non-literati alike.

Yet the richness of its language, the subtlety of its arguments, and its undeniable intelligence and self-consciousness defy the classification of popular culture . . .[2]

Byatt is an intellectual writer using a reader-friendly form which derives from the tradition of domestic realism, whatever reservations Byatt may have had about this tradition when she first began to write.[3]

One of the most fruitful ways of approaching the 'mind/body problem' in Byatt's work is through her own account, in her introduction to *Passions of the Mind*, of her unfinished doctoral dissertation on religious allegory in the seventeenth century. She writes:

Before I abandoned it, this project had narrowed itself to a discussion of temptations in gardens between *The Faerie Queene* and *Paradise Regained*, between the Bower of Blisse, the serpent's address to Eve, and Satan's temptation of the incarnate Christ, the Word in human form, in the wilderness. It is not too much to say that this unwritten work, with its neoplatonic myths, its interest in the incarnation, in fallen and unfallen (adequate and inadequate) language to describe reality, has haunted both my novels and my reading patterns ever since.[4]

The (absent) thesis would seem to be concerned with two types of split or division, and with an imagined, lost origin. And I would suggest that the whole of Byatt's work is structured around two interlocking 'fall' myths. The first is that of the fall into language. We are now probably most familiar with the Lacanian, psychoanalytic version of that myth, in which it is argued that we fall from a primary state of wordless union with the mother into separation, loss and language. Byatt, however, grafts her reading of Foucault onto her reading of Renaissance literature and of T. S. Eliot to come up with an alternative myth. This is the myth of a fall from an original, Adamic state of grace in which words and things were fused, into a post-Babel state in which words and things have split apart and language has become shifting and unstable. Byatt here brings together biblical story, Eliot's influential account of the 'dissociated sensibility', and Foucault's analysis of sixteenth-century language in *Les Mots et les choses*.[5] In an essay called 'Still Life: *Nature Morte*', she quotes the following pertinent passage from Foucault:

In its raw sixteenth-century historical state, language is not an arbitrary system; it is deposited in the world and is part of the world, both because things themselves hide and reveal their enigma like a language and because words offer themselves to men as things to be deciphered.[6]

A little later, Foucault writes:

In its original form, when it was given to man by God himself, language was an absolutely certain and transparent sign for things, because it resembled them. The names of things were lodged in the things they designated, just as strength is written in the body of the lion, regality in the eye of the eagle, just as the influence of the planets is marked upon the brows of men: by the form of similitude. This transparency was destroyed at Babel as a punishment for men.[7]

Les Mots et les choses was published in 1966, and Foucault's post-structuralist thought seems to have fed particularly into Byatt's *roman fleuve* which begins with *The Virgin in the Garden* (*Babel Tower* is, of course, the most recently published volume in this sequence). However, all her fiction is preoccupied with the felt disjunction between word and thing, a disjunction which can in a sense be seen as analogous to the mind–body split which is worked out more elaborately in her second 'fall' myth.

This is the more familiar and perhaps universal myth of a fall from primal innocence into sin, sexual division, procreation and death. *Paradise Lost* is perhaps the most important pre-text here – it was to have been central to Byatt's projected doctoral thesis, and it seems to haunt, productively, her writing. In this respect, it is worth remembering how clearly Milton articulates the distinction between man's capacities and those of woman, for example in *Paradise Lost* Book 4, ll.296–99:

> Not equal, as their sex not equal seemed;
> For contemplation hee and valour formed,
> For softness shee and sweet attractive Grace,
> Hee for God only, shee for God in him.[8]

The terms of female existence described in *Paradise Lost* are precisely those which Beauvoir finds deeply inscribed in *twentieth-century*

Western culture: 'destined to the male from childhood, habituated to seeing in him a being whom she cannot possibly equal, the woman . . . will dream of transcending her being towards one of these superior beings'.[9]

However, it is the iconography of *Paradise Lost* rather than its doctrinal content which is most important to Byatt, especially the image of the paradisal garden with its trees and flowers, and the figures of Eve and the serpent, which are conjoined in Christian mythology as Eve becomes identified with sexuality, the body and death. Milton, of course, alludes constantly to Classical myth in *Paradise Lost*, and Byatt is particularly interested too in the overlap between the Christian myth of the Fall and the Classical myth of Ceres and Proserpine, or Demeter and Persephone. As we shall see, Eve's paradisal garden, Proserpina's 'faire field of Enna' and the Virgilian underworld to which she descends become central images in Byatt's fiction. Bringing together aspects of Classical mythology, Old Norse and Breton myth and the Christian story, Byatt explores the complex ways in which these founding myths articulate and shape the experience of women.

Byatt's first two novels are pre-texts for the tetralogy which began with *The Virgin in the Garden*. *The Shadow of the Sun* and *The Game* are self-reflexively 'about' the situation Byatt found herself in when she first began to write – excluded, she felt, from dominant male models of creativity, but dissatisfied with the woman's novel as she saw it. *The Shadow of the Sun* was first published in 1964, the same year as Sylvia Plath's *The Bell Jar*, a text with which it shares many characteristics. Byatt's novel offers a sustained critique of the gendered nature of philosophy and aesthetics and explores the damaging effects of this on a young woman who wishes to write. The sun-metaphor around which the text is organized takes us back, as Byatt points out in her preface, to Neoplatonic creation myths, where the sun is the male Logos, or mind, which penetrates inert Hyle, or matter, and brings it to life and form.[10] *The Shadow of the Sun*, as much as Irigaray's *Speculum*, thus offers a critique of the Western metaphysical tradition in which, as Irigaray puts it, 'Any Theory of the "Subject" Has Always Been Appropriated by the "Masculine"',[11] and in which intellection and creativity of any kind always operate *against* inert (female) matter. In this tradition, matter is stripped of all life, form and shaping power:

An Ideal-Principle approaches and leads Matter towards some desired dimension, investing this underlie with a magnitude from itself. *Matter neither has the dimension nor acquires it; all that shows upon it of dimension derives from the Ideal-Principle.*[12]

Byatt also mentions in her introduction the impact of Coleridge, who, reworking the imagery of Plato in post-Copernican terms, 'saw the human intellect as a light like the moon, reflecting the light of the primary consciousness, the Sun'. Needless to say, Anna, the heroine of the novel, cannot aspire even to this moon-like status. Her name, echoing that of Anna Brangwen, points to another influence which shapes the novel, that of D. H. Lawrence. Byatt refers to his short story 'Sun' as a version of the Neoplatonic creation myth, the central female character in it being fecundated by the sun: we might also remember the more sinister story 'The Woman Who Rode Away', in which a European woman is sacrificed to the Aztec sun-god. This story ends with an endorsement of '[t]he mastery that man must hold, and that passes from race to race'. In the Cambridge of the 1950s (which was Byatt's Cambridge), the more troubling aspects of such a philosophy went unnoticed: in his 1955 study *D. H. Lawrence: Novelist* Leavis simply reads this story in terms of 'the intensity and profound seriousness of Lawrence's interest in human life'.[13]

In *The Shadow of the Sun*, Henry Severell (the name suggesting both several selves and a willingness to sever all human ties) is the exemplary Coleridgean artist-figure, absorbing and reflecting the light and energy of the primary imagination/the sun, containing it without being destroyed by it. His visions of light, visual images rendered in words, are both metaphors for and instances of what Coleridge called 'the highest . . . intuitive knowledge':[14]

> And still the light poured, heavy, and white, and hot, into the valley before him and collected, molten and seething, on the corn beneath him; he could hear it thundering into the silence; and still he had to see, so that his cone was now an hourglass funnel, opening both ways, and the wide light all pressed and weighed in the point of intersection which was himself.[15]

Anna wants to have this kind of vision too: she thinks of Henry in terms reminiscent of seventeenth-century devotional verse as having 'strange knowledge adhering to him, the shreds of another brighter world'. However, the vision which Byatt gives Anna is not even secondary, like Henry's, but tertiary. While Henry is in Coleridge's terms a moon reflecting the light of the sun, Anna is a mirror reflecting, in turn, the light of the moon. In one of the most remarkable passages in the novel, Anna is in the bathroom, which already functions in this text as a specifically female space, long before Byatt writes in *Possession* about Melusine, whose monstrous body is discovered as she bathes. Looking at light reflected in mirrors and through water, in what seems a drowned, under-water world (a metaphor which is also important in *Possession*), Anna sees an intense pattern of brightness:

> [I]t was a drowned world, a sunken secret world, with pillars and planes of light shining gently in its corners and the odd brightness of a tap, or the sliver of light along the edge of the basin, winking like living creatures, strange fish suspended and swaying in the darkness ... Shadows of light, Anna thought ... She carried [the glass] across to the window and held it so that light was directed and split through the water onto the floor of the bath. The circle of brightness opened like a flower, with crisp, spinning petals ... she said to herself, turning the glass round and round ... "I can do something with this. Oh, I can do something with this, that matters." (pp. 133–4)

What is interesting is that Anna *has* her vision, and it is specifically a vision of a flower, with 'crisp, spinning petals'. For Byatt the flower, from Milton's 'bright consummate flow'r' of the intellect to Mallarmé's 'l'absente de tous bouquets', represents art itself.[16] Anna's flower thus represents the possibility of a woman's art. It can and does exist, but is vulnerable because of its difference and potentially limited by its connection with the domestic sphere (it is notable that Anna's vision takes place inside the house, not outside in the fields, like her father's).

In the novel, Anna is placed somewhere between her father, the ideal type of the artist, and a married woman friend, Margaret, who has given herself up completely to 'the feminine mystique'. Powerfully exploring these two extremes, Byatt contrasts Henry's capacity for visionary consciousness, which brings him 'such a happiness that he trembled for it' and Margaret's subjection to the vision of others. In chapter 28, Henry is in the garden, gazing down into the dark purple trumpet of a gloxinia and thinking, appropriately enough, of the imperial Tyrian purple, and of Aldous Huxley on the visionary potential of film. Henry is able to lose himself in the visual world and can create precisely out of his 'lack of sense of proportion'. In the chapter which follows, Margaret, an abandoned wife, is looking at pictures in *Vogue*, huge blow-ups of a painted mouth, an eye, a fingernail. At first they seem to have 'the jewelled glitter of the medieval heaven', but as Margaret gazes these fragments of the commodified, fetishized female body become intolerable to her:

> The mouth was dead vegetable, the eye a dead hairy animal, the nail dead worm. Margaret experienced again, more violently, the sensation she had brushed in the bath, that she was falling apart, that bits of her were separate and falling irretrievably away. (pp. 181–2)

Walter Benjamin writes of fashion that it 'prostitutes the living body to the inorganic world. In relation to the living it represents the rights of the corpse. Fetishism, which succumbs to the sex-appeal of the inorganic, is its vital nerve'.[17] In this passage, Byatt represents a woman so identified with fashion and the feminine mystique that she is almost a corpse, her body composed of petrified fragments. Or as Margaret thinks in the bath, her body is 'residue', mere inorganic matter.

Anna Severell can be read as offering some kind of middle way between these two extremes. She is neither unaware of other human beings, like Henry, nor reduced to a fetish of femininity, like Margaret, and her creative aspirations, however vague, point the way to a different (female?) art. Yet Byatt's first novel ends with Anna's pregnancy, and with the suggestion that she has lost her capacity for vision because of it, because she is *'femina gravida*, weighed down, weighed down' (p. 289). Anna feels betrayed by her biology and by contemporary cultural expectations that she should expend her energy 'at the kitchen sink' (as opposed to writing about it).

Byatt's next novel, *The Game* (1967) has *two* women writers as central characters, torn halves of an ideal whole. Cassandra Corbett is a don and keeper of a private journal; her sister Julia is a well-known woman's novelist. Cassandra, Byatt has said in an interview, is a better writer than Julia, because she sees writing as artifice.[18] That is, she is aware that language is not transparent, that it has

its own, metaphorical life. Nonetheless, she is a failed writer because she lives too much in the imagination, denying the reality
of the body and of the physical world. As her priest remarks,
Cassandra has 'only a very tenuous connection with reality': she
has made the outer world into 'a network of symbols', and has
cultivated her enclosed 'walled-garden skills at the expense of any
others she might have had'.[19] Julia, by contrast, sees writing as
simple description of an unproblematic reality, and devotes herself
to chronicling the mundane, exploring 'in loving detail the lives
of those trapped in comfort by washing-machines and small children' (p. 47). Julia does not feel cut off from the physical world,
but is aware that she has not fully developed her imaginative powers.
She has too eagerly embraced limitation: 'It's true what they say
about me, I remain on a level of complaining about facts' (p. 122).
Byatt has also retrospectively described Julia's kind of writing in
terms of 'self-indulgent creation, the "waste fertility" with which
Comus tempts the Lady'.[20]

Like *The Shadow of the Sun*, *The Game* is principally structured
around myth and metaphor. One key myth is that of Cassandra.
When she was at Cambridge, Byatt wrote the story of Cassandra
'over and over', and through the character Cassandra in *The Game*
she explores its significance. Cassandra was the daughter of Priam
and Hecuba, loved by Apollo, the sun god and also the god of the
muses. When she rejected Apollo, he punished her by rendering
her gift of prophecy (given to her by snakes) useless. She predicted
the fall of Troy, but her warnings went unheeded: she was subsequently raped by Ajax, taken away by Agamemnon and finally killed
by Agamemnon's wife Clytemnestra. The most significant aspect of
the myth for Byatt is that it is Cassandra's rejection of the god
Apollo which silences her, or renders her speech useless. Transpos-
ing this story into the terms of her novel, Byatt seems to suggest
that the woman writer must, so to speak, traffic with Apollo, that
is, she must not shy away from either intellectual or sexual knowledge. The character Cassandra, living as she does in the closed gardens
of her imagination and her virginity, is, as she is aware, quite sterile:

Cassandra who was Apollo's priestess, and – since she refused
intercourse with the Lord of the Muses, and was thus no artist –
incapable of communication. Unrelated to the world of objects
around her. (Apollo, besides being Lord of the Muses, was God

of Light and thus doubly rejected for some impossible chastity.) Cassandra, like myself, like myself, a specialist in useless knowledge. (p. 141)

Another governing myth or story which was important to Byatt as a child and which is referred to in many of her novels is that of the Lady of Shalott. Immediately after the passage in her journal quoted above, Cassandra identifies herself with the lady:

The Lady of Shalott, also. The web, the mirror, the knight with the sun on him, reflected in the mirror and woven into the web. I am half sick of shadows. A poem a great deal more intelligent than we commonly give it credit for. (p. 141)

Tennyson's adventurous and prescient poem functions for Byatt as an allegory of a *simultaneous* fall into sexuality and fall into language. Enclosed in her tower and her garden ('a space of flowers'), the virgin lady weaves an imitative tapestry, perceiving without words: in Byatt's terms her thought is primary thought. Lancelot's intrusion into her world is a kind of rape: bringing the light of the sun and the force of his sexual energy into her shadow-world, he metaphorically takes her virginity, 'cracking' the mirror, and also causes the web of (pictorial) language to break free of the world of things:

> Out flew the web and floated wide;
> The mirror crack'd from side to side;
> 'The curse is come upon me,' cried
>   The Lady of Shalott.

Byatt's gloss on the poem confirms its resonance as an allegory for a sexually and linguistically fallen and divided state. Speaking of her heroines she has said:

They're all the Lady of Shalott: that's another image which is so deep in my very early childhood. It's to do with the thing that all my books are about: the sensuous life, childbearing, therefore men, therefore danger, and making things by yourself of exquisite beauty which can be accused of being unreal. All my books are about the woman artist – in that sense, they're terribly feminist books – and they're about what language is.[21]

The third and most important myth/symbol in *The Game* is the biblical myth of the Fall/the image of the serpent. The serpent figures largely in the novel. Simon Moffitt, the central male character, has spent his life studying snakes, and Cassandra and Julia, both of whom have been in love with him, are drawn back into his world when after years in the jungle he returns to England to present a series of television programmes about his work. Watching Simon – who has tempted her – and the vivid televisual images of snakes, Cassandra reflects on the meaning of the serpent for her:

> The serpent is traditionally . . . a symbol for our horror at finding ourselves necessarily embodied. *It is the brute.* A creature reduced to a mouth and a stomach. On thy belly shalt thou go, etc. In the myth of Psyche, Psyche's curiosity discovers Eros embodied as a serpent. The neo-Platonic interpretation is that this curiosity has transformed spiritual love to bodily lust. The limiting, debasing animal functions. (p. 24)

For Cassandra, the serpent represents the horror of embodiment, specifically female embodiment. She goes on to quote Coleridge's poem 'Psyche', in which the earth-bound serpent deforms and kills the things on which it feeds – just like a lover, she thinks. Yet, as one of the epigraphs of the novel reminds us, for Coleridge the serpent was also an image of the imagination, 'for ever varying and for ever flowing into itself – circular, and without beginning or end'. Julia also associates the serpent with the imagination, so that each sister sees in the serpent that which she repudiates, Julia the imagination, Cassandra the life of the body. In its elusiveness, the serpent thus represents the ambiguous nature of knowledge itself, which can be either intellectual or carnal. Ideally, we might think, it would be both, so that soul and body, butterfly and serpent would be one. Analogously, if Cassandra and Julia were to merge, if the torn halves were to be united, they would be the complete artist. Or would they? In *The Game* Byatt begins to explore the ambiguity of the ideal of completeness. In conversation with Simon, Cassandra remarks that what we 'crave – in love, or death' is 'completeness', and she also suggests that 'one must come together, body and soul, imagination and senses, for one's dissolution' (p. 199). The implication is that completeness and wholeness, much as we desire them, can be *deadly* (hence Cassandra's suicide): life and creativity may depend on incompleteness and division. This complex issue is more fully explored in *The Virgin and the Garden*, *Still Life* and *Possession*.

The Virgin and the Garden (1978) explores the theme of the woman artist implicitly rather than explicitly, as neither of the main female characters is an artist. But like *The Game*, the novel is structured around the lives of two sisters who take very different paths in their attempts to reconcile the life of the mind and the life of the body. Stephanie and Frederica Potter are New Elizabethans, educated young women of the 1950s, affronting their destiny. What is striking is that in the novel Byatt places far more emphasis on the first Queen Elizabeth than on the second. We might think that Elizabeth II, queen and mother, would offer a role model for the young Potter sisters, but she is seen as a weak 1950s stereotype, a 'young wife and mother' who lacks any grip on power. Elizabeth I is important for Frederica precisely because she is a powerful woman. Frederica, who is still at school when the novel begins, is 'typecast' as the young Elizabeth in Alexander Wedderburn's play *Astraea*, a verse-drama which explores the iconography of the Virgin Queen. Frederica physically resembles Elizabeth and adopts some of the same strategies for survival.

Both Byatt's novel and Alexander's play draw on an article by Frances Yates, 'Queen Elizabeth I as Astraea', which explores the identification of Elizabeth with Astraea, the just virgin of the golden age, and with Virgo, the sign of the month of August. Yates's article is thus concerned with the ambiguity of Elizabeth as a figure who represents symbolically both a virgin (even, potentially, the Virgin Mary) and the goddess of harvest and fruitfulness (Ceres). She argues that the complex construction of Elizabeth-as-icon reflected, and to some extent resolved on a symbolic level, the political and religious conflicts of the period. In one particularly interesting passage she writes:

> The complex and opposite mythological ingredients of Elizabeth Virgo as a symbol are thus a suitable reflection of the conflicts and antitheses which the Elizabethan settlement tried to evade. Her 'imperial peace' covered, *not without deep internal strains*, divided religious opinions.[22]

What is suggestive in relation to Byatt's novel is the idea of a rhetorical resolution which does not really address underlying conflict. Like Elizabeth I, Frederica uses rhetoric to knit together an image

which makes some sense of her contradictory position. Just as Elizabeth deployed rhetoric to link female virginity and imperial power,
so Frederica uses language to pull together her conflicting identities as unsexed mind and desiring woman. For both Elizabeth and
Frederica, there is a cost, hinted at in the violent image of 'quar-
tering' which Alexander associates with Elizabeth:

> He had, he told [Frederica], pouring sherry, taken the red and
> white from the little poem about Elizabeth the Virgin he had
> incorporated into his text.
>   *Under a tree I saw a Virgin sit.*
>   *The red and white rose quatered in her face.*
> Quartered had made him think of hanging and drawing there, as well
> as heraldry, and so the red and white, blood and stone, had grown.[23]

Both Elizabeth and Frederica deal with conflict by separation and
repression: Frederica's term for this is 'lamination'. At one point in
the novel, when she is feeling particularly oppressed by her unsat-
isfactory relationship with Alexander, Frederica takes the bus to
Goathland, and after an inconclusive sexual encounter with a doll
salesman, hits upon the idea of lamination as a counter to the
confusing and contradictory experiences of her day:

> One could let all these facts and things lie alongside each other
> like laminations, not like growing cells. This laminated knowl-
> edge produced a powerful sense of freedom, truthfulness and even
> selflessness . . . She sensed that the idea of lamination could pro-
> vide both a model of conduct and an aesthetic that might suit
> herself and prove fruitful. It would, she decided, as in the event
> it did, take years to work out the implications. (pp. 209–10)

Byatt is explicit about the way in which 'lamination' can be a solution to the 'mind/body problem':

> I remember thinking of [lamination] as a strategy for survival
> when I was Frederica's age, in the sense that I thought you could
> possibly manage to be both at once, a passionate woman and a
> passionate intellectual, and efficient, if you could just switch gear
> and switch gear from one to the other, but if you let them all
> run together organically, something messy would occur and you
> would get overwhelmed.[24]

It is not necessarily a good solution, particularly in the longer term, but it enables Frederica to survive. This is important to Byatt, who has also said that *The Virgin in the Garden* is connected with 'a very early desire I had as a child to substitute female myths for Christianity'.[25] Flawed as they are, Elizabeth and Frederica are images of female agency and power – Frederica may not run a country, but she does pick her way through the mire of family life to achieve 'extraordinarily excellent' A level marks and escape to Cambridge.

If Frederica is Queen Elizabeth in the metaphorical scheme of the novel, Stephanie, her elder sister, is Mary Queen of Scots, who marries, sinks and dies, as Byatt observes. Stephanie rhymes with Persephone, and the myth of Demeter and Persephone (or Ceres and Proserpine) is central to this novel and to all Byatt's work from this point on. Luce Irigaray has written about Demeter and Persephone in relation to the mother–daughter relationship which has been, in her view, occulted and repressed in our culture. For Irigaray, the relationship between Demeter and Persephone is an allegory for the possibility of (re)productive, woman-to-woman relationships:

> Carried off by the god of the underworld – or darkness – Kore-Persephone will be given back to her mother during the spring and summer months so that the world can maintain its fertility. The mother agrees to be fertile *with her daughter*.[26]

Byatt's reading of the story is closer to its mythological roots, in which Demeter and Persephone are essentially one figure, the earth-goddess who is maternal and who must go to the underworld in order to create and preserve life. While feminist readers, including Beauvoir and Irigaray, have seen the myth as evoking a lost (ideal) matriarchal culture, for Byatt it functions as a profound and resonant image for the processes and effects of heterosexual love for women. We have seen that she speaks of 'the sensuous life, childbearing, therefore men, therefore danger': for her, the myth of Ceres and Proserpine suggests the way in which the experience of sexual love can be, for women, a kind of descent into the underworld. Whether as a result of the ways in which the female body has been culturally coded, or in part because of the specific nature of female sexual anatomy, Byatt's women experience sex and orgasm in terms of an engulfment in physical experience, a movement into an unseen and potentially dangerous interior world which nonetheless has its own vivid shapes and contours.

Another intertext which overlaps with and draws on the myth of Ceres and Proserpine is *The Winter's Tale*, which is linked in the novel with Stephanie and with her mother, Winifred. Winifred's son is conceived after a discussion with her husband about *The Winter's Tale* in which Winifred identifies strongly with Hermione's suffering – 'All the years of her womanhood gone, and her two children, one dead, one vanished, and no feelings required but gratitude and joy' (p. 86). Later, when she in turn is pregnant, Stephanie notices an allusion to Hermione in Alexander's play which is lost on the rest of the audience. The two women, who are alike in many ways, identify with Hermione because she represents the abjected maternal pregnant body. One could argue that in *The Winter's Tale* it is Hermione's pregnancy, rather than her lively conversation with Polixenes, which is such an affront to king and court that she must be banished and subsequently punished by the death of her son and the protracted absence of her daughter. Hermione and Perdita are also of course identified with Ceres and Proserpine: Perdita alludes to the myth in her flower speech, much recited by Frederica in Byatt's novel – 'O Proserpina,/ For the flowers now, that, frighted, thou lett'st fall/ From Dis's waggon!' (*The Winter's Tale*, IV, III).

Julia Kristeva is one of the few feminist theorists to have written about the pregnant female body, and her understanding of pregnancy as an excess within, and to some extent a threat to, culture seems to accord with Byatt's view. In the essay 'Stabat Mater' Kristeva writes:

> Although it concerns every woman's body, the heterogeneity that cannot be subsumed in the signifier nevertheless explodes violently with pregnancy (the threshold of culture and nature) and the child's arrival (which extracts woman out of her oneness and gives her the possibility – but not the certainty – of reaching out to the other, the ethical). Those particularities of the maternal body compose woman into a being of folds, a catastrophe of being that the dialectics of the trinity and its supplements would be unable to subsume.[27]

The mis-match between the experience of pregnancy and the teachings of the Church (the 'dialectics of the trinity') is a key issue for Stephanie later in the novel.

Stephanie's role as Ceres-Proserpine is made explicit in the text, particularly in a key episode when she cycles home from school after taking a class on Keats's 'Ode on a Grecian Urn', a poem which itself alludes to a sacrificial rite. Just before she leaves the school, she is given a bunch of primroses, the flowers which in some accounts Proserpine was gathering when she was carried off to the underworld. Following the path home, Stephanie is about to go down into a hollow when Daniel, the local curate, rises up before her: gloomy Dis. 'Into the crater from the other side, ponderously manoeuvring, came a large black figure on a massive black bicycle. As though... he had simply risen up from the sooty laurels the other side of the crater' (p. 80). Not long afterwards, overcome by the force of Daniel's desire, Stephanie agrees to marry him. In a dense and moving passage, Byatt evokes Stephanie's feelings as Daniel makes love to her after their wedding:

> [S]he had the thought, in words, that this was truly the only time in her life when her attention had all been gathered in one place – body, mind, and whatever dreams or makes images. Then the images took over. She had always a very vague imagining of the inner spaces of her body, dark interior flesh, black-red, red-black, flexible and shifting, larger than she imagined herself from outside, with no kind of graspable perspective, no apparent limits... This inner world had its own clear landscape. It grew with precise assurance, light out of dark, sapphire rising in the black-red, wandering in rooted caverns... coming out into fields of flowers, light green stalks, airy leaves, bright flowers moving and dancing... They have their own lights, Virgil said of his underworld... and the light... shone through flower stalk and running water, in the rippling heads of the flowers and corn, a sunless sea brimming with its own shining... She was this world and walked in it, strayed lingering and rapid between the line of leaves and the line of sand and the line of the fine water, the line perpetually glittering and falling, perpetually renewed. (pp. 281–2)

Female interior space is imaged as an interior garden, fluid and immeasurable, and sexual experience here creates a sense of illimitability which is precisely not dissolution. The images of flowers rising out of the warm dark, of the corn and of the sea, suggest the way in which sex is inextricably connected, at this point in Stephanie's life, with fertility and with the potential for growth in her and in the wider physical world. The use of Virgil, conflating the underworld

of Classical mythology and the fertile female body, further establishes a connection between sex and death which is important to
Stephanie: it is emphatically pagan and affirmative, emphasizing
renewal and rebirth rather than Christian repudiation of the body.[28]

Byatt has said that in this novel 'I wanted to substitute a female
mythology for a male one. The male mythology is the Dying God
and Resurrection. The female one is birth and Renaissance'.[29] Through
Stephanie, she develops a mythology which challenges the Christian emphasis on transcendence. At Easter, for example, Stephanie
thinks how much she prefers pagan Spring festivals, with their
emphasis on the sap rising in this world, to the Christian emphasis on death and resurrection:

> Birth was a real miracle... and resurrection would be a greater
> one, if believed, but the blood we drink, the shadowy, temporary
> Form outside the spiced tomb, are neither believed nor needed as
> the song of the heavens at the Birth is believed and needed...
> [T]he English mind was secretly horrified by glassy sea, crystal
> walls... and throne of the New Jerusalem where Spring would never
> come again because there was neither grass nor winter. (p. 155)

Later, when she is herself pregnant, she works in Daniel's church,
which is dedicated to St Bartholomew, to cover up a reproduction
of Michelangelo's portrait of the martyr in the Sistine Chapel.
Michelangelo depicts St Bartholomew – to whom he gives his own
features – casting off his earthly body in disgust. Stephanie dislikes
this intensely, and decides to 'embower' and 'obscure' this image
in a cloud of wild cut flowers, lovingly detailed by Byatt – 'white
umbellifers and marguerites, green hellebore and sprays of dogroses'.
Through such contrasts, the novel offers a critique of a Christian
mythology (and a masculine aesthetic) which prefers the dream of
life after death to the reality of embodied life. There is also a suggestion, as there is in Kristeva's essay 'Stabat Mater', that the
perspective of (actual or potential) maternity brings a different inflection to our understanding of mortality. For example, Kristeva
describes the mother's sense of her relation to her child in terms
which suggest an acceptance of individual death in the light of
species survival: 'such an other has come out of myself, which is
yet not myself but a flow of unending germinations'.[30]

Stephanie's sexual experiences with Daniel, which take her into
her own interior garden, bring her nearer to a sense of complete-

ness than any other of Byatt's characters. She experiences a sense of unity which is neither a specious image (like Frederica's imaginary sense of herself), nor bound up with a drive towards dissolution and death (as it is for Cassandra in *The Game*). It is, rather, an intense experience of 'being-in-the-world', in Heideggerian terms. Such experience is continued in *Still Life* (1985) through the birth of her son, which gives Stephanie a moment of ecstasy which is also entirely bound up with *this* world:

> "There," she said to him, and he looked, and the light poured through the window, brighter and brighter, and his eyes saw it, and hers, and she was aware of bliss, a word she didn't like, but the only one. There was her body, quiet, used, resting: there was her mind, free, clear, shining: there was the boy and his eyes, seeing what? And ecstasy.[31]

The use of sun-imagery in the context of childbirth offers an implicit critique of Platonic idealist thought.

Yet Stephanie is gradually worn down by being 'sunk in biology'. She cannot think, because of the demands of childcare. In the antenatal clinic, she reads Wordsworth and thinks about the relationship between words and things: the result of her fierce concentration is that she fails to help another woman who subsequently loses her baby. After her son's birth, she makes another effort to go to the local library to work on the Immortality Ode, and offers a significant rereading of Wordsworth's poem. Whereas conventional criticism emphasizes metaphors of transcendence in the poem, Stephanie concentrates instead on images of depth, in particular the 'varying deeps' of stanza VIII – 'the eternal deep', 'the darkness of the grave'. She sees in these 'a Wordsworthian vision of a darkness that was life and thought', and goes on to consider his sense of the depths of the earth to which the root of a plant must reach, if it is to live (p. 155). She shows that his poem produces an earthly countermythology that balances, and perhaps undermines, the myth of the divinely transcendent origins of life. What Stephanie thus does is to find and inscribe her own (female) underworld, source of life and renewal, in a visionary rereading of Wordsworth's text. But whatever the strength of her insight, and whatever the pleasure it gives her, she cannot sustain it because she has to get back to her son. She is torn between William (Wordsworth) and her son William, a state which Byatt describes very precisely: 'Stephanie, her mind on the platonic aspects of the "Immortality Ode", her body extremely anxious about William, came through the front door' (p. 156–7). William and his needs prevail, of course. Stephanie's dilemma is a text-book example of the 'mind-body problem', a problem which in Byatt's view feminism has failed to solve:

> [T]he feminist movement, whatever its virtues, has not produced any satisfactory answer to what I see as the major biological/ intellectual problem of women ... this problem is what to do with the fact that you're a childbearing animal and that, whatever the feminists say, the nurturing of small children is a female thing.[32]

While in this statement Byatt seems to take a biologically determinist view of the female role, in her fiction she gives full weight to the cultural determinants of bodily identities. Indeed, it is precisely this sense of the extraordinarily complex interplay between the body and culture which gives the portrait of Stephanie its interest and power.

In the scheme of the novel Stephanie's death is on one level determined by classical mythology. As we have seen, Stephanie/ Persephone represents the maternal figure who must go underground in order to be fertilized and produce new life. The myth is important to Byatt because it suggests the loss of self in maternity which has been explored above, a loss which is a kind of death, though it brings renewal. However, Stephanie's death also seems to be determined by a scientific law which decrees, in the narrator's words, that 'as the immortal life of the genotype is transmitted, some say, so the phenotype, the individual body, becomes redundant, dispensable: it is economic for it to age, cease to function, die' (p. 237). The narrative perspective in *Still Life* is bleaker than that in *The Virgin in the Garden* because the redemptive aspects of the Ceres and Proserpine myth have become intertwined with a more reductive, neo-Darwinian discourse. From this point of view it is interesting that while Stephanie's daughter Mary, as her name suggests, represents the possibility of rebirth and renewal, the narrator casts a shadow over this image. Describing a different Mary in a nativity play, s/he warns that as they watch:

> Parents are moved because childhood is so swift and vanishing. They are perhaps also more darkly moved by some threat in the

law of flesh and blood itself... Not only childhood vanishes: men and women, having handed on their genes, are superfluous... Mary looks protectively at the doll: Mary's mother looks, moved and protective, at Mary's childish body and soft face. And time runs on. (p. 41)

While Stephanie is sunk in biology, Frederica, the survivor, continues to laminate. At Cambridge she compartmentalizes her life and is 'confident and inventive about categorizing people' (p. 120). She has some men as friends, some as lovers, but sees none of them whole. This 'splitting' mechanism is a response to her own fear and vulnerability, and is Frederica's way of resisting her cultural conditioning as a woman. Byatt writes that Frederica 'was conditioned to desire to be abject. This desire was reinforced by the behaviour of Rosamond Lehmann's heroines' (p. 127). Byatt mentions Lehmann several times in the novel, and in its Cambridge sections *Still Life* can be seen as a reworking of *Dusty Answer*, a reworking in which the heroine struggles with her (culturally determined) impulse to surrender herself entirely to an ideal lover. Frederica holds out for a long time, having sex on her own terms (it is significant that when she plays the Lady in *Comus*, she ends up speaking the lines of both Comus and the Lady: she is always her own seducer). She 'falls' in the end, yielding to Nigel Reiver, who comes upon her in her room when she is curled up in bed with period pains, reading Proust, Racine and Plato. Through comic juxtaposition, Byatt makes the same point as Irigaray about Plato's refusal to recognize the material/maternal origins of human life:

Frederica... then turned to Plato's myth of the fire in the cave. Her own gas fire boiled and bubbled sporadically; she could feel hot gouts of blood welling out. (p. 290)

When she finally sleeps with Nigel, Frederica loses her grip of herself, of 'separate Frederica', but it is an experience which she finds not only pleasurable but also frightening. Unlike Stephanie, she continues to find the loss of autonomy and of boundaries rather terrifying, closer to dissolution than to renewal.

Despite Frederica's determination to hold on to the things of the mind, in *Still Life* intellectual and artistic issues are almost exclusively a male preserve. While Stephanie tries to think about words and things and fails, Alexander Wedderburn writes a successful play addressing questions of representation in literature and the visual arts. While Frederica is unable to draft a coherent PhD proposal, Raphael Faber, a male don, discourses eloquently on the dissociation of sensibility and the separation of language and things, citing the now-familiar image of Mallarmé's 'l'absente de tous bouquets' (p. 203). It is the fall into sexuality, rather than the fall into language, which preoccupies the female characters, but even on the question of sexual division, the text offers only a male perspective, that of Freud. An eminent grammarian refers to Freud's discussion of sexual division in a conversation with Alexander about the attractions of still life painting:

> In Freud's myth the peace of the inanimate came before the striving of life, and the peace of the Aristophanic hermaphrodite before the constructions and cell-divisions of Eros. In Freud's vision things secretly resent the calling to life of light: they wish to return to the state in which they were – instincts are conservative, "every organism wishes to die only after its own fashion". Maybe we could see our fascination for still life – or *nature morte* – in these terms? Maybe the kind of lifeless life of *things* bathed in light is another version of the golden age – an impossible stasis, a world without desire and division? (p. 179)

This view of the sexual instincts as an arbitrary development or a kind of accident is also important, as we have seen, in Drabble's *The Realms of Gold*. In *Still Life*, the notion of art itself as a return to the inorganic – the 'lifeless life of things' – is both fascinating and deeply troubling. It offers a vision of the ideal for which we strive (the garden, in Byatt's personal mythology) which is also a vision of death. As Freud so persuasively puts it:

> It would be in contradiction to the conservative nature of the instincts if the goal of life were a state of things which had never yet been attained. On the contrary, it must be an *old* state of things, an initial state from which the living entity has at one time or other departed and to which it is striving to return.[33]

Against Freudian and neo-Darwinian theory, however, we can set an image which suggests a different perspective. The narrator of *Still Life* tells us that:

The germ of this novel was a fact which was also a metaphor: a young woman, with a child, looking at a tray of earth in which unthinned seedlings on etiolated pale stalks died in the struggle for survival. She held in her hand the picture of a flower, the seed packet with its bright image. Nasturtium, Giant Climbing, mixed. (p. 237)

In the novel, this experience is also Stephanie's. A poor gardener because she cannot bring herself ruthlessly to thin out seedlings, she manages at length to cover her cottage in a blaze of nasturtiums, scarlet and orange, ivory and mahogany-red. Looking at them, she thinks of Jack and the Beanstalk:

Stephanie watched them lift in the early light, fold into limp triangles at night, and was put in mind of Jack and the Beanstalk, the prosaic and angry mother who had been given a few seeds in exchange for a cow and had stood at the foot of a brilliant ladder into the sky. (p. 228)

What Stephanie sees is a seamless continuity between the seeds in the earth and the flower of the children's story, itself as magical as the beanstalk it describes, itself a work of art. There is no division for Stephanie here between the material world and the life of the mind, and it is because they are one that both real flowers and flowers of the mind are beautiful and redemptive. No other character in the novel matches the depth of Stephanie's insight – which is, of course, never articulated by her.

In *Still Life* male artists and thinkers experience life in terms of negative divisions: Stephanie does not. She is, as Byatt has said in interview, a visionary, someone with an extraordinary depth of understanding. However, Stephanie does not become an artist and has no intention of intervening in the public sphere. One of the paradoxes of the novel is thus that no female character in it achieves what Byatt has achieved, that is, no female character becomes an artist who successfully incorporates female experience into her work. Byatt's next and most popular novel, *Possession* (1990) has such a female artist figure, but one who achieves her artistic success at enormous cost. She has to give up her daughter (partly because of Victorian social codes, but also to preserve a space in which to write), and receives almost no public recognition in her lifetime. In exploring Christabel La Motte's nineteenth-century problems, Byatt

is also perhaps expressing some of her own anxiety about the consequences of producing a female-centred art. She is on record, of
course, as disliking classification as a 'woman writer', fearing that
this may prevent her writing being judged 'on merit' – which of
course begs the question of who determines 'merit'.[34] Nonetheless,
the fact that her work is unambiguously centred on female experience must have caused her some concern about its critical reception.

Possession represents Byatt's first explicit engagement with the kind
of feminist theory which would advocate and defend a specifically
female art. Her use of the Melusine myth in the novel was suggested by a talk she heard Irigaray give, and she subsequently read
the published version of the lecture, 'Femmes Divines' (reprinted
in *Sexes and Genealogies*). In *Possession*, Byatt parodies French feminism, or at least bastardized versions of it such as that offered by
Leonora Stern, an American feminist critic who first appears in the
novel enveloping the twentieth-century heroine, Maud Bailey 'in
large warm arms, in musky perfume, in soft spreading breasts'.[35]
Leonora reads Christabel LaMotte's poetry through a hotchpotch
of ideas taken from Cixous and Irigaray, as in this passage from
her book *Motif and Matrix in the Poems of LaMotte*:

> Cixous has remarked that many women experience visions of
> caves and fountains during the orgasmic pleasures of auto-eroticism
> and shared caresses. It is a landscape of touch and double-touch,
> for as Irigaray has showed us, all our deepest 'vision' begins with
> our self-stimulation, the touch and kiss of our two lower lips,
> our *double sex*. (p. 244)

Leonora goes on to provide an analysis of the landscape of the
poetry as representing female auto-eroticism and lesbian desire,
incorporating in passing an overblown account of Charlotte Brontë's
first encounter with the sea in terms of female orgasm. French feminist
thought appears in such a version as simplistic and misleading,
almost as a form of lesbian propaganda. Cixous and Irigaray are
presented as feminists who privilege lesbian relationships (as Leonora
does) and who unproblematically *endorse* cultural myths which identify woman with the generative earth and with the fluid sea.

This is not just to parody but to misrepresent Irigaray, whose
thinking in 'Femmes Divines' seems in fact extraordinarily close to
Byatt's in *Possession*. For example, 'Femmes Divines' begins with a
meditation on our relation to the elements, 'the material condi-

tions of existence', and goes on to explore the complex relationship between physical or material 'facts' and the cultural and
mythological forms which both express and shape them. Tracing
some of the means by which we construct our identity in the material/
cultural world, Irigaray contests the way in which women have
been identified with the earth and water and also seen as bestial,
half-human. She writes of:

> The impotence, the formlessness, the deformity associated with
> women, the way they are equated with something other than
> the human and split between the human and the inhuman (half-
> woman, half-animal) . . . forced to comply with models that do
> not match them, that exile, double, mask them, cut them off
> from themselves and from one another, stripping away their ability
> to move forward into love, art, thought.[36]

Possession is concerned with precisely such 'deforming' myths, in
particular myths like that of Melusine which have developed around
the figure of the creative woman. Christabel La Motte is such a
woman, a poet who at first aligns herself (like Cassandra in *The
Game*) with the Lady of Shalott. She lives in seclusion in what we
assume to be a lesbian relationship with another artist, and values
the enclosed and protected space in which she makes her art, affirming
that although women are taught to dread 'the terrible tower' sur-
rounded by thickets, 'within its confines we are free' (p. 137). Nonetheless, like all Byatt's characters she falls (as Byatt puts it, reviving
a dead metaphor, she 'falls heavily in love'), and after a brief but
passionate affair with the poet Randolph Ash, flees to Brittany where
her child is born in secret. Her daughter is brought up by her sister,
and Christabel returns to live as a dependent in her family home.
Her daughter does not love her, but sees her as a 'sorcière, a spinster
in a fairy tale'.

Christabel's major work is a long poem, 'The Fairy Melusine',
based on the myth recounted by the medieval writer Jean d'Arras
and published in 1478. Melusine is a fairy with supernatural powers
who must live with a mortal man in order to die a natural death.
She finds this man in Raymond, who promises never to spy on her
and never to visit her on Saturdays, when she changes into a snake
from the waist down. If his gaze falls upon her then she will lose
her appearance as a woman. Of course the prohibition is broken.
Raymond spies upon Melusine in her bath, denounces her publicly

and condemns her to eternal life as a snake, separating her from her children. The significance of Melusine for Byatt seems to be twofold. On the one hand, she is clearly a descendent of the figure of Eve, half-woman, half-serpent, her monstrous form expressing the horror of embodiment. This is clearly within the Christian tradition of repudiation of the fallen body and identification of it and the material world with women. From such a perspective the myth can be read as intensely misogynist, representing women as gross and sinful beings who can only be redeemed through marriage to a man. Randolph Ash highlights this aspect of it in a letter to Christabel, quoting a description of the Melusines from the sixteenth-century writer Paracelsus: 'It is thought they live without rational souls in fantastic bodies, that they are nourished by the mere elements, and at the final Judgement will pass away with these, unless they may be married to a man' (p. 172). However, Melusine can also be read, as she is by Christabel, as representing not the monstrosity common to all women, but specifically the monstrosity of the creative woman. In this respect, the bestial Melusine can be compared with the bird-woman Fevvers in Carter's *Nights at the Circus* (1984). For Melusine's supernatural powers are intensely creative: during the period of her marriage she brings great prosperity and happiness to her kingdom. Christabel writes of her interest in this second aspect of the fairy-woman:

> I am interested in other visions of the fairy Melusine – who has two aspects – an Unnatural Monster – and a most proud and loving and *handy* woman. Now there is an odd word – but no other seems to suffice – all she touched was well done – her palaces squarely built and the stones set on rightly, her fields full of wholesome corn. (p. 174)

La Motte also speaks of the freedom and pleasure Melusine had in her own private space, free from the gaze of men – 'Who knows what Melusina was in her freedom with no eyes on her?'

For both Byatt and Irigaray, the figure of Melusine poses a problem. On the one hand, the image of woman as monstrous ties her to the physical world and denies her intellectual and spiritual life. The negative charge of such an image must be resisted. On the other hand, the trope of monstrosity reflects a truth about the difference of women's experience, a difference which can be a source of strength, and which needs to be expressed. From this point of view, 'monstrosity' has positive aspects, particularly from the point of view of the woman artist. Irigaray seems to suggest this when she writes:

> In the enigmas formed by the popular or the literary imagination, in the monsters produced by culture, we may seek a sense of the darkest part of our becoming.[37]

In *Possession*, Byatt also links the figure of Melusine with that of Ceres-Proserpine. Writing to Ash about the nature of Melusine, Christabel suggests that she was 'not only Ghoul – but a kind of goddess of Foison – a French Ceres, it might be' (p. 174). Just as Christabel here fuses the figures of Melusine and Ceres, so in her novel Byatt brings together the Melusine myth, which she connects with the woman artist, and the Ceres-Proserpine myth which she habitually connects with the sexual life of women. It is in fact Randolph Ash who is particularly interested in Ceres and Proserpine. He reads Vico's analysis of the myth, and in his poem 'The Garden of Proserpina' brings together classical, Norse and Christian mythology, offering a powerful and illuminating meditation on the intertwining of language, metaphor and myth in the structuring of human reality. But it is Christabel who recognizes, in her last letter to Ash, that she herself represents both Melusine and Ceres, artist and mother. She has written a poem which she knows is good ('I think she *will not die*, my Melusine, some discerning reader will save her?'), and she has a daughter who is happy and carefree ('a happy soul – a sunny creature').

In the last few pages of the novel, Ash sees his and Christabel's daughter Maia in similarly dual terms, as having both a 'fairy' (Melusine) and an 'earth mother' (Ceres-Proserpine) inheritance: 'There,' he said, crowning the little pale head. 'Full beautiful, a fairy's child. Or like Proserpine' (p. 510). But what strikes the reader is that while Ash sees Maia/May (mother of the muses/mother of corn) whole and entire in this paradisal moment, somewhere Christabel is suffering. The cost to her of being both artist and mother has been inordinate. Her daughter does not know her or like her, and her (female) art is not recognized. Something of the same pattern also seems to be emerging in the lives of the twentieth-century characters in the novel, Roland and Maud. It is Roland who after the excitements of the literary-detective plot gains access to a hitherto forbidden garden and begins to name and to write, confidently, whereas Maud seems exhausted and bowed down by her inheritance from Christabel. Through the slightly *distraite* figure of Maud, the novel thus suggests the difficulties which continue to face the intellectual/creative woman. Maud will not experience exactly the same problems as Christabel, but she still feels that she is a divided being. She hides away her corn-blonde hair, for example, because she feels that her physical beauty contradicts her intellectual position and authority. The mind–body problem, evidently, is still there.

6
Anita Brookner: The Principle of Hope

Brookner's novels are primarily concerned with romantic love, and while her fiction offers a partial critique of the assumptions which underlie popular romance, it also endorses 'romantic hopefulness' as an essential condition of life. Her protagonists are often academic women with attachments both to the intellectual life and to an old-fashioned model of femininity in which a woman waits to be discovered, looking her best, 'by a man who has battled across continents, abandoning whatever he may have had in his in-tray, to reclaim [her]'.[1] Her work thus explores a particular aspect of the mind–body problem, the conflict between an investment in intellectual life and an investment in an ideal of femininity in which woman functions as the passive object of male desire. In exploring this conflict, Brookner is doing more than disclosing a pathetic disparity between the intellectual sophistication and emotional naivety of her heroines. They are not so much naive as innocent and hopeful, and this is the most interesting aspect of Brookner's treatment of romance. Most feminist analysis of romance has explored it from a psychoanalytic point of view. Janice Radway's classic study *Reading the Romance*, for example, draws on the work of Nancy Chodorow in order to argue that the function of popular romance is to offer vicarious nurturance to women who, typically, spend their lives in nurturing others.[2] Such a perspective, while illuminating, fails to acknowledge the wider social implications and possibilities of the romance structure. Making exactly this point, Bridget Fowler suggests that the work of Ernst Bloch, which draws on both Marxist and Freudian thought, offers a more fruitful starting point for thinking about romance.[3] In his eclectic study *The Principle of Hope*, Bloch explores the utopian impulses present in a wide range of literary and cultural forms. Bloch understands utopia not as an impossible ideal, but as a real and concrete goal. Rejecting much earlier philosophy for its preoccupation with the past, Bloch focuses on the 'Not-Yet-Conscious', on the anticipatory and progressive strands of thought which are always present and which '[look] in the world itself for what can help the world'.[4]

In discussing utopias, Bloch goes on to make a distinction between 'nightdreams' and 'daydreams' which is particularly helpful for an understanding of Brookner's fiction. For Bloch, the nightdream provides 'fictitious fulfilments of an unconscious wishful fantasy' and it is essentially archaic and infantile. By contrast, the daydream offers the vision of a possible future world order: 'daydream imaginative creations do not blow soap-bubbles, they open windows, and outside them is the daydream world of a possibility which can at any rate be given form' (p. 98). In its regressive and conservative aspects the nightdream can be linked with formulaic popular fiction (including romance), which provides the reassurance of the stable and the known. By contrast, the daydream is for Bloch an essential component of all great works of art, which are always orientated towards the future and the unknown. Yet the distinction between nightdream and daydream is by no means absolute, for between the level of the dreamer and that of the daydreamer there can be an exchange. Bloch argues that '[a]rchaic material can communicate with waking imagination' because many night-dreams are undischarged and unfinished, and thus 'demand day-dream, forward intention'. So that

> The insight . . . that archaic brooding can be utopian in reality finally explains the possibility of a merging of night-dreams and daydreams, gives *the explanation and dissolution* of a partially possible *merging of the dream-games*. (p. 102, Bloch's italics)

Brookner's fiction both enacts and scrutinizes such a 'merging of the dream-games'. Her fiction incorporates elements of nightdream and daydream, with allusions to both formulaic romance and to high culture – such hybridity being, as I have argued, entirely characteristic of the woman's novel.

Through this 'merging of the dream-games' Brookner explores the tension between what she calls the 'archaic female longings' of her characters and their rational understanding of their position as independent, late-twentieth-century women. In doing this, she does not condemn such archaic longing, but rather, in line with Bloch's argument, disentangles those aspects of it which are genuinely utopian and which can be aligned with a 'principle of hope' which finds expression for Brookner in a vision of 'the ideal of love'. While such an ideal may have its origins in private need, it develops in Brookner's work into a vision with a strongly social and ethical dimension, into what Bloch calls a 'waking dream with world-extension'.

Dr Ruth Weiss, the heroine of Brookner's first novel *A Start in Life* (1981), has an appearance and character which are 'exactly half-way between the nineteenth and twentieth centuries'.[5] She may appear to be something of a throwback, yet the point of the novel is to explore the extent to which many late-twentieth-century women still identify with and internalize 'structures of feeling', in Raymond Williams's phrase, usually associated with earlier social formations. Brookner's work suggests that the structuring of desire has remained relatively stable despite changes in the organization of social and sexual life: *A Start in Life* explores the way in which popular culture, in particular, maintains such structures of feeling. Both Ruth's mother Helen and her housekeeper are addicted to romance, which continues to suggest that the point of a woman's life is to be 'rescued' by a man who will then relieve her of all responsibility for her existence. Brookner underlines this via her description of the helpless and ineffectual Helen's reading:

> She had got to the part where the governess, maddened by despair at the rakish ne'er-do-well younger son's forthcoming engagement to the neighbouring squire's daughter, has rushed out into the night and is about to be discovered sobbing on the moor . . . Deserting the glittering lights of the ballroom, the ne'er-do-well, his black curls streaming in the wind, finds a tiny fragile figure all but spent with exhaustion. Cradling her roughly in his arms, he realizes that she is his own true love . . . Helen sighed unconsciously as the door of the ballroom opened on to the stormy night. *Why had nobody ever done as much for her?* (pp. 119–20, my italics)

Through pastiche, the narrative distances itself from such an enervating view of love, and yet the heroine, Ruth, develops an ideal of love which is not unrelated to such popular structures. It is the strength of the novel to reveal in this way the underlying connections between popular and legitimate discourses of love. Ruth's conscious ideal is exactly the kind which, Anthony Giddens has argued, emerged in the late-eighteenth century in response to widespread changes in the structure of marriage and family life. Giddens distinguishes romantic love from *'amour passion'*, the latter being the kind of passionate love which detaches the lovers from the routines of everyday life. Romantic love, by contrast, offers a kind of *realistic* project for the future, a narrative of hope. Crucially, it offers to resolve the conflict between desire and social obligation by aligning love and sexuality with legitimacy and marriage. It offers, Giddens argues, both reparation and transcendence:

> [I]t presumes . . . a meeting of souls which is reparative in character. The other, by being who he or she is, answers a lack which the individual does not even necessarily recognize – until the love relation is initiated. And this lack is directly to do with self-identity: in some sense, the flawed individual is made whole.
>   Romantic love . . . produces triumph, a conquest of mundane prescriptions and compromises.[6]

On this level, romance in *A Start in Life* functions as a true ideal, promising a (limited) space of reciprocity within an alienated capitalist society. Yet Brookner also shows the disjunction between Ruth's conscious belief in love as mutually redemptive and her unconscious investment in patterns of behaviour which are more regressive. At one crucial point, as her older lover watches her planning their life together, the narrator writes:

> He was wise enough to know that the kindest way to treat a scholar and a person of some dignity and courage is to pretend that she is none of these things and to accord her the nurture and protection expected by less independent women. Ruth . . . was, indeed, already thinking like the ordinary woman invented by Duplessis. Plates, she thought, knives and forks . . . (p. 135)

Brookner further suggests the complexity of Ruth's situation through her use of *Eugénie Grandet* (1833) as an intertext. In her youth, Ruth has identified strongly with Balzac's virtuous and tragic heroine, only to reject her in young adulthood, believing that happiness only comes to those who are active and predatory, not passive and mild like Eugénie. Ruth trains herself to be a 'bad winner' rather than a 'good loser', but fails in her endeavour, ultimately sacrificing a love affair to her duty to look after her ailing parents. What is most interesting about Balzac's novel in relation to Brookner's is its dramatization of two conflicting views of marriage. Eugénie's love for her cousin Charles represents pure romantic love. She dreams of a marriage with him which will be reparative and restorative, and which will be uncontaminated by expedient or material considerations. Charles, on the other hand, has no difficulty in separating love from marriage, viewing the latter simply as a means of advancing his position in society. As he writes to Eugénie in the letter which destroys all her hopes, 'Love, in marriage, is just a wild dream. I know now – I have learned from experience – that it is advisable to obey all the social laws and conform with all the social conventions when one marries.'[7] While Balzac does not comment on the gendered nature of these conflicting perspectives, Brookner's novel emphasizes the ease with which the male characters are able to separate love and marriage, seeing them as by no means necessarily connected.

Her male characters are also only too happy to fall into a pattern of behaviour whereby their desires and needs are met by more than one woman. Richard Hirst, Ruth's first love, is a particularly unpleasant example, bestowing his handsome presence in return for well-cooked meals and financial help for his work as a student counsellor. The role of food in his relationship with Ruth is particularly instructive, and indeed the role of food is fascinating throughout Brookner's fiction, which offers a kind of social and cultural analysis of eating and its discontents. Melanie Klein has argued that the psychological structure of eating always retains traces of our earliest experiences of nurture. These experiences will always contain elements of conflict and frustration, for the child can never have continuous satisfaction in so far as 'the baby never has uninterrupted possession of the breast'.[8] As the child develops, '[g]reedy, erotic and destructive phantasies and feelings have for their object the inside of the mother's body. In his imagination the child attacks it, robbing it of everything it contains and eating it up'. This gives rise to further conflicting feelings of love, hatred and guilt: it is crucial that the child should reconcile these feelings in order that they should be able to form good relationships in adult life. It could be argued that some of the curious attitudes towards food exhibited by Brookner's heroines are connected with such early conflicts. Klein's interest in the link between food and knowledge is also pertinent for a reading of Brookner's fiction. Melitta Schmideberg, Klein's daughter, developing Klein's work on the relation to eating and the relationship to the wider world, has argued that 'the incorporative function of eating is a model for later intellectual comprehension'.[9] Arguing that inhibition in eating can lead to intellectual inhibition, she also observes that in other cases, 'intellectual acquisition is felt to be less real and less aggressive, thus calling for less anxiety, than the actual consumption of food'. Could this be why Brookner's heroines, while they betray extreme anxiety over eating, typically find intellectual and creative life a welcome distraction from such bodily preoccupations?

In a key scene in *A Start in Life*, Ruth cooks dinner for Richard, spending the whole day preparing the meal and cooking the rice several times over as Richard is extremely late. When he finally arrives, much of the meal is ruined, and she has to give all the food to Richard, pretending that she is not hungry. After he has gone, she spends a night 'made sleepless by misery and hunger'. Her relationship to her beautiful and demanding mother is an anxious one, and it is as though her reluctance to take food for herself, and her anxiety to provide it for the men she loves, is connected with some unresolved guilt over taking food – and indeed taking her life – from the mother whom she imagines to be far more worthy and precious than herself.

Ruth's start in life (the title comes from another novel by Balzac, *Un Début dans la vie*) leads not to the romance for which she longs but to a reversal of roles in which she cares for her ageing parents. In this respect, the novel offers an unsparing view of the true terrors of domestic life for those who cannot exact service from others but must render it. It also offers a critique of the depiction of suffering in the works of the 'Old Masters' which is particularly suggestive in relation to the function of the 'woman's novel'. Ruth has been bathing her mother:

> She felt a sudden wave of fury, which she directed against all painters of martyrdoms and depositions. 'About suffering, they were never wrong, the Old Masters,' said Auden. But they were. Frequently. Death was usually heroic, old age serene and wise. And of course, the element of time, that was what was missing. Duration. How many more nights would she have to undress her mother, only to dress her again in the morning? (pp. 169–70)

The poem Ruth is thinking of is Auden's 'Musée des Beaux Arts', in which the central image is that of Icarus falling into the green sea. It is no accident that this image of a failed male drive to transcendence should accompany the indictment of an artistic tradition which includes both the 'Old Masters' and the poetry of Auden. What Brookner's text suggests is that this tradition rests on a disavowal of the life of the body and of the realities of suffering and decrepitude, with their exhausting dimensions of duration and repetition. In an interview, Brookner has also expressed a similar unease about the relation between 'great art' and the realities of life: 'I think the lessons taught in great books are misleading. The commerce in life is rarely so simple and never so just.'[10] Of course, this is the central theme of *A Start in Life*: the discrepancy between the expectations created by great literature and the reality of daily life. In dramatizing this discrepancy, Brookner raises a fundamental question. All artistic representation must depend on selection, but what is at stake is the principle of selection, and therefore the nature of the artistic *form* which will – Brookner passionately believes – 'save us all'. Might the appropriate form be that of the 'woman's novel', attentive as it is *both* to the ideal and to the experience of embodied life?

Brookner's next novel, *Providence* (1982), also explores the complex relationship between 'the lessons taught in great books' and 'the commerce in life'. In this novel, the picture is further complicated by Brookner's exploration of the connections between Romanticism and romance, that is, between an artistic movement which is part of 'high' cultural tradition and a structure of feeling which is more usually associated with popular cultural forms. The heroine, Kitty Maule, is an academic engaged on a temporary basis in a small provincial university. During the course of the novel she is working on a public lecture on 'The Romantic Tradition', and is also taking a weekly class on Benjamin Constant's novel *Adolphe* (written in 1806, first published in 1816). Brookner herself seems to view the Romantic movement with some disquiet. When asked in interview what attracted her as an art historian to the eighteenth century she replied:

> The Enlightenment, and the fact that it might just have come out right. The Romantic movement came along and bowled it all over. I do like a rational world, rational explanations and good humour and fearlessness.[11]

What appeals to Kitty about *Adolphe* is the fact that it is, as she points out, 'a yardstick for the shift in consciousness between the eighteenth and the nineteenth centuries'.[12] In his 'Preface' to the second edition of the novel, Constant places nineteenth-century romantic feeling and suffering within a moral framework which derives from the eighteenth century. As Kitty points out, '[t]he hero of *Adolphe* experiences pain through his conscience. He does not explain it as a general rule. What we have here is a moment of supreme morality' (p. 48). Feeling is kept within social and moral bounds. However, the Romantic period was one in which there was a weakened sense of 'communal enterprise' and an increased emphasis on individual freedom. In *Providence*, largely through the very careful selection of quotations from *Adolphe*, Brookner suggests that the danger for the Romantic hero, for whom Adolphe is a prototype, is of a conflict between the drive to individual self-fulfilment and the need to retain ties with others.[13] Such ties are most obviously available through the structure of romantic love, a structure which is in many ways in conflict with *Romantic* ideals.

Giddens has described the ways in which the ideal of romantic love developed in the Romantic period at a period when women were subordinated in the home and indeed secluded in it. But whereas feminist historians have argued that the ideology of romantic love was for this reason oppressive, offering an illusion of control in a situation of dependency, Giddens argues the reverse, suggesting that the development of ideas about romantic love was also 'an expression of women's power, a contradictory assertion of autonomy in the face of deprivation'.[14] It is likely that Brookner (who has often distanced herself from feminist thought) would agree with Giddens on this point, particularly as Giddens's analysis emphasizes the constructive, ethical components of the ideal of romantic love. In her fiction there is certainly a powerful affirmation of the ideal of romantic love from the woman's point of view, while there is, equally, a sense that the male characters – often self-styled Romantic heroes – are simply unable to measure up to this ideal. In *Providence*, for example, Kitty views Maurice, the man she loves, as a heroic figure, seeing in him all the qualities she would wish to possess herself:

His brilliance and ease, his seeming physical invulnerability, the elevated character of his decisions, the distances he covered, his

power of choice and strength of resolve, cast him in the guise of
the unfettered man, the mythic hero, the deliverer. (p. 91)

Nonetheless, from the very beginning of the novel there are sug-
gestions that Maurice may not be all that Kitty thinks he is. At
one point Kitty is humbled by his apparent 'passion for the absolute'
in French cathedrals, aware that while visiting them she herself
would be calculating 'the moment at which she might have crept
out to the patisserie' (p. 22). When she and Maurice do eventually
visit the cathedral of Saint-Denis, this gap between Maurice's 'transcendent' ideals and Kitty's simple physical needs is cruelly amplified
as Maurice prays to a stone Madonna, quite indifferent to Kitty's
physical and emotional distress (she is tearful and fatigued, and
finds the cathedral oppressive, 'a vast necropolis'). Maurice is in truth
egotistical and self-deluding, his faith more a faith in his own worth
than a faith in God. He certainly has no desire for a relationship
with a woman which would engage all his faculties and desires. Indeed, at the terrible denouement of the novel, it turns out that he
has been having an affair with a student, the aptly-named Miss
Fairchild, while drawing on Kitty for intellectual companionship (and
indeed food). He compartmentalizes his feelings and uses different
women for different needs, just as in the nineteenth century, Giddens
argues, men dealt with the tension between romantic love and *amour
passion* 'by separating the comfort of the domestic environment
from the sexuality of the mistress or whore'.[15]

Through the use of Romantic intertexts and through Kitty's experiences, Brookner thus explores the cultural and historical
connections between Romanticism and the ideal of romantic love.
What the text seems to suggest is that there has been a continuing
tension over the last two hundred years between male investment
in an ideal of independent self-worth and female investment in an
ideal of self-realization through mutuality in love. The point is made
– albeit in comic terms – in a scene in which Kitty, travelling to
Paris, meets a schoolteacher named Pascoe, a 'remarkably handsome'
man with 'a Byronic head'. While Pascoe notices that Kitty is 'very
pretty', and wants her to have dinner with him for that reason, he
shows no interest in her life or in her opinions. Kitty, by contrast,
is willing to think about him and to try to see his good points,
only to conclude that all her efforts will be in vain, for he is 'impossibly self-absorbed. A Romantic hero, she decided' (p. 108).

Like Ruth in *A Start in Life*, Kitty spends an inordinate amount of time cooking for the man she loves, while she herself has difficulty in eating. She finds it easiest to eat if she can distract herself from the physicality of the process by reading or listening to the radio. In this novel, the psychology of self-starvation is explored in depth and explicitly linked with Kitty's relationship with her mother. Kitty's eating difficulties have, we are told, increased since her mother's death:

> It had been a strange and peaceful death, her mother collapsed in her chair, one small hand trailing through some fragments of walnut shell. The faintly sour smell of her grandmother's discarded fruit peel was still in Kitty's nostrils, as well as the sight of her grandfather, with tears pouring down his face, crying, 'Marie-Thérèse! Marie-Thérèse!' ... Kitty Maule could never sit down to a hearty plateful of food without hearing the plaint, 'Marie-Thérèse! Marie-Thérèse!' Her throat would close and a faint trembling would start in her hands. (p. 17)

In this memorable scene, appetite for life and food is pulled sharply back as death infects life, the 'sour' fruit peel and dried-up walnut shells merging with what has so suddenly become the waste material, the cast-off, dead body of the mother. This is both a scene of abjection and a scene which stages that sense of guilt at taking life from the mother also evident in *A Start in Life*.

While a Kleinian perspective on what we would now call Kitty's 'eating disorder' would emphasize her sense of guilt (and repressed aggression) towards her mother, and would see her move to the intellectual life as a deflection of such guilt, a Kristevan analysis focusing on the nature of abjection would lead to a rather different interpretation. For Kristeva, abjection is primarily to do with the mother, because it is the uncertain boundary between the infant and the maternal body which provides the earliest experience of separation and of individual identity. As the infant has the first glimmers of its own separate identity, it views the mother's body with a mixture of horror and fascination: this profound mingling of horror and fascination is, in effect, the experience of abjection. Kristeva suggests in *Black Sun* that while male children are able to move out of abjection via an eroticization of the female body, female children often remain trapped in the orbit of the mother, forever mourning the lost a/object, the maternal body.

For Kristeva, the most powerful images of abjection are food loath-ing, and the corpse. In *Powers of Horror* she writes that food loathing is 'perhaps the most elementary and most archaic form of abjection. When the eyes see or the lips touch that skin on the surface of milk . . . I experience a gagging sensation and, still farther down, spasms in the stomach'. The corpse 'upsets even more violently the one who confronts it as fragile and fallacious chance'.[16] Clearly, both food loathing and the corpse are bound together in the scene quoted above, a scene which is literally sickening. Yet could it be that despite the 'unpleasure' contained in that scene, Kitty's repeated rejection of food represents a wish to return to the state of abjection, precisely because it is a state which returns her in some measure to her mother? In such a reading it would be longing, and not guilt, which drives her self-denial, a longing for escape from a life in which she cannot find self-realization in a relation-ship of romantic love.

Hotel du Lac (1984) offers a further analysis of romantic love. The fact that the novel is dedicated to Rosamond Lehmann bears wit-ness to Brookner's sense of continuity, to her view that what might be called the 'psychic structure' of romance has remained relatively unchanged during the twentieth century. It is also significant that the central character is named Edith Hope, the surname suggesting a link between Bloch's defence of popular culture in *The Principle of Hope* and Brookner's understanding of popular romance, an under-standing which recognizes the utopian elements embedded even in the most formulaic of romances.

Edith Hope is a writer of popular romances with names like *Be-neath the Visiting Moon, The Stone and the Star, The Sun at Midnight*. She is intelligent and discriminating: a professor's daughter, she looks like Virginia Woolf, 'remarkably Bloomsburian'. From such a position of cultural advantage, she is entirely able to deconstruct popular romance, analysing its functions of compensation and wish-fulfilment. In an analysis which anticipates the points which were to be made by feminist critics in the later 1980s, Edith argues that popular romance is structured around the myth of the tortoise and the hare:

"Now you will notice, Harold, that in my books it is the mouse-like unassuming girl who gets the hero, while the scornful temptress with whom he has had a stormy affair retreats baffled from the fray, never to return. The tortoise wins every time. This

is a lie, of course," she said, pleasantly, but with authority...
"In real life, of course, it is the hare who wins. Every time."
(p. 27)

Edith goes on to make the important point, however, that while
romantic fiction may lie, the 'lie' is a complex one. The implication of the fiction Edith writes is not merely that despite her lack
of physical beauty the heroine will get her man: it is that she will
get the hero because her *virtue* will be rewarded. The hero will see
past deceptive appearances and will recognize the heroine's patience
and fidelity. This is why Edith can write, at the end of the book,
that while her lover may have thought that she wrote her stories
'with that mixture of satire and cynical detachment that is thought
to become the modern writer in this field', he would have been
wrong: 'I believed every word I wrote' (p. 181). The word 'believed'
has a particular meaning here. It suggests Edith's commitment
to an *ideal* of romantic love in which two people come together
without strategy, as Brookner puts it in an interview.[17] In a conversation with a guest at the hotel, Edith defends such love as necessary
to life, and also distinguishes it from *amour passion*. Her ideal is of
a reparative love in which love leads to domesticity. As she tells
Mr Neville:

"My idea of absolute happiness is to sit in a hot garden all day,
reading, or writing, utterly safe in the knowledge that the person I love will come home to me in the evening. Every evening."
(p. 98)

The idea/l of domesticity is crucial for Brookner, and it is this
which underlies the haunting topography of the novel. The hotel
of the title is one to which Edith has been banished by her friend
Penelope, after her spectacular failure to turn up to her own wedding to the kind and sensible Geoffrey Long. The hotel is known
as a discreet refuge for those 'whom life had mistreated' or those
who have offended against social codes in some way, and it is popu-
lated almost entirely by women. The anonymity of the hotel painfully
underlines the fact that all these women are, as Edith notes, cast-
off or abandoned, therefore homeless. Even the hotel's decor is grey
and lifeless, and against its neutral tones the image of the home,
for which these women long, burns brightly. It is interesting that
Bloch, who writes so warmly about common dreams, also focuses

on the house or home, which he links with ideal marriage. In *The Principle of Hope* he writes:

> The house is itself a symbol, and indeed an open one despite all its closedness; it has as its background the goal-hope of the home-land-symbol, which persists throughout most wishful dreams and stands at the end of all. (p. 326)

The 'utopian nimbus' of marriage is linked by Bloch with the 'cryptic wishful symbol of the house', and he goes on to fuse this with the image of 'the great sea voyage which marriage can be ... which does not end with old age, not even with the death of one partner' (p. 327). In *Hotel du Lac*, Brookner offers a terrifying reversal of this image of the 'great sea-voyage' when Edith goes on a boat trip with Mr Neville. As they set out, Edith begins to ponder the significance of the journey:

> Ships, she knew, were often used by painters as symbols of the soul, sometimes of the soul departing for unknown shores. Of death, in fact. Or, if not of death, not of anything very hopeful. Ship of fools, slave ship, shipwreck, storm at sea: such representations, even if not expert, working on that fear that lies dormant even in the strongest heart, upset the nerves and the balance, for such was their intention. Edith, once again, felt unsafe, distressed, unhoused. (p. 160)

In this brief passage, the motifs of the voyage, of the house and of hope are deftly woven together. This is a journey away from hope (and indeed away from Edith's own surname), as it is on this excursion that Mr Neville (whose name rhymes, of course, with devil), tempts Edith with the offer of marriage, in a union of 'shared interests' and of 'companionship' (p. 167). So desolate is Edith at this point that she almost agrees, only to be 'saved' by her realization that while he is proposing to her, Mr Neville is also having an affair with Jennifer Pusey. Immediately, Edith decides to leave the hotel, sending a telegram to her lover with the message 'Coming home', which she subsequently modifies to 'Returning', in deference to her sense that her own small house is not a 'home' in the fullest sense.

Edith's lover, David, is a figure familiar in Brookner's novels. He is married to a good-looking but demanding woman, and comes to

Edith for sex and (again) food. Edith spends a good deal of time cooking for him, not for herself:

> Anxious, in her nightgown, she would watch him, a saucepan of baked beans to hand. Judging the state of his appetite with the eye of an expert, she would take another dish and ladle on to his plate a quivering mound of egg custard. 'Food fit for heroes,' he would sigh contentedly . . . (p. 29)

The interlinked motifs of greed and self-denial are important in this novel, and are explored most fully through the figures of the other female guests at the hotel. One, Monica, a woman of 'extra-ordinary slenderness', is a self-confessed bulimic:

> Monica has what is politely referred to as an eating problem: at least that is how she refers to it . . . What it means in practice is that she messes her food around distastefully in the dining room, already slightly off-colour from acute and raging boredom, and ends up smuggling most of it down to Kiki [her dog], who is seated on her lap. In between meals she can be seen in a café near the station eating cakes. (p. 80)

The eating disorder may well be linked with Monica's fear of having a child. Her husband has sent her to the hotel with instructions to 'get herself into working order' so that she can produce an heir, but while Monica wants a child she may also (in the context of marriage to an apparently unfeeling and brutish husband), fear pregnancy as an invasion both of her body and of her self. Maud Ellmann quotes an anorexic patient who makes exactly these connections:

> One of Helmut Thoma's anorectic patients sees food and impregnation as identical because they both entail a violation of her self-identity: "Bottle – child – disgust, if I think of it – injections – the idea that there is something flowing into me, into my mouth or into the vagina, is maddening – integer, integra, integrum occurs to me – untouchable – he does not have to bear a child – a man is what he is – he does not receive and he does not give".[18]

At the other extreme from Monica, who despite/because of her beauty takes up as little bodily space as possible, are the Puseys, mother and daughter, with their avidity and greed in relation to food, sex and money. While Monica has been injured emotionally in a way which is not entirely clear to Edith, the Puseys are entirely successful predators, hares rather than tortoises. Edith regards Mrs Pusey as a creature from an 'alien species', and understands that the differences between Mrs Pusey and herself are differences of appetite:

> For in this charming woman ... Edith perceived avidity, gross-ness, ardour. It was her perception of this will to repletion and to triumph that had occasioned her mild feeling of faintness when she watched Mrs Pusey and Jennifer eating their dinner. She had also perceived a difference of appetite, one that seemed to carry an implicit threat to her own. (p. 39)

This 'difference of appetite' is crucial. The Puseys are among those who successfully pursue their appetite for food, sex and money, and their success depends on their being able to ingest others in accordance with their need. Edith, and indeed Mr Neville, have an appetite for words. Brookner underlines the transpositions which can take place between the pleasures of food/the body and the plea-sures of words/the mind, when she describes Edith's pleasure in listening to Mr Neville:

> He was a man of few words, but those few words were judi-ciously selected, weighed for quality, and delivered with expertise. Edith, used to the *ruminative* monologues that most people con-sider to be adequate for the purposes of rational discourse ... leaned back in her chair and smiled. The *sensation* of being en-tertained by words was one which she encountered all too rarely. People expect writers to entertain *them*, she reflected. They con-sider that writers should be *gratified* simply by performing their task to the audience's satisfaction. (p. 91, my italics)

Both Edith and Mr Neville savour language, but in *Hotel du Lac* as in Brookner's other fiction it is only the male character who is able to satisfy both his appetite for words and his physical desires. Mr Neville (like Richard and like Maurice in earlier texts) does this by compartmentalizing his needs, taking conversation from Edith and sex from Jennifer. Brookner's female characters, on the other hand, seek to reconcile mind and body through a redemptive relation-ship of romantic love. Failing to achieve this, they reject what might be called 'unredeemed' physical appetites, opting for the pleasures of words (involving deferral and substitution) over the pleasures of things (associated with gratification outside an ethical context). Such a rejection of the 'unredeemed' body can, of course, be linked with the cultural coding of the female body in terms of immanence described by Beauvoir in *The Second Sex*.

Brookner's later novels have continued to explore the question of romance and have, increasingly, placed it within the context of an entire life-span. The title of *Brief Lives* (1990) paradoxically suggests an interest in such a longer-term view. The novel charts the life of Fay Langdon from childhood to old age, with a particular emphasis in the opening chapters on the ways in which Fay's expectations of love have been shaped by popular culture. Like Angela Carter, Brookner emphasizes the influence which the cinema (the 'dream factory') had in the construction of feminine identity in the inter-war years. Unlike Carter, who is fascinated by the more daring and sexually ambiguous figures of Garbo and Dietrich, Brookner stresses the importance of Hollywood musical comedies, with their down-to-earth but spirited heroines who journeyed via virtuous love to the haven of marriage:

> There would, inevitably, be an offer of marriage, for they were very moral tales. A girl won through by charm, or personality, not by influence, while if the hero ever had any base idea of seduction he was soon reformed by the virtue demonstrated by the object of his fascination – it was never, ever, passion – until such time as the knot was tied.[19]

Fay's ideas have also been formed through the reading of popular fiction, especially the books that her mother brought home from Boots Lending Library, 'simple honest stories'. For Fay and her mother these were 'a source of endless pleasure, an integral part of Sunday, with nothing harsh or disturbing to tell us, and always a happy ending ... that interval before it got too dark to read seemed to me – still seems to me – magical' (p. 16). As Bloch might have pointed out, here the religious content of Sundays has been replaced by popular daydreams with a utopian and ethical dimension.

The element of the daydream is also present in the songs Fay sings. Before her marriage, she has had a successful career as Fay Dodsworth, singing 'the lighter sort of ballad', songs with titles like 'Only Make-Believe', 'You Are My Heart's Delight' and 'I'll be

Loving You Always'. Her particular song is 'Arcady'. As Fay points out, these songs are not just escapist, but are also powerful expressions of hope. They are also expressions of *belief* in a secular world. Or as Bloch puts it:

> Everybody's life is pervaded by daydreams: one part of this is just stale, even enervating escapism . . . but another part is provocative, is not content just to accept the bad which exists, does not accept renunciation. (p. 3)

For Fay, the longing for love is, inevitably, bound up with the ideal of marriage. She falls in love with Owen Langdon, the most beautiful man she has ever seen, but from the first he inspires fear in her because he is 'impossibly handsome' and therefore, she thinks, too good for her. His physical beauty and his tendency to 'existential boredom' make it seem unlikely that he will ever really settle down, whereas for Fay, 'falling in love was a lifelong commitment, and the prospect of marriage a solemn undertaking' (p. 27). For her, marriage is a secular sacrament. However, Fay's expectations of marriage remain largely unfulfilled. The image of the house/home functions as a register of the emotional depth of her relationships, and a painful contrast is apparent between her childhood home and the house she lives in with Owen. Fay spends her entire married life in a house designed by Owen's first wife, decorated 'in dark harsh colours, indigo, sage green, and the brooding red of claret'. The dark and sombre colours suggest a tomb-like incarceration, and this impression is deepened through the description of Owen's bedroom, which has echoes of the description of the red-room in *Jane Eyre*.[20] Brookner writes:

> Everything was spotless, excessive, and chilly. Owen's bed, which seemed to me twice the normal size, had a white satin coverlet with sculptured edges to match the white satin padded and buttoned bedhead. (p. 25)

Such a room holds no promise of sexual pleasure or emotional warmth, but presages the death of love and indeed literal death – Owen, like Mr Reed in *Jane Eyre*, dies relatively young. In contrast to all this, Fay's childhood home is 'my natural, my only home . . . it enshrined so much love, love that could never come again' (p. 67).

Fay's marriage is not a complete failure. She and Owen are mis-matched, for she is quiet and reflective, while he is 'brazen' and 'emotionally inarticulate', giving all his energy to money-making rather than to love. Yet they remain faithful to each other, *well*-matched in that each mourns the death of their original love for the other. Fay is convinced that 'he loved me as much as he was capable of loving a woman, in conditions of intimacy, and for life' (p. 57). However, the difference between this novel and Brookner's earlier fiction is that here she seems to suggest that the ideal of romantic love continuing into marriage can never be fulfilled. Indeed, Fay judges her initial, adulatory love for Owen to have been 'in a sense inauthentic'. It is an interesting word, calling up Beauvoir's critique of 'idolatrous love' in *The Second Sex*. Beauvoir argues that:

> An authentic love should accept the contingence of the other with all his idiosyncrasies, his limitations, and his basic gratu-itousness. It would not pretend to be *a mode of salvation*, but a human inter-relation. Idolatrous love attributes *an absolute value* to the loved one, a first falsity that is brilliantly apparent to all outsiders.[21]

In *Brief Lives* the suggestion is that 'idolatrous love' is an illusion to which women are particularly prone. Fay reflects that 'women throughout the ages have felt dissatisfied with what is available, the friendlier varieties of love which are natural to the human race' (p. 56). The implication is that the love is in some sense connected with the dissatisfaction (which is, of course, Beauvoir's point). Thus in this novel, the ideal of romantic love seems to be giving way to a more prosaic view of the possibilities offered by marriage.

The word 'authentic' crops up again in connection with Fay's adulterous affair with Charlie Morton, which begins after Owen's death. Looking back on the affair, Fay reflects that 'Adultery is not noble . . . Even when there is real love, authentic love, it is not the sort in which one rejoices' (p. 102). It is not clear at this point whether Fay is claiming 'authenticity' for her love for Charlie, but after his death she certainly disclaims it:

> Those who survive an adulterous love affair are retrospectively amazed at the flimsiness of the structure that supported it. In time they see that it cannot be granted the status of a love affair

at all, that it was in fact *a simulacrum*, sometimes negligent, sometimes hasty, usually hidden. (p. 178, my italics)

Indeed, none of the relationships in *Brief Lives* can be 'granted the status of a love affair', and the very possibility of successful adult love is called into question.

In this novel, Brookner begins to explore the origins of love in childhood attachments. Freud, of course, argues that adult relationships are always in a sense re-stagings of a child's earliest relationships, the most important of which is with the mother. He writes, for example, that '[t]here are . . . good reasons why a child sucking at his mother's breast has become the prototype of every relation of love. The finding of an object [of desire] is in fact a refinding of it.'[22] Freud also argues that what he calls 'the finding of an object' – that is, the development of the individual's adult sexual desires – depends on a 'diphasic' process, that is, a process taking place in two stages. The first is connected with infancy and concerns the 'affectionate current' of sexual life. The second is connected with puberty and concerns the 'sensual current' of sexual life. Writing from a male perspective, Freud highlights the possibility that these two currents may fail to merge, and indeed it is precisely such a disjunction between what Freud calls 'admiration and respect', and sexual desire, which characterizes Brookner's male heroes.[23]

Freud also argues that 'we must reckon with the possibility that something in the nature of the sexual instinct itself is unfavourable to the realization of complete satisfaction'. The object of sexual desire is, by definition, always an inadequate substitute for what has been lost:

> Psychoanalysis has shown us that when the original object of a wishful impulse has been lost as a result of repression, it is frequently represented by an endless series of substitute objects none of which, however, brings full satisfaction.[24]

Fay Langdon expresses exactly this sense that one can never recapture the sense of loving and of being loved that one experiences in childhood. After her mother's death she reflects that:

> I should never again be all the world to anyone, as it says in the song. Normally I despise women who claim never to have got over their parents' death, or who affirm that their fathers

were the most perfect men who had ever lived. I despise them, but I understand them. How can any later love compensate for the first, unless it is perfect? (p. 69)

Through a brief incident which follows these reflections, Brookner reinforces this melancholy view of human attachments. Fay visits the hairdresser, and witnesses a rite of passage, a little girl having her hair cut for the first time. While this could be read in (Freudian) terms as the child's first recognition of her own (and her mother's) castrated state, the text focuses on the child's sense of rupture from her mother, and her 'passionate attempt to re-enter her mother, the arms locked around the woman's neck'. Fay has tears in her eyes, 'seeing that closeness, of which only a sorrowful memory remained in my own life'. This opens up into a view of the whole sweep of life, as Fay reflects that adult love is merely a 'doomed' attempt to recapture the 'primal spontaneity' of childhood feeling. When adult love fails, nothing is left in prospect but the slow and inevitable decay and decline of the body – it is on this occasion that the hairdresser suggests for the first time that Fay should dye her hair, which is losing its colour.

The novel ends with Fay's meditation on the 'profound' and 'sophisticated' truths expressed in the popular songs she used to sing. She finds them painful because they remind her of 'the durability, the hopelessness of desire, as if underneath all experience lurks the child's bewilderment. Why do you not love me? say the songs.' But the melancholy which they, and the novel, convey is not simply a function of the failure to find love. Even if love is found, Fay suggests, it can never satisfy, for:

the act of love is finite and ... what is being voiced is not only the disappointment of this but one's exacerbated need for permanent transformation, exacerbated, that is, by the act of love itself. (p. 216)

In contrast to *Hotel du Lac*, in which Edith Hope affirms her commitment to the ideal of love, *Brief Lives* thus seems to suggest that love – adult love – cannot redeem us. The implication of this later novel is that neither women nor men can find transcendence in love, and that the pursuit of such love – the pursuit of 'permanent transformation' – should not be the goal of life. Nonetheless, Fay cannot help but continue to think in these terms, and to look forward to a future which involves a man. As narrator, she points out that although it may seem ridiculous for a woman of her 'advanced years' to think of the future, 'I imagine that one always does and always will, and even in one's last days one will be wondering what is to come' (p. 216).

A Family Romance (1993) incorporates these bleaker perspectives into a text which ends on a more positive note of affirmation. The title points us straight to Freud's essay 'Family Romances' (1909), in which he explores the common childish fantasy that we have been adopted and that our real parents are far more noble than the ones with whom we are living. Freud links this fantasy with the child's need to avenge himself (the child is male throughout Freud's account) against parents who may have slighted him in some way. However, Freud points out that the fantasy also represents the child's wish to return to an earlier stage in his relations with his parents, a stage in which he had absolute belief in them. He writes:

> Indeed the whole effort at replacing the real father by a superior one is only an expression of the child's longing for the happy, vanished days when his father seemed to him the noblest and strongest of men and his mother the dearest and loveliest of women.[25]

The child's early love for its parents is a major theme of this novel, which explores a network of relationships in the extended family of Jane Manning. The theme surfaces first in the story of Jane's maternal grandmother Toni, who grew up – appropriately enough – in Vienna. The central relationship of Toni's girlhood is with her widowed father, whom she adores. Aspects of this relationship reflect Freud's insights into the complex relationship between father and daughter. In his early work, Freud argued that whenever hysteria was present, it could be traced back to an experience of abuse directed against the hysteric in childhood. However, his so-called 'seduction theory' does not necessarily assume actual abuse, as he emphasized that his interest was in the 'scene' of seduction, and he repeatedly stressed the primacy of psychic over material reality. Toni is described as 'hysterical', and her frantic need for her father's approval seems to be connected with an imagined seduction which she both fears and desires. This seems the more likely in the context of her repressed awareness of her father's sexual relationship with their housekeeper, Frau Zimmermann, which she suspects 'with fear and indignation'.[26] It is this element of fear which complicates Toni's need for her father and which makes it slightly different from the more straightforward Oedipal desire which Freud described in his later work.[27]

It is, perhaps, the element of fear that leads Toni, later, to rebuff her husband and to invest all her energy in a (safer) love for her son:

> Here was a golden child made in her own image. With the same astonishing lack of understanding which had led her to perch on her father's knee and lay her head on his shoulder she trained the boy to be her consort. (pp. 31–2)

The 'symbiosis' between mother and son is, however, damaging to Hugo, for it compromises, in turn, his ability to love a woman other than his mother, or to love a woman with a love which differs from that he feels for his mother. His good-humoured mildness is not enough for his wife, Dolly, whose story is at the heart of the novel. Dolly's most striking characteristic is her capacity for hope and expectation, which contrasts sharply with the melancholy stoicism exhibited by Toni during the last years of her life. Dolly's marriage to Hugo does little to satisfy her, and after his death she is reduced to a life of tedious bridge-playing with other women. Nonetheless, she retains her drive to fulfilment, turning up her face to others, even in middle-age, 'as others might make a wish, with a longing for happiness, a trust that if certain words were imparted, certain promises made, all her dreams would come true' (p. 56). At this stage in her life, she still maintains contact with Jane's mother Henrietta, her sister-in-law. Jane sees this relationship in terms of simple financial exploitation (Henrietta, like her mother before her, supports Dolly financially). However, after her mother's death, Jane realizes that there has been more to the relationship than this. Her mother has met more than financial need: she has also had the insight to stand in, in part, for the person who is lacking in Dolly's life, and has played her part as 'an admirer, an adherent, without once demonstrating anything less than perfect good faith'. When Jane's mother dies, and Dolly is upset not so much by Henrietta's death as by Jane's failure to tell her about it straight away, Jane is forced to reassess the situation:

> Because I had considered Dolly well able to take care of herself I had failed to ask certain questions. "What do you need? Whom do you love? Whom do you miss? What do you share? And with whom do you share it?" Because I needed someone to ask these questions of me I became aware of the questions themselves. "What do you lack?" I thought; that was the most fundamental question of all. (p. 134)

The question of lack runs through all Brookner's fiction, as signalled most obviously in the punning title of *Hotel du Lac*. It is tempting to make a familiar move and to link lack with Lacan, and indeed the narrator in *A Family Romance* makes a classically Lacanian distinction between need and lack in relation to Dolly. However, Brookner's interest is not quite in the founding lack which Lacan hypothesizes – that lack which propels us into the symbolic order and which for Lacan takes on an almost metaphysical dimension. Rather, Brookner works within a Freudian paradigm which attaches more weight to a child's early experiences, in order to uncover the attachments and needs which structure her characters' subjectivity. Her archaeology of Dolly's personality discloses that Dolly's deepest need is not to love, but to be loved:

> When I had last seen her she was flirtatious, impatient: I had thought her in love, then. Now I see that my reasoning was frivolous, that Dolly's need for love was more archaic than this, that what she wanted was to be thought of as a loveable person. She wanted to demonstrate that she was worthy of love, of any kind of love, of all kinds. And if she clung to this supposed lover of hers, she was willing to cling no less to myself, grotesque though this may seem. (p. 133)

This leads us to one of the most interesting and problematic aspects of Brookner's treatment of romantic love. Edith, in *Hotel du Lac*, describes a woman's dream of being reclaimed by a man who has battled across continents to find her, and in this novel too the ideal scene for the woman in love involves extreme passivity – throughout the text Dolly's cry is 'love me, save me'. Thinking about Dolly, Jane expresses her sense of an underlying conflict in many women's lives between their 'archaic female longings' and the realities of adult life:

> Led by her need for money she had perhaps overlooked or even
> buried that longing, that desire for fulfilment, for obedience, for
> a man's protection, archaic female longings which will not be
> banished, but which survive long after compromises have been
> reached and reality acknowledged. Many a woman knows that
> on the level of her most basic imaginings she has not been sat-
> isfied. (p. 122)

At the end of the novel this conflict is brought into sharper focus.
Jane has become a successful writer for children: we loop back to
the title, for Freud's implication in 'Family Romances' is that fairy
stories and children's stories are precisely family romances, fantasies
which give expression to the hopes and fears engendered by family
life. As a successful writer, Jane defends the traditional story against
the politically correct stories that contemporary children encounter.
She links the politically correct with a rationality that exists 'somewhere in the region of exasperation'. The feminists whom she meets
advocate rational marriages based on 'sharing', but Jane cannot bear
the thought of 'sharing household chores with some cheerful fellow
in jeans and a shirt ironed by himself'. She prefers 'the fairy-tale
version, and will prefer it until I die, even though I may be destined
to die alone' (p. 212). For Jane, the fairy-tale version of romance
finds its fullest expression in 'Sleeping Beauty'. While she asks herself
whether the story is in some sense a trap, 'designed to keep women
passive and expectant', she also analyses it in these terms:

> Beauty had only awoken because her prince had tried so hard to
> reach her; difficult to ignore the evidence of this. And she had
> been wounded in the first place by a spindle, the symbolism of
> which was easy to discern. Were we dealing here with a highly
> moral tale, which was in more ways than one an allegory of
> true love and a warning against mere physical curiosity? (p. 208)

The choice of Sleeping Beauty is significant. While Jane suggests
that it is a 'moral tale', and while there is clearly a connection
between the concept of 'true love' in the fairy tale and the concept of
romantic love as it appears in Brookner's earlier novels, there are darker
elements in Sleeping Beauty. As Jane herself points out, its symbolism
suggests loss of virginity punished by a kind of living death, and
the princess is only brought back to life through the heroic efforts
of the prince. Sleeping Beauty is thus, it could be argued, another

version of the Fall myth, in which a woman's curiosity leads to sexual knowledge, depravity and death, to a state of *déréliction* from which she can only be redeemed by a Christ-like male figure.

The novel ends with Jane's gallant acceptance of her role as the focus of Dolly's undiminished hope. Like her mother, she must play the part of Dolly's 'adherent', and she resolves not to let Dolly down – 'I shall follow the adventure through to the end, I hope with honour, and even after she is gone I shall continue to see her at the window, waving to me ardently, as if I were her best beloved' (p. 218). The analysis of the mechanisms of displacement in Dolly's life is incisive, and the bleakness of the perspective is counterbalanced by Jane's heroic willingness to maintain, on some level, 'romance' in her aunt's life. Nonetheless, Jane's broader endorsement of structures of feeling which place women in positions of passivity is disquieting. Freud goes so far as to link passivity with masochism in the 'Three Essays on the Theory of Sexuality':

> [T]he term masochism comprises any passive attitude towards sexual life and the sexual object, the extreme instance of which appears to be that in which satisfaction is conditional upon suffering physical or mental pain at the hands of the sexual object.[28]

There is an element of masochism in Jane's choice of a single life, and in her identification with the comatose Sleeping Beauty. It could indeed be argued that there is a strand of masochism running throughout Brookner's fiction, expressed most obviously through the self-abnegation of her gifted heroines but also evident in an undercurrent of dislike or distaste for the female body. Brookner's heroines often seek to rid themselves of their own body through self-starvation and/or seek redemption from gross female embodiment via the mediation of an ideal man, often a true believer (a Christian). Her fiction thus dramatizes a conflict between mind and body, between rational understanding and archaic longing, which remains in her view a fundamental feature of many women's lives. Hence, she writes, 'the look of cheerful forbearance which is the most recognisable expression on the face of the average woman, whereas if questioned she would confess to a certain mystification. Why must it be like this?' Brookner suggests that it is to her characters' credit that in the face of this mystification they maintain their longing ('the only honest quality of all men', according to Bloch) and their 'hope of a happy end' (p. 123).

Notes

Introduction

1   Rosalind Coward, '"This Novel Changes Lives": Are Women's Novels Feminist Novels? A Response to Rebecca O'Rourke's Article "Summer Reading"', *Feminist Review* 5 (1980), reprinted in full in Elaine Showalter (ed.), *The New Feminist Criticism* (London: Virago, 1986) and in part in Mary Eagleton (ed.), *Feminist Literary Theory: A Reader* (Oxford: Blackwell, 1986, second edition 1996).

2   Elaine Showalter (ed.), *The New Feminist Criticism* (London: Virago, 1986), pp. 230–1.

3   Maroula Joannou, *'Ladies, Please Don't Smash These Windows': Women's Writing, Feminist Consciousness and Social Change 1918–38* (Oxford: Berg, 1995), p. 128. Subsequent references are incorporated into the text.

4   Following Joannou, I define 'feminist', used as an adjective, in terms of a 'disposition to question patriarchal attitudes', while 'feminine' denotes the behaviour expected of women (which of course varies from culture to culture).

5   Nicola Beauman, *A Very Great Profession: The Woman's Novel 1914–1939* (London: Virago, 1983, reprinted with new foreword 1995), p. 5.

6   Olga Kenyon, *Women Novelists Today: a Survey of English Writing in the Seventies and Eighties* (Brighton: Harvester Press, 1988), p. 149.

7   See A. S. Byatt, *Passions of the Mind: Selected Writings*, first published 1991 (London: Vintage, 1993), p. 268; *The Shadow of the Sun*, first published 1964 (London: Vintage, 1991), p. xii.

8   Interview with Anita Brookner in Olga Kenyon, *Women Writers Talk* (Oxford: Lennard Publishing, 1989), p. 22.

9   Hilary Radner, 'Extra-Curricular Activities: Women Writers and the Readerly Text', in Mary Lynn Broe and Angela Ingram (eds), *Women's Writing in Exile* (Chapel Hill and London: University of North Carolina Press, 1989), p. 252. Subsequent references are incorporated into the text.

10   See Roland Barthes, *The Pleasure of the Text*, trans Richard Miller (London: Cape, 1976).

11   Hilary Radner, '"Out of Category": The Middlebrow Novel', in *Shopping Around: Feminine Culture and the Pursuit of Pleasure* (London: Routledge, 1995), pp. 105–15.

12   Margaret Drabble, *The Millstone*, first published 1965 (Harmondsworth: Penguin, 1968), p. 68.

13   For an account of women's education in this period see Jane McDermid, 'Women and Education', in June Purvis (ed.), *Women's History: Britain, 1850–1945* (London: UCL Press, 1995), pp. 107–30.

14   Figures taken from Deirdre Beddoe, *Back to Home and Duty: Women Between the Wars, 1918–1939* (London: Pandora, 1989), pp. 45–6.

15 Figures taken from Janette Webb, 'The Ivory Tower: Positive Action for Women in Higher Education', in Angela Coyle and Jane Skinner (eds), *Women and Work: Positive Action for Change* (London: Macmillan, 1988), p. 106.
16 Beauman, p. 11.
17 A. S. Byatt, *Passions of the Mind*, p. 268.
18 Cate Haste, *Rules of Desire: Sex in Britain World War 1 to the Present* (London: Pimlico, 1992), p. 89. Subsequent references are incorporated into the text.
19 See Victoria Glendinning, *Elizabeth Bowen: Portrait of a Writer*, first published 1977 (London: Phoenix, 1993), pp. 57–9.
20 Quoted in Haste, *Rules of Desire*, p. 290.
21 Sheila Rowbotham, *Woman's Consciousness, Man's World* (Harmondsworth: Penguin, 1973), p. 91.
22 Rosamond Lehmann, *The Swan in the Evening: Fragments of an Inner Life* (London: Collins, 1967), p. 68.
23 On this see Celia Lury, *Consumer Culture* (Cambridge: Polity Press, 1996), p. 143.
24 Christine Battersby, *The Phenomenal Woman: Feminist Metaphysics and the Patterns of Identity* (Cambridge: Polity Press, 1998), p. 48. Subsequent references are incorporated into the text.
25 Luce Irigaray, *Speculum of the Other Woman*, trans. Gillian C. Gill (Ithaca: Cornell University Press, 1985), p. 307.
26 Luce Irigaray, *An Ethics of Sexual Difference*, trans. Carolyn Burke and Gillian C. Gill (London: the Athlone Press, 1993), pp. 6–7. Subsequent references are incorporated into the text.
27 Luce Irigaray, 'Questions to Emmanuel Levinas', in Margaret Whitford (ed.) *The Irigaray Reader* (Oxford: Blackwell, 1991), p. 180.
28 I am grateful to Andrea Peterson for drawing this aspect of Battersby's argument to my attention.
29 Elizabeth Grosz, *Volatile Bodies: Toward a Corporeal Feminism* (Bloomington and Indianapolis: Indiana University Press, 1994), pp. 15–19.
30 Judith Butler, *Gender Trouble: Feminism and the Subversion of Identity* (London: Routledge, 1990), p. x.
31 Judith Butler, *Bodies that Matter: On the Discursive Limits of "Sex"* (London: Routledge, 1993), pp. 10–11.
32 Rosi Braidotti, *Patterns of Dissonance: A Study of Women in Contemporary Philosophy* (Cambridge: Polity Press, 1991), p. 120.
33 Julia Kristeva, 'Stabat Mater', in Kelly Oliver (ed.), *The Portable Kristeva* (New York: Columbia University Press, 1997), p. 327.
34 Interview with Anita Brookner in Olga Kenyon, *Women Writers Talk*, p. 15.
35 Lehmann, p. 68.
36 Glendinning, p. 59.
37 Elizabeth Taylor, *At Mrs Lippincote's*, first published 1945 (London: Virago, 1988), pp. v–vii.
38 Janet Todd (ed.), *Women Writers Talking* (London: Holmes & Meier, 1983), p. 176.
39 Ibid., p. 186.
40 Interview with Anita Brookner in John Haffenden, *Novelists in Interview* (London: Methuen, 1985), p. 73.

Chapter 1   Rosamond Lehmann

1   Rosamond Lehmann, *The Swan in the Evening* (London: Collins, 1967), p. 67.
2   Woolf knew Rosamond Lehmann and had read *Dusty Answer*. See *The Diary of Virginia Woolf*, vol. III, ed. Anne Olivier Bell (London: Hogarth Press, 1980), pp. 314–15.
3   *The Diary of Virginia Woolf*, vol. III, ed. Anne Olivier Bell, pp. 200–1.
4   Quoted in Virginia Woolf, *Women and Fiction: The Manuscript Versions of A Room of One's Own*, transcribed and edited by S. P. Rosenbaum (Oxford: Blackwell, 1992), p. xviii.
5   Rosamond Lehmann, *Dusty Answer*, first published 1927 (London: Flamingo, 1996), p. 303. Subsequent references are incorporated into the text.
6   See Hilary Radner, 'Extra-Curricular Activities: Women Writers and the Readerly Text', in Mary Lynn Broe and Angela Ingram (eds), *Women's Writing in Exile* (Chapel Hill and London: University of North Carolina Press, 1989).
7   Hélène Cixous and Cathérine Clement, *The Newly Born Woman*, trans. Betsy Wing (Manchester: Manchester University Press, 1986), p. 64.
8   See Judy Simons, *Rosamond Lehmann* (London: Macmillan, 1992), pp. 25–6.
9   Toril Moi, *Simone de Beauvoir: The Making of an Intellectual Woman* (Oxford: Blackwell, 1994), p. 277, n. 26.
10   Simone de Beauvoir, *The Second Sex*, first published 1949 (Harmondsworth: Penguin, 1972), p. 653, my emphasis. Subsequent references are incorporated into the text.
11   Judy Simons, *Rosamond Lehmann*, p. 26.
12   Rosamond Lehmann, *The Weather in the Streets*, first published 1936 (Harmondsworth: Penguin, 1972), p. 125. Subsequent references are incorporated into the text.
13   Rosamond Lehmann, *The Ballad and the Source* (London: Book Society in association with Collins, 1944), p. 133. Subsequent references are incorporated into the text.
14   See Nancy Chodorow, *The Reproduction of Mothering: Psychoanalysis and the Sociology of Gender* (Berkeley: University of California Press, 1978).
15   Rosamond Lehmann, 'The Future of the Novel', quoted in Sydney Janet Kaplan, *Feminine Consciousness in the Modern British Novel* (Chicago: University of Illinois Press, 1975), p. 112.
16   See the essays collected in Melanie Klein, *Love, Guilt and Reparation and Other Works, 1921–1945* (London: Virago, 1988).
17   Rosamond Lehmann, *The Echoing Grove*, first published 1953 (London: Flamingo, 1996), p. 137. Subsequent references are incorporated into the text.
18   See Alison Light, 'Introduction', in *Forever England: Femininity, Literature and Conservatism Between the Wars* (London: Routledge, 1991).
19   See Margaret Whitford, *Luce Irigaray: Philosophy in the Feminine* (London: Routledge, 1991), p. 47, for a discussion of these ideas.
20   Janet Watts, 'Introduction' to Rosamond Lehmann, *A Sea-Grape Tree*, first published 1976 (London: Virago, 1982, repr. 1993). This edition has a 'Postscript' by Rosamond Lehmann.
21   Judy Simons, *Rosamond Lehmann*, p. 131.

22 Whitford, *Luce Irigaray: Philosophy in the Feminine*, p. 147.

23 Luce Irigaray, 'The Bodily Encounter with the Mother' in Margaret Whitford (ed.), *The Irigaray Reader* (Oxford: Blackwell, 1991), pp. 44–5.

24 Ibid., p. 46.

25 Whitford, *Luce Irigaray: Philosophy in the Feminine*, p. 142.

26 Ibid., p. 147.

27 Luce Irigaray, 'Questions to Emmanuel Levinas', in Whitford (ed.), *The Irigaray Reader*, p. 180.

28 Luce Irigaray, 'He Risks Who Risks Life Itself', in Whitford (ed.), *The Irigaray Reader*, p. 216.

Chapter 2   Elizabeth Bowen

1 Gilles Deleuze and Felix Guattari, *A Thousand Plateaus: Capitalism and Schizophrenia*, trans. Brian Massumi (London: Athlone Press, 1988). Subsequent references will be incorporated into the text.

2 Elizabeth Grosz, 'A Thousand Tiny Sexes: Feminism and Rhizomatics', in Constantin V. Boundas and Dorothea Olkowski (eds), *Gilles Deleuze and the Theater of Philosophy* (London: Routledge, 1994).

3 Gilles Deleuze and Claire Parnet, *Dialogues*, trans. Hugh Tomlinson and Barbara Habberjam (London: Athlone Press, 1987), p. 74.

4 Grosz, p. 196.

5 Elizabeth Bowen, *To the North*, first published 1932 (Harmondsworth: Penguin, 1945), p. 155. Subsequent references are incorporated into the text.

6 Gilles Deleuze, *Nietzsche and Philosophy*, p. 70, quoted in John Hughes, *Lines of Flight: Reading Deleuze with Hardy, Gissing, Conrad, Woolf* (Sheffield: Sheffield Academic Press, 1997).

7 Aurelia Armstrong, 'Some Reflections on Deleuze's Spinoza: Composition and Agency', in Keith Ansell Pearson (ed.), *Deleuze and Philosophy: The Difference Engineer* (London: Routledge, 1997), p. 56.

8 Elizabeth Bowen, *The House in Paris*, first published 1935 (Harmondsworth: Penguin, 1946), p. 166. Subsequent references are incorporated into the text.

9 Compare John Hughes's important point about the orphan as an outsider-figure in nineteenth-century literature. See *Lines of Flight*, p. 15.

10 Elizabeth Bowen, *The Death of the Heart*, first published 1938 (London: Jonathan Cape, 1972), p. 22. Subsequent references are incorporated into the text.

11 Grosz, p. 195.

12 Deleuze and Parnet, *Dialogues*, p. 89.

13 Elizabeth Bowen, *The Heat of the Day*, first published 1949 (London: Jonathan Cape, 1949), p. 187. Subsequent references are incorporated into the text.

14 Andrew Bennett and Nicholas Royle, *Elizabeth Bowen and the Dissolution of the Novel: Still Lives* (London: Macmillan, 1995), p. 106.

15 Elizabeth Bowen, *A World of Love*, first published 1955 (London: Jonathan Cape, 1955), p. 224. Subsequent references are incorporated into the text.

16 Quoted from *Time* magazine on the cover of the Penguin Modern Classics edition of the novel (Harmondsworth: Penguin, 1983).

Chapter 3 Elizabeth Taylor

1 Luce Irigaray, *Speculum of the Other Woman*, trans. Gillian C. Gill (Ithaca: Cornell University Press, 1985).
2 Rosi Braidotti, *Patterns of Dissonance* (Cambridge: Polity Press, 1991), p. 253.
3 Margaret Whitford, *Luce Irigaray: Philosophy in the Feminine* (London: Routledge, 1991), p. 102.
4 Patsy Stoneman, *Brontë Transformations: The Cultural Dissemination of Jane Eyre and Wuthering Heights* (Hemel Hempstead: Prentice Hall/Harvester Wheatsheaf, 1996), p. 146.
5 Elizabeth Taylor, *Palladian*, first published 1946 (London: Virago, 1985), p. 166. Subsequent references are incorporated into the text.
6 See Hilary Radner, 'Extra-Curricular Activities: Women Writers and the Readerly Text', in Mary Lynn Broe and Angela Ingram (eds), *Women's Writing in Exile* (Chapel Hill and London: University of North Carolina Press, 1989).
7 It is interesting in relation to the genesis of *Palladian* to note that the film of *Rebecca* came out in the same year as *Pride and Prejudice*, as did that of *Wuthering Heights*, with Laurence Olivier playing the male lead in all three films.
8 See Laura Mulvey, 'Visual Pleasure and Narrative Cinema', in *Visual and Other Pleasures* (London: Macmillan, 1989); see also *Angela Carter's Curious Room* (London: BBC1 Omnibus Video, 1992).
9 Virginia Woolf, *The Waves*, first published 1931 (Oxford: Oxford University Press, 1992), p. 170.
10 Elizabeth Taylor, *A Wreath of Roses*, first published 1949 (London: Reprint Society, 1950), pp. 45–6. Subsequent references are incorporated into the text.
11 Luce Irigaray, *The Ethics of Sexual Difference*, quoted in Whitford, p. 47.
12 Angela Carter, *The Passion of New Eve*, first published 1977 (London: Virago, 1982), p. 5.
13 Julia Kristeva, 'Women's Time' in Kelly Oliver (ed.), *The Portable Kristeva* (New York: Columbia University Press, 1997), p. 364.
14 Ibid., p. 296.
15 Elizabeth Taylor, *A Game of Hide and Seek*, first published 1951 (London: Book Club, 1951), p. 7. Subsequent references are incorporated into the text.
16 Jacqueline Rose, 'Sexuality in the Reading of Shakespeare: *Hamlet* and *Measure for Measure*', in Cyrus Hoy (ed.), the Norton Critical Edition of *Hamlet* (New York and London: W. W. Norton, 1992), p. 279.
17 Quoted in Nicola Beauman, *A Very Great Profession: The Woman's Novel 1914–39* (London: Virago, 1995), pp. 204–5.
18 Virginia Woolf, 'Professions for Women' in Michèle Barrett (ed.) *Virginia Woolf: Women and Writing* (London: Women's Press, 1988), p. 62.
19 Elizabeth Taylor, *The Sleeping Beauty*, first published 1953 (London: Virago, 1982), p. 1. Subsequent references are incorporated into the text.
20 Braidotti, p. 253, as above.

21 Luce Irigaray, *This Sex Which Is Not One*, trans. Catherine Porter (Ithaca: Cornell University Press, 1985), pp. 133–4.
22 Robert Liddell, *Elizabeth and Ivy* (London: Peter Owen, 1986), p. 96.
23 Christine Battersby, *The Phenomenal Woman: Feminist Metaphysics and the Patterns of Identity* (Cambridge: Polity Press, 1998), p. 2.
24 Elizabeth Taylor, *The Wedding Group*, first published 1968 (London: Virago, 1985), p. 48.
25 For the connection with Eric Gill, see chapter 7 of his *Autobiography* (London: Jonathan Cape, 1940). See also John Crompton, 'All Done By Mirrors: Reflectivity in the Novels of Elizabeth Taylor (1912–1975)', unpublished PhD thesis, University of Hull, 1992.
26 Battersby, p. 7.
27 Quoted in Elizabeth Jane Howard's introduction to the Virago edition of *The Wedding Group*, p. ix.

Chapter 4   Margaret Drabble

1 Seyla Benhabib, *The Reluctant Modernism of Hannah Arendt* (Thousand Oaks, London, New Delhi: Sage Publications, 1996), p. 135.
2 Arendt is referred to in *The Gates of Ivory*, first published 1991. (Harmondsworth: Penguin, 1992), p. 13, and her book *The Burden of Our Time* (London: Secker & Warburg, 1951) appears in the bibliography.
3 Christine Battersby, *The Phenomenal Woman: Feminist Metaphysics and the Patterns of Identity* (Cambridge: Polity Press, 1998), p. 7 (her italics).
4 Hannah Arendt, *The Human Condition* (Chicago and London: University of Chicago Press, 1958), p. 9. Subsequent references are incorporated into the text.
5 Benhabib, p. 108.
6 Simone de Beauvoir, *The Second Sex*, first published 1949 (Harmondsworth: Penguin, 1972), p. 449.
7 Margaret Drabble, *The Waterfall*, first published 1969 (Harmondsworth: Penguin, 1971), p. 9. Subsequent references are incorporated into the text.
8 Margaret Drabble, *The Needle's Eye*, first published 1972 (Harmondsworth: Penguin, 1973), p. 246. Subsequent references are incorporated into the text.
9 Margaret Drabble, *The Realms of Gold*, first published 1975 (Harmondsworth: Penguin, 1977), pp. 97–8. Subsequent references are incorporated into the text.
10 See the interview with Margaret Drabble in Janet Todd (ed.), *Women Writers Talking* (New York and London: Holmes & Meier, 1983), p. 167.
11 See Elizabeth Fox-Genovese, 'The Ambiguities of Female Identity: A Reading of the Novels of Margaret Drabble', *Partisan Review* 46:2, 1979, p. 243.
12 Margaret Drabble, *The Middle Ground*, first published 1980 (Harmondsworth: Penguin, 1981), p. 39. Subsequent references are incorporated into the text.
13 See Eve Kosofsky Sedgwick, *Between Men: English Literature and Male Homosocial Desire* (New York: Columbia University Press, 1985) for the development of this idea.
14 Battersby, p. 201.

15 Morton Schoolman, 'Introduction', Benhabib, p. xxi, my italics.
16 Margaret Drabble, *The Radiant Way*, first published 1987 (Harmondsworth: Penguin, 1988), p. 17. Subsequent references are incorporated into the text.
17 Julia Kristeva, 'Women's Time' in Kelly Oliver (ed.), *The Portable Kristeva* (New York and Chichester: Columbia University Press, 1997), p. 360.
18 See Jacqueline Rose, 'Margaret Thatcher and Ruth Ellis' in *Why War? – Psychoanalysis, Politics, and the Return to Melanie Klein* (Oxford: Blackwell, 1993).
19 See the interview with Margaret Drabble in Olga Kenyon (ed.), *Women Writers Talk* (Oxford: Lennard Publishing, 1989), p. 37.
20 Sigmund Freud, 'From the History of an Infantile Neurosis' in *Collected Papers*, vol. III (London: Hogarth Press, 1925), p. 517.
21 See Sedgwick, as above, and Luce Irigaray, 'Women on the Market' in *This Sex Which Is Not One*, trans. Catherine Porter (Ithaca: Cornell University Press, 1985), p. 171.
22 Nicole Ward Jouve, *'The Streetcleaner': The Yorkshire Ripper Case on Trial* (London and New York: Marion Boyars Publishers, 1986).
23 'Medusa's Head' in *The Standard Edition of the Complete Psychological Works of Sigmund Freud*, vol. XVIII (London: Hogarth Press, 1955), p. 273.
24 Margaret Drabble, 'Women Writers as an Unprotected Species' in Judy Simons and Kate Fullbrook (eds), *Writing: A Woman's Business* (Manchester and New York: Manchester University Press, 1998), p. 165.
25 Benhabib, p. 136.

Chapter 5   A. S. Byatt

1 Interview with A. S. Byatt in Nicholas Tredell, *Conversations with Critics* (Manchester: Carcanet Press, 1994), p. 60.
2 Hilary Radner, 'Extra-Curricular Activities: Women Writers and the Readerly Text', in Mary Lynn Broe and Angela Ingram (eds), *Women's Writing in Exile* (Chapel Hill and London: University of North Carolina Press, 1989), p. 256.
3 In her Introduction to *The Shadow of the Sun*, for example, Byatt writes that 'the underlying shape of [the novel] is dictated by Elizabeth Bowen and Rosamond Lehmann, and a vague dissatisfaction with this state of affairs'. See *The Shadow of the Sun*, first published 1964 (London: Vintage, 1991), p. xii.
4 A. S. Byatt, *Passions of the Mind: Selected Writings*, first published 1991 (London: Vintage, 1993), p. 3.
5 See T. S. Eliot's essay 'The Metaphysical Poets' in Frank Kermode (ed.), *Selected Prose of T. S. Eliot* (London: Faber & Faber, 1975) and Michel Foucault, *The Order of Things: An Archaeology of the Human Sciences*, first published as *Les Mots et les choses* in 1966 (London: Routledge, 1997).
6 A. S. Byatt, *Passions of the Mind*, pp. 16–17 (her translation).
7 Michel Foucault, *The Order of Things*, p. 36.
8 John Milton, *Paradise Lost* (Harmondsworth: Penguin, 1989), pp. 86–7.
9 Simone de Beauvoir, *The Second Sex*, first published 1949 (Harmondsworth: Penguin, 1972), p. 653.

10 A. S. Byatt, Introduction to *The Shadow of the Sun*, p. xiv.
11 Luce Irigaray, *Speculum of the Other Woman*, trans. Gillian C. Gill (Ithaca: Cornell University Press, 1985), p. 133.
12 Ibid., pp. 176–7, my italics. Irigaray quotes directly from Plotinus here.
13 F. R. Leavis, *D. H. Lawrence: Novelist*, first published 1955 (Harmondsworth: Penguin, 1976), p. 332.
14 S. T. Coleridge, *Biographia Literaria* (London: J. M. Dent, 1984), p. 139.
15 A. S. Byatt, *The Shadow of the Sun*, p. 15. Subsequent references are incorporated into the text.
16 See *Paradise Lost*, V, ll. 479–85:

> So from the root
> Springs lighter the green stalk, from thence the leaves
> More airy, last the bright consummate flow'r
> Spirits odorous breathes: flow'rs and their fruit
> Man's nourishment, by gradual scale sublim'd
> To vital Spirits aspire, to animal,
> To intellectual.

See also Stéphane Mallarmé, *Oeuvres Complètes*, p. 859 for a discussion of the perfect Idea of a flower, the 'idée même et suave, l'absente de tous bouquets'.
17 Walter Benjamin, 'Paris – the capital of the nineteenth century', in *Charles Baudelaire: A Lyric Poet in the Era of High Capitalism*, trans. Harry Zohn (London: Verso, 1983), p. 166.
18 A. S. Byatt, in Tredell, p. 66.
19 A. S. Byatt, *The Game*, first published 1967 (London: Vintage, 1992), p. 18. Subsequent references are incorporated into the text.
20 Interview with A. S. Byatt in Janet Todd (ed.), *Women Writers Talking* (New York and London: Holmes & Meier, 1983), p. 186.
21 A. S. Byatt in Tredell, p. 66.
22 Frances Yates, 'Queen Elizabeth I as Astraea' in *Astraea: The Imperial Theme in the Sixteenth Century* (London and Boston: Routledge & Kegan Paul, 1975), p. 87, my italics.
23 A. S. Byatt, *The Virgin in the Garden*, first published 1978 (Harmondsworth: Penguin, 1981), p. 102. Subsequent references are incorporated into the text.
24 See A. S. Byatt in Tredell, p. 69.
25 Ibid., p. 71.
26 Luce Irigaray, *Sexes and Genealogies*, trans. Gillian C. Gill (New York and Chichester: Columbia University Press, 1993), p. 79.
27 Julia Kristeva, 'Stabat Mater' in Kelly Oliver (ed.), *The Portable Kristeva* (New York and Chichester: Columbia University Press, 1997), pp. 327–8.
28 The line Byatt ascribes to Virgil, 'They have their own lights', seems to be a reminiscence of the description of the Homes of the Blest in *Aeneid* VI, ll. 640–1, which the Penguin translation gives as 'Here an ampler air clothes the plains with brilliant light, and always they see a sun and stars that are theirs alone' (p. 166). I am grateful to Gill Spraggs for this reference.

29 See A. S. Byatt in Todd, p. 193.
30 *The Portable Kristeva*, p. 329.
31 A. S. Byatt, *Still Life*, first published 1985 (Harmondsworth: Penguin, 1986), p. 94. Subsequent references are incorporated into the text.
32 See A. S. Byatt in Tredell, pp. 61–2.
33 *The Standard Edition of the Complete Psychological Works of Sigmund Freud*, vol. XVIII (London: Hogarth Press, 1955), p. 38.
34 See A. S. Byatt in Todd, p. 187.
35 A. S. Byatt, *Possession: A Romance*, first published 1990 (London: Vintage, 1991), p. 310. Subsequent references are incorporated into the text.
36 Luce Irigaray, *Sexes and Genealogies*, p. 64.
37 Ibid., p. 59.

Chapter 6   Anita Brookner

1   Anita Brookner, *Hotel du Lac*, first published 1984 (London: Triad/Panther Books, 1985), p. 27. Subsequent references are incorporated into the text.
2   See Janice Radway, *Reading the Romance* (Chapel Hill: University of North Carolina Press, 1984).
3   See Bridget Fowler, *The Alienated Reader: Women and Popular Romantic Literature in the Twentieth Century* (Hemel Hempstead: Harvester Wheatsheaf, 1991), chapter 2.
4   Ernst Bloch, *The Principle of Hope*, first published 1959, vols 1–3, trans. N. and S. Plaice and P. Knight (Oxford: Blackwell, 1986), p. 3. Subsequent references are incorporated into the text.
5   Anita Brookner, *A Start in Life*, first published 1981 (London: Triad/Granada, 1982), p. 8. Subsequent references are incorporated into the text.
6   Anthony Giddens, *The Transformation of Intimacy: Sexuality, Love and Eroticism in Modern Societies* (Cambridge: Polity Press, 1992), p. 45.
7   Honoré de Balzac, *Eugénie Grandet*, trans. Marion Ayton Crawford (Harmondsworth: Penguin, 1976), p. 234.
8   Melanie Klein, 'Weaning', in *Love, Guilt and Reparation and Other Works 1921–1945*, with a new introduction by Hanna Segal (London: Virago, 1988), p. 295.
9   Melitta Schmideberg, 'Intellectual Inhibition and Eating Disorders', trans. Robert Gillett and Jacqueline Rose, in Jacqueline Rose, *Why War? – Psychoanalysis, Politics, and the Return to Melanie Klein* (Oxford: Blackwell, 1993), p. 264.
10 Interview with Anita Brookner in John Haffenden, *Novelists in Interview* (London: Methuen, 1985), p. 66.
11 Ibid., p. 63.
12 Anita Brookner, *Providence*, first published 1982 (Harmondsworth: Penguin, 1991), p. 131. Subsequent references are incorporated into the text.
13 She quotes, for example, this passage from the Preface (the translation is provided by one of Kitty's students):

'"But when one sees the anguish that results from these broken attachments, the painful astonishment of a deceived soul, that mistrust that succeeds perfect trust ... one feels, then, that there is something sacred in the heart that suffers because it loves; one discovers how deep are the roots of the affection one thought to inspire without sharing it; and if one overcomes what one calls weakness, it is by destroying in oneself all that was generous, by tearing up all that was faithful, by sacrificing all that was noble and good."'(p. 47)

14 Giddens, p. 43.
15 Ibid.
16 Kelly Oliver (ed.), *The Portable Kristeva* (New York and Chichester: Columbia University Press, 1997), pp. 230–1.
17 Interview with Anita Brookner in Olga Kenyon, *Women Writers Talk* (Oxford: Lennard Publishing, 1989), p. 15.
18 Maud Ellmann, *The Hunger Artists: Starving, Writing and Imprisonment* (London: Virago, 1993), p. 44.
19 Anita Brookner, *Brief Lives*, first published 1990 (Harmondsworth: Penguin, 1991), p. 12. The title comes from John Aubrey's seventeenth century *Brief Lives*. Subsequent references are incorporated into the text.
20 See *Jane Eyre*, chapter 2:

A bed supported on massive pillars of mahogany, hung with curtains of deep red damask, stood out like a tabernacle in the centre ... Out of these deep surrounding shades rose high, and glared white, the piled-up mattresses and pillows of the bed, spread with a snowy Marseilles counterpane.

21 Simone de Beauvoir, *The Second Sex*, first published 1949 (Harmondsworth: Penguin, 1972), p. 664, my italics.
22 Sigmund Freud, 'Three Essays on the Theory of Sexuality', reprinted in *The Pelican Freud Library*, vol. 7 (Harmondsworth: Penguin, 1977), pp. 144–5.
23 Ibid., p. 119.
24 Sigmund Freud, 'On the Universal Tendency to Debasement in the Sphere of Love', *Pelican Freud Library*, vol. 7, p. 258.
25 Sigmund Freud, 'Family Romances', *Pelican Freud Library*, vol. 7, pp. 224–5.
26 Anita Brookner, *A Family Romance*, first published 1993 (Harmondsworth: Penguin, 1994), p. 30. Subsequent references are incorporated into the text.
27 See Sigmund Freud, 'Female Sexuality', *Pelican Freud Library*, vol. 7, pp. 367–92.
28 Sigmund Freud, 'Three Essays on the Theory of Sexuality', *Pelican Freud Library*, vol. 7, p. 71.

Bibliography

Primary Sources

Bowen, Elizabeth, *To the North*, first published 1932 (Harmondsworth: Penguin, 1945).

Bowen, Elizabeth, *The House in Paris*, first published 1935 (Harmondsworth: Penguin, 1946).

Bowen, Elizabeth, *The Death of the Heart*, first published 1938 (London: Jonathan Cape, 1972).

Bowen, Elizabeth, *The Heat of the Day* (London: Jonathan Cape, 1949).

Bowen, Elizabeth, *A World of Love* (London: Jonathan Cape, 1955).

Brookner, Anita, *A Start in Life*, first published 1981 (London: Triad/Granada, 1982).

Brookner, Anita, *Providence*, first published 1982 (Harmondsworth: Penguin, 1991).

Brookner, Anita, *Hotel du Lac*, first published 1984 (London: Triad/Panther Books, 1985).

Brookner, Anita, *Brief Lives*, first published 1990 (Harmondsworth: Penguin, 1991).

Brookner, Anita, *A Family Romance*, first published 1993 (Harmondsworth: Penguin, 1994).

Byatt, A. S., *The Shadow of the Sun*, first published 1964 (London: Vintage, 1991).

Byatt, A. S., *The Game*, first published 1967 (London: Vintage, 1992).

Byatt, A. S., *The Virgin in the Garden*, first published 1978 (Harmondsworth: Penguin, 1981).

Byatt, A. S., *Still Life*, first published 1985 (Harmondsworth: Penguin, 1986).

Byatt, A. S., *Possession: A Romance*, first published 1990 (London: Vintage, 1991).

Drabble, Margaret, *The Millstone*, first published 1965 (Harmondsworth: Penguin, 1968).

Drabble, Margaret, *The Waterfall*, first published 1969 (Harmondsworth: Penguin, 1971).

Drabble, Margaret, *The Needle's Eye*, first published 1972 (Harmondsworth: Penguin, 1973).

Drabble, Margaret, *The Realms of Gold*, first published 1975 (Harmondsworth: Penguin, 1977).

Drabble, Margaret, *The Middle Ground*, first published 1980 (Harmondsworth: Penguin, 1981).

Drabble, Margaret, *The Radiant Way*, first published 1987 (Harmondsworth: Penguin, 1988).

Lehmann, Rosamond, *Dusty Answer*, first published 1927 (London: Flamingo, 1996).

Lehmann, Rosamond, *The Weather in the Streets*, first published 1936 (Harmondsworth: Penguin, 1972).

Lehmann, Rosamond, *The Ballad and the Source* (London: Book Society in association with Collins, 1944).

Lehmann, Rosamond, *The Echoing Grove*, first published 1953 (London: Flamingo, 1996).

Lehmann, Rosamond, *A Sea-Grape Tree*, first published 1976 (London: Virago, 1982, repr. 1993).

Lehmann, Rosamond, *The Swan in the Evening: Fragments of an Inner Life* (London: Collins, 1967).

Taylor, Elizabeth, *Palladian*, first published 1946 (London: Virago, 1985).

Taylor, Elizabeth, *A Wreath of Roses*, first published 1949 (London: Reprint Society, 1950).

Taylor, Elizabeth, *A Game of Hide and Seek*, first published 1951 (London: Book Club, 1951).

Taylor, Elizabeth, *The Sleeping Beauty*, first published 1953 (London: Virago, 1982).

Taylor, Elizabeth, *The Wedding Group*, first published 1968 (London: Virago, 1985).

Secondary Sources

Arendt, Hannah, *The Human Condition* (Chicago and London: University of Chicago Press, 1958).

Arendt, Hannah, *The Burden of Our Time* (London: Secker & Warburg, 1951).

Armstrong, Aurelia, 'Some Reflections on Deleuze's Spinoza: Composition and Agency', in Keith Ansell Pearson (ed.), *Deleuze and Philosophy: The Difference Engineer* (London: Routledge, 1997).

Balzac, Honoré de, *Eugénie Grandet*, trans. Marion Ayton Crawford (Harmondsworth: Penguin, 1976).

Barrett, Michèle (ed.) *Virginia Woolf: Women and Writing* (London: Women's Press, 1988).

Barthes, Roland, *The Pleasure of the Text*, trans. Richard Miller (London: Cape, 1976).

Battersby, Christine, *The Phenomenal Woman: Feminist Metaphysics and the Patterns of Identity* (Cambridge: Polity Press, 1998).

Beauman, Nicola, *A Very Great Profession: The Woman's Novel 1914–1939* (London: Virago, 1983, reprinted with new foreword 1995).

Beauvoir, Simone de, *The Second Sex*, first published 1949 (Harmondsworth: Penguin, 1972).

Beddoe, Deirdre, *Back to Home and Duty: Women Between the Wars, 1918–1939* (London: Pandora, 1989).

Benhabib, Seyla, *The Reluctant Modernism of Hannah Arendt* (Thousand Oaks, London, New Delhi: Sage Publications, 1996).

Benjamin, Walter, 'Paris – the capital of the nineteenth century', in *Charles Baudelaire: A Lyric Poet in the Era of High Capitalism*, trans. Harry Zohn (London: Verso, 1983).

Bennett, Andrew and Nicholas Royle, *Elizabeth Bowen and the Dissolution of the Novel* (London: Macmillan, 1995).

Bloch, Ernst, *The Principle of Hope*, first published 1959, vols 1–3, trans. Plaice, N. and S., and P. Knight (Oxford: Blackwell, 1986).

Boundas, Constantin V. and Dorothea Olkowski (eds), *Gilles Deleuze and the Theater of Philosophy* (London: Routledge, 1994).

Braidotti, Rosi, *Patterns of Dissonance: A Study of Women in Contemporary Philosophy* (Cambridge: Polity Press, 1991).

Broe, Mary Lynn and Angela Ingram (eds), *Women's Writing in Exile* (Chapel Hill and London: University of North Carolina Press, 1989).

Brontë, Charlotte, *Jane Eyre*, first published 1847 (Oxford: World's Classics, 1993).

Brontë, Charlotte, *Villette*, first published 1853 (Oxford: World's Classics, 1990).

Brontë, Emily, *Wuthering Heights*, first published 1847 (Oxford: World's Classics, 1995).

Butler, Judith, *Bodies that Matter: On the Discursive Limits of "Sex"* (London: Routledge, 1993).

Butler, Judith, *Gender Trouble: Feminism and the Subversion of Identity* (London: Routledge, 1990).

Byatt, A. S., *Passions of the Mind: Selected Writings*, first published 1991 (London: Vintage, 1993).

Carter, Angela, *The Passion of New Eve*, first published 1977 (London: Virago, 1982).

Chodorow, Nancy, *The Reproduction of Mothering: Psychoanalysis and the Sociology of Gender* (Berkeley: University of California Press, 1978).

Cixous, Hélène and Cathérine Clement, *The Newly Born Woman*, trans. Betsy Wing (Manchester: Manchester University Press, 1986).

Coleridge, S. T., *Biographia Literaria*, first published 1817 (London: J. M. Dent, 1984).

Constant, Benjamin, *Adolphe*, trans. Leonard Tancock (Harmondsworth: Penguin, 1964).

Coward, Rosalind, '"This Novel Changes Lives": Are Women's Novels Feminist Novels? A Response to Rebecca O'Rourke's Article "Summer Reading"', *Feminist Review* 5 (1980), reprinted in full in Elaine Showalter (ed.), *The New Feminist Criticism* (London: Virago, 1986).

Coyle, Angela and Jane Skinner (eds), *Women and Work: Positive Action for Change* (London: Macmillan, 1988).

Crompton, John, 'All Done By Mirrors: Reflectivity in the Novels of Elizabeth Taylor (1912–1975)', unpublished PhD thesis, University of Hull, 1992.

Deleuze, Gilles and Claire Parnet, *Dialogues*, trans. Hugh Tomlinson and Barbara Habberjam (London: Athlone Press, 1987).

Deleuze, Gilles and Felix Guattari, *A Thousand Plateaus: Capitalism and Schizophrenia*, trans. Brian Massumi (London: Athlone Press, 1988).

Du Maurier, Daphne, *Rebecca*, first published 1938 (London: Arrow Books, 1992).

Eagleton, Mary, *Feminist Literary Theory: A Reader* (Oxford: Blackwell, 1986, second edition 1996).

Eliot, T. S, 'The Metaphysical Poets' (1921) in Frank Kermode (ed.), *Selected Prose of T. S. Eliot* (London: Faber & Faber, 1975).

Ellmann, Maud, *The Hunger Artists: Starving, Writing and Imprisonment* (London: Virago, 1993).

Foucault, Michel, *The Order of Things: An Archaeology of the Human Sciences*, first published as *Les Mots et les choses* in 1966 (London: Routledge, 1997).

Fowler, Bridget, *The Alienated Reader: Women and Popular Romantic Literature in the Twentieth Century* (Hemel Hempstead: Harvester Wheatsheaf, 1991).

Fox-Genovese, Elizabeth, 'The Ambiguities of Female Identity: A Reading of the Novels of Margaret Drabble', *Partisan Review* 46:2 (1979).

Freud, Sigmund, 'From the History of an Infantile Neurosis' in *Collected Papers*, vol. III (London: Hogarth Press, 1925).

Freud, Sigmund, 'Medusa's Head' in *The Standard Edition of the Complete Psychological Works of Sigmund Freud*, vol. XVIII (London: Hogarth Press, 1955).

Freud, Sigmund, 'Three Essays on the Theory of Sexuality' in *The Pelican Freud Library*, vol. 7 (Harmondsworth: Penguin, 1977).

Freud, Sigmund, 'Family Romances', *Pelican Freud Library*, vol. 7.

Freud, Sigmund, 'On the Universal Tendency to Debasement in the Sphere of Love', *Pelican Freud Library*, vol. 7.

Freud, Sigmund, 'Female Sexuality', *Pelican Freud Library*, vol. 7.

Giddens, Anthony, *The Transformation of Intimacy: Sexuality, Love and Eroticism in Modern Societies* (Cambridge: Polity Press, 1992).

Gill, Eric, *Autobiography* (London: Jonathan Cape, 1940).

Glendinning, Victoria, *Elizabeth Bowen: Portrait of a Writer*, first published 1977 (London: Phoenix, 1993).

Grosz, Elizabeth, 'A Thousand Tiny Sexes: Feminism and Rhizomatics', in Constantin V. Boundas and Dorothea Olkowski (eds), *Gilles Deleuze and the Theater of Philosophy* (London: Routledge, 1994).

Grosz, Elizabeth, *Volatile Bodies: Toward a Corporeal Feminism* (Bloomington and Indianapolis: Indiana University Press, 1994).

Haffenden, John, *Novelists in Interview* (London: Methuen, 1985).

Haste, Cate, *Rules of Desire: Sex in Britain World War I to the Present* (London: Pimlico, 1992).

Howard, Elizabeth Jane, 'Introduction' to Elizabeth Taylor, *The Wedding Group* (London: Virago, 1968).

Hoy, Cyrus (ed.), the Norton Critical Edition of *Hamlet* (New York and London: W. W. Norton, 1992).

Hughes, John, *Lines of Flight: Reading Deleuze with Hardy, Gissing, Conrad, Woolf* (Sheffield: Sheffield Academic Press, 1997).

Ingman, Heather, *Women's Fiction Between the Wars: Mothers, Daughters and Writing* (Edinburgh: Edinburgh University Press, 1998).

Irigaray, Luce, *Speculum of the Other Woman*, trans. Gillian C. Gill (Ithaca: Cornell University Press, 1985).

Irigaray, Luce, *This Sex Which Is Not One*, trans. Catherine Porter (Ithaca: Cornell University Press, 1985).

Irigaray, Luce, *An Ethics of Sexual Difference*, trans. Carolyn Burke and Gillian C. Gill (London: Athlone Press, 1993).

Irigaray, Luce, *Sexes and Genealogies*, trans. Gillian C. Gill (New York and Chichester: Columbia University Press, 1993).

Irigaray, Luce, 'The Bodily Encounter with the Mother' in Margaret Whitford (ed.), *The Irigaray Reader* (Oxford: Blackwell, 1991).

Irigaray, Luce, 'Questions to Emmanuel Levinas', in Margaret Whitford (ed.) *The Irigaray Reader*.

Irigaray, Luce, 'He Risks Who Risks Life Itself', in Whitford (ed.), *The Irigaray Reader*.

Joannou, Maroula, *'Ladies, Please Don't Smash These Windows': Women's Writing, Feminist Consciousness and Social Change 1918–38* (Oxford: Berg, 1995).

Kaplan, Sydney Janet, *Feminine Consciousness in the Modern British Novel* (Chicago: University of Illinois Press, 1975).

Kenyon, Olga, *Women Novelists Today: a Survey of English Writing in the Seventies and Eighties* (Brighton: Harvester Press, 1988).

Kenyon, Olga, *Women Writers Talk* (Oxford: Lennard Publishing, 1989).

Klein, Melanie, *Love, Guilt and Reparation and Other Works, 1921–1945* (London: Virago, 1988).

Kristeva, Julia, *Black Sun: Depression and Melancholia*, trans. Leon S. Roudiez (New York: Columbia University Press, 1989).

Kristeva, Julia, 'Stabat Mater' in Kelly Oliver (ed.), *The Portable Kristeva* (New York and Chichester: Columbia University Press, 1997).

Kristeva, Julia, 'Women's Time' in Kelly Oliver (ed.), *The Portable Kristeva*.

Leavis, F. R., *D. H. Lawrence: Novelist*, first published 1955 (Harmondsworth: Penguin, 1976).

Liddell, Robert, *Elizabeth and Ivy* (London: Peter Owen, 1986).

Light, Alison, 'Introduction', in *Forever England: Femininity, Literature and Conservatism Between the Wars* (London: Routledge, 1991).

Lury, Celia, *Consumer Culture* (Cambridge: Polity Press, 1996).

Mallarmé, Stéphane, *Oeuvres Complètes* (Paris: Gallimard, 1945).

McDermid, Jane, 'Women and Education', in June Purvis (ed.), *Women's History: Britain, 1850–1945* (London: UCL Press, 1995).

Milton, John, *Paradise Lost* (Harmondsworth: Penguin, 1989).

Moi, Toril, *Simone de Beauvoir: The Making of an Intellectual Woman* (Oxford: Blackwell, 1994).

Mulvey, Laura, 'Visual Pleasure and Narrative Cinema', in *Visual and Other Pleasures* (London: Macmillan, 1989).

Oliver, Kelly (ed.), *The Portable Kristeva* (New York and Chichester: Columbia University Press, 1997).

Pearson, Keith Ansell (ed.), *Deleuze and Philosophy: The Difference Engineer* (London: Routledge, 1997).

Purvis, June (ed.), *Women's History: Britain, 1850–1945* (London: UCL Press, 1995).

Radner, Hilary, 'Extra-Curricular Activities: Women Writers and the Readerly Text', in Mary Lynn Broe and Angela Ingram (eds), *Women's Writing in Exile* (Chapel Hill and London: University of North Carolina Press, 1989).

Radner, Hilary, '"Out of Category": The Middlebrow Novel', in *Shopping Around: Feminine Culture and the Pursuit of Pleasure* (London: Routledge, 1995).

Radway, Janice, *Reading the Romance* (Chapel Hill: University of North Carolina Press, 1984).

Rose, Jacqueline, 'Sexuality in the Reading of Shakespeare: *Hamlet* and *Measure for Measure*', in Cyrus Hoy (ed.), the Norton Critical Edition of *Hamlet* (New York and London: W. W. Norton, 1992).

Rose, Jacqueline, 'Margaret Thatcher and Ruth Ellis' in *Why War? – Psychoanalysis, Politics, and the Return to Melanie Klein* (Oxford: Blackwell, 1993).

Rowbotham, Sheila, *Woman's Consciousness, Man's World* (Harmondsworth: Penguin, 1973).

Schmideberg, Melitta, 'Intellectual Inhibition and Eating Disorders', trans. Robert Gillett and Jacqueline Rose, in Jacqueline Rose, *Why War? – Psychoanalysis, Politics, and the Return to Melanie Klein*.

Schoolman, Morton, 'Introduction' to Seyla Benhabib, *The Reluctant Modernism of Hannah Arendt*.

Sedgwick, Eve Kosofsky, *Between Men: English Literature and Male Homosocial Desire* (New York: Columbia University Press, 1985).

Showalter, Elaine (ed.), *The New Feminist Criticism* (London: Virago, 1986).

Simons, Judy, *Rosamond Lehmann* (London: Macmillan, 1992).

Simons, Judy and Kate Fullbrook (eds), *Writing: A Woman's Business* (Manchester and New York: Manchester University Press, 1998).

Stoneman, Patsy, *Brontë Transformations: The Cultural Dissemination of Jane Eyre and Wuthering Heights* (Hemel Hempstead: Prentice Hall/Harvester Wheatsheaf, 1996).

Taylor, Elizabeth, 'Autobiographical Sketch', reprinted as a preface to *At Mrs Lippincote's*, first published 1945 (London: Virago, 1988).

Todd, Janet (ed.), *Women Writers Talking* (London: Holmes & Meier, 1983).

Tredell, Nicholas, *Conversations with Critics* (Manchester: Carcanet Press, 1994).

Virgil, *The Aeneid*, trans. W. F. Jackson Knight (Harmondsworth; Penguin, 1958).

Ward Jouve, Nicole, *'The Streetcleaner': The Yorkshire Ripper Case on Trial* (London and New York: Marion Boyars Publishers, 1986).

Watts, Janet, 'Introduction' to Rosamond Lehmann, *A Sea-Grape Tree*.

Webb, Janette, 'The Ivory Tower: Positive Action for Women in Higher Education', in Angela Coyle and Jane Skinner (eds), *Women and Work: Positive Action for Change* (London: Macmillan, 1988).

Whitford, Margaret (ed.), *The Irigaray Reader* (Oxford: Blackwell, 1991).

Whitford, Margaret, *Luce Irigaray: Philosophy in the Feminine* (London: Routledge, 1991).

Woolf, Virginia, *Mrs Dalloway*, first published 1925 (Oxford: World's Classics, 1992).

Woolf, Virginia, *The Waves*, first published 1931 (Oxford: World's Classics, 1992).

Woolf, Virginia, *The Years*, first published 1937 (Oxford: World's Classics, 1992).

Woolf, Virginia, *A Room of One's Own; Three Guineas*, first published 1929; 1938 (Oxford: Oxford University Press, 1992).

Woolf, Virginia, *Women and Fiction: The Manuscript Versions of A Room of One's Own*, transcribed and edited by S. P. Rosenbaum (Oxford: Blackwell, 1992).

Woolf, Virginia, *The Diary of Virginia Woolf*, vol. III, ed. Anne Olivier Bell (London: Hogarth Press, 1980).

Woolf, Virginia, 'Professions for Women' in Michèle Barrett (ed.), *Virginia Woolf: Women and Writing* (London: Women's Press, 1988).

Yates, Frances, 'Queen Elizabeth I as Astraea' in *Astraea: The Imperial Theme in the Sixteenth Century* (London and Boston: Routledge & Kegan Paul, 1975).

Index